NOAH'S ARK

Writing **Architecture** series

A project of the Anyone Corporation; Cynthia Davidson, editor

NOAH'S ARK

ESSAYS ON ARCHITECTURE

HUBERT DAMISCH

EDITED AND WITH AN INTRODUCTION BY ANTHONY VIDLER

TRANSLATED BY JULIE ROSE

THE MIT PRESS

CAMBRIDGE, MASSACHUSETTS

LONDON, ENGLAND

This translation was made possible in part by a grant from the Graham Foundation for Advanced Studies in the Fine Arts.

This book was set in Filosofia and Trade Gothic by the MIT Press. Printed and bound in the United States of America.

Library of Congress Cataloging-in-Publication Data

Names: Damisch, Hubert, author. | Vidler, Anthony, editor. | Rose, Julie, 1952– translator.
Title: Noah's ark : essays on architecture / Hubert Damisch ; Edited and introduction by Anthony Vidler ; Translated by Julie Rose.
Description: Cambridge, MA : The MIT Press, 2016. | Series: Writing architecture | Includes bibliographical references and index.
Identifiers: LCCN 2015038269 | ISBN 9780262528580 (pbk. : alk. paper)
Subjects: LCSH: Architecture—Philosophy.
Classification: LCC NA2500 .D33513 2016 | DDC 720.1—dc23 LC record available at http://lccn.loc.gov/2015038269

10   9   8   7   6   5   4   3   2   1

CONTENTS

SOURCES

The essays collected here are sometimes partly rewritten, often-times translated (sometimes anew) by the award-winning translator Julie Rose, and edited by Anthony Vidler. The prologue first appeared as "L'Arche de Noé" in *Revue Critique* 43 (January–February 1987). Chapter 1, "Aujourd'hui, l'architecture," first appeared as in *Le temps de la réflexion*, no. 2 (1981). Chapter 2, "The Column, the Wall," was published in French and English in *Architectural Design* 49 (1979), in a special issue on Leon Battista Alberti edited by Joseph Rykwert. Chapter 4 first appeared as "La Colonnade de Perrault et les fonctions de l'ordre classique" in *L'urbanisme de Paris et l'Europe, 1600–1680*, edited by Pierre Francastel (1969). Chapter 5 was first published as "L'architecture raisonnée," the preface to *L'architecture raisonné: Extraits du Dictionnaire de l'architecture française* (1964). A previous translation appeared in *Architectural Design* 50, nos. 3–4 (1980), a special issue on Viollet-le-Duc. Chapter 6 first appeared as "Du structuralisme au fonctionnalisme" in *A la rescherché de Viollet-le-Duc*, edited by Geert Bekaert (1980). Chapter 7, "Ledoux with Kant," was originally published as the preface to the French translation of Emil Kaufmann's *De Ledoux à Le Corbusier: Origine et développement de l'architecture autonome* (1981). It was translated by Erin Williams and previously appeared in *Perspecta* 33, a special issue titled "Mining Autonomy" (2002). Chapter 8 first appeared as "L'autre 'Ich' ou le désir du vide: Pour un tombeau d'Adolf Loos" in *Critique* 31, nos. 339–340 (August–September 1975). The translation here, by John Savage, was published first in *Grey Room* 1 (Autumn 2000). Chapter 9 first appeared as "Ornamento" in *L'Enciclopedia Einaudi*, vol. 10 (1980).

Chapter 10, "Against the Slope: Le Corbusier's La Tourette," first appeared in English, translated by Julie Rose, in *Log* 4 (Winter 2005). Chapter 11 first appeared as "La plus petite différence" in *Mies van der Rohe: Sa carrière, son héritage et ses disciples*, an exhibition catalogue published by Centre Georges Pompidou (1987). Chapter 12 appeared as "Le parti du détail" in *Jean Prouvé: Constructeur 1901–1984*, published by Centre Georges Pompidou (1990). Chapter 13 is a compilation of four essays that first appeared in the *Any* book series, published by the Anyone Corporation with the MIT Press: "How We Deal with History," in *Anyhow* (1998); "Three Minus Two, Two Plus One: Architecture and the Fabric of Time," in *Anytime* (1999); "The Offense of Wandering," translated by Mortimer Schiff, in *Anymore* (2000), and "Anything But," in *Anything* (2001). Chapter 14, "Blotting Out Architecture? A Fable in Seven Parts," translated by Julie Rose for publication in *Log* 1 (Fall 2003), was first given as the lecture "Effacer l'architecture" at the Canadian Centre for Architecture in Montreal in May 2003.

INTRODUCTION

I keep thinking of myself as some sort of displaced philosopher. The issue of displacement is, in any sense, crucial to my work. According to Gilles Deleuze, philosophy has mostly to do with inventing concepts. In that sense, I am not a philosopher: I do not invent concepts, but I try to displace them. For instance, the concept of structure is of great interest, when dealt with in artistic terms. I first became interested in architecture because architecture provides us with an open series of structural models.
—Hubert Damisch[1]

The following essays, written between 1963 and 2005, represent Hubert Damisch's forays into architectural theory. Organized roughly according to the chronology of their subject matter, they span the period between the Renaissance and the present, a period of architecture's emergence as a "discipline" with all the attendant problems of "origin" (Noah's Ark or Adam's House?), "structure" (abstract model of relations between the elements, or supporting framework?), "meaning" (communicative sign or silent system?), and, with increasing industrialization, "material" (building fabric or essential nature?).

These questions and more permeate Damisch's reflections, which are not so much couched in terms of theoretical pronouncements or historical exegeses but rather read as what he calls in another preface "a set of exercises." In the case of the previous collection, under the title *Skyline*, Damisch's "exercises" were primarily (as his subtitle *The Narcissistic City* indicates) concerned with the imaginary, symbolic realms explored by psychoanalysis. In the present collection, the preoccupation is less with Freud or Lacan (although the presence of a modern subject is always lurking close to the surface) as it is with the general idea of "structure," construed both physically and mentally and analyzed in terms introduced by structuralists both anthropological and linguistic, from Claude Lévi-Strauss to Roland Barthes.

However, Damisch differs from many who have tried to *apply* structuralism to architecture, forcing architecture to conform to the combinatory rules of language, and from those who would *read* architecture as a language, with the result that its elements are isolated as so many words and phrases. His aim is both more philosophical (to think of architecture in another key than that of its internal disciplinary forms) and less systematic (as he constructs a kind of parallel universe for architectural thought). Here, the conjunction that appears often in his titles—*with*—is symptomatic: His aim is not to treat architecture *and* philosophy, structure, semiology, nor to develop a philosophy *of* architecture, but to discuss, to formulate a discourse of architecture *with* philosophy. The title of one of the essays in this collection, "Ledoux with Kant," thus does not imply that Ledoux ever read Kant, or that his architecture might be analyzed according to Kantian aesthetics, but that the juxtaposition of the two might reveal important and hitherto unexplored questions. In this sense, architecture would be as important for the analysis of philosophy as philosophy would be for architecture.

Philosophy and architecture have had an uncertain partnership since Plato's excoriation of Pericles's Acropolis as a mark of Athenian decadence and Socrates's indifference; he who by all accounts was the son of a stonemason and trained as one himself was only concerned to make sure that the "builder" stuck to his trade and was refused full citizenship with all the other trades. It was left to Vitruvius, hardly a philosopher, to piece together a few fragments of Greek wisdom into a story of "origins" (from wood to stone) and a theory of design (*concinnitas, firmitas, venustas*) that has continued to haunt architecture. If, since then, architecture was noticed in philosophical discourse, it was more as a useful analogy—its apparent "rational" structure a paradigm for philosophical argument (Descartes) or as an abstract model for construing "judgment" (Kant).

It was not until the late eighteenth and early nineteenth centuries, and with the still problematic inclusion of architecture (a mixed art) among the other (fine) arts within the subgenre of philosophy named "aesthetics" by Baumgarten, that architecture entered into discussions of origin and ontology with its own supposed autonomy. Thus, Hegel saw it as the first, symbolic step toward philosophical emancipation, rapidly to be overtaken by sculpture, painting, and poetry. Schelling, following the historiographical line of progress outlined by Hegel, assessed architecture in terms of its internal and implicitly external forces; Nietzsche used its decline and fall from grace as an expressive art as a sign of the loss of primal rhetorical energy; and Heidegger attempted to resituate its origin as an indestructible monument to presence.

Meanwhile, nonphilosophers and architects, from the abbé Laugier to Viollet-le-Duc and Gottfried Semper, began the process of reformulating the Vitruvian notion of origin, through ever more sophisticated versions of structural and ornamental history, with the legacy to the twentieth century of a bifurcated discipline caught between the literal model of structure (the reinforced concrete Maison Dom-ino or the Miesian steel frame) and a vague, quasi-Neoplatonic version of typology that put this model to work in various programmatic contexts.

In this discursive impasse, one that was replicated in the many other disciplinary discourses analyzed by Michel Foucault, the disruptions forced by Derrida and Lacan into the notion of structure and sign opened the way to a rethinking of the very idea of a "structural" model, whether of origin, center, or foundation—a rethinking paradoxically founded on the refutation of the model of structuralist anthropology proposed by Lévi-Strauss. In "Structure, Sign, and Play" (1965), Derrida highlighted the dilemma of "doing without the concepts of metaphysics in order to shake metaphysics," of questioning the notion of a centered structure and a central signified when no syntax or lexicon exists outside the history of metaphysics: "We can pronounce not a single destructive proposition which has not already had to slip into the form, the logic, and the implicit postulations of precisely what it seeks to contest."[2] This problematic, which Derrida found to be sustained in the anthropology of Lévi-Strauss, was (slowly enough) taken on by critics of the mythic structures of architecture. Gradually, through many interesting but properly illegitimate misreadings, the equally mythic model of "Deconstructivism" was born—but not without the intervention of a second destruction, one operated by Lacan on the notion of the subject, one already destabilized, as Derrida notes, by "the Freudian critique of self-presence, that is, the critique of consciousness, of the subject, of self-identity and of self-proximity or self-possession,"[3] and that, extended by Lacan, displaced the apparently fixed position of the viewing subject.

Asked by Denis Hollier some years ago how he might define himself ("Historian of art? Antihistorian of art? Theorist of art? Philosopher of art?"), Hubert Damisch referred to two major influences on his education: the phenomenologist Merleau-Ponty and the art historian Pierre Francastel. In Merleau-Ponty's seminars, he encountered "the question of the unconscious," the "perception of history," and "structuralism," as it was then being developed by Lévi-Strauss. From Francastel, he absorbed the social history of art and an interest in art and technique. In a sense, we can read Damisch's subsequent work—on painting, film, and architecture—as a long and complex meditation and response to these two thinkers, in a vein, as he states, that explores as much what they rejected as what they put forward. In this reflection, the problematic that emerged for Damisch was "the perception that there are questions that emerge from within the historical field that can be posed in historical terms but that history itself cannot answer. That's what absorbed me: how is it that history can pose questions that it nonetheless cannot answer?"[4]

Another answer would perhaps be that, as a philosopher concerned with attacking fundamental questions of the arts, Damisch has taken a route that avoids the usual traps of the field. Rather than use the various arts as analogical props for thought (Descartes on architecture, for example, as a model of rational argument), or absorbing them in an attempted general theory of aesthetics (Baumgarten, Schelling, Hegel, etc.), he is engaged in unpacking the different practices from the inside, so to speak, as if they possessed their own peculiar form of philosophical thinking—as if, as he has often said, they "thought themselves." Which would be one way of saying that his analysis is truly structural—and constructing a structural model is for him a primary task of the analyst. However, such a model, as he has emphasized again and again, is not a static and unmoving object in itself; it is rather an instrument used to *displace* the object—in Damisch's terms, a *theoretical object*: "A theoretical object is something that obliges you to do theory; we could start there. Secondly, it's an object that obliges you to do theory but also furnishes you with the means of doing it. . . . Third it's a theoretical object because it forces us to ask ourselves what theory is. It is posed in theoretical terms; it produces theory; and it necessitates a reflection on theory."[5] Once constructed, however, this theoretical object itself produces effects; the very act of producing it "displaces" the objects of analysis.

An observer of clouds, miasmas, uncertain perspectives, of the disturbing psychic undercurrents of beauty, and the heterogeneity of vision, Hubert Damisch would seem to be an unlikely theorist of architecture. Something as firm, formed, stable, fixed, and unshifting as architecture would hardly appeal, let alone respond, to the interrogation of the *informe*, the unseen, and the unthought—the subjects, indeed, that are habitually attributed to Damisch. Yet, from the outset, without much fanfare, and with no treatise or book to advertise the fact, this detective of the elusive has been elaborating, through incisive and regularly published essays, a theory of architecture. Rather, on the surface at least, he has been interrogating other, historical theories of architecture in such a way that, if read systematically and preferably consecutively in the chronological order of their subject matter, an emergent theory of architecture might be discerned—one that, while not pretending to operative or instrumental status, nevertheless construes the subject in a radical frame, a frame that if allowed will shift the nature of architectural understanding or, as Damisch prefers, architectural "thinking."

"What is *thinking* in painting, in forms and through means proper to it," asks Damisch in another context, that of his investigation of another "origin," that of perspective.[6] In a work completed contemporaneously, the preface to the French edition of Emil Kaufmann's book *Von Ledoux bis Le Corbusier*, Damisch poses the same question, but to architecture, precisely through the "forms and through means proper to it."[7] In the case of painting, Damisch has demonstrated that *perspectiva artificialis* allows the painter not simply to "show" but also to "think" by means of an apparatus that is epistemologically akin to the sentence in language. Perspective organizes "point of view, vanishing point, and distance point, and the other corollary points designating here, there, and over there—which is sufficient to make it possible to speak, again nonmetaphorically, of a geometry of the sentence that would have its analogue in the figurative register." In this sense, perspective, like the sentence, "assigns the subject within a previously established network that gives it meaning, while at the same time opening up the possibility of something like a statement in painting."[8]

What, then, might provide such an apparatus for architecture, one that might allow it to *think* and even, despite its supposed abstraction, to make a statement something akin to a sentence? Certainly, the "origin" of geometry, in the same way as the "origin" of perspective for painting, provides a partial answer for architecture. Even as Greek geometry purified itself (in Husserl's terms) of all anthropomorphism, so architecture in Ledoux's hands purified itself of organic metaphor, bodily embodiment, and the imitation of antiquity. The process of "autonomization of form" construed columns as cylinders bereft of human proportions, villas as cubes denied all Palladian attributes save that of their diagrammatic nine-square plans, and houses that "spoke" solely through geometrical alphabetization. Beyond this specifically eighteenth-century model, Damisch develops a set of conditions that reach into the posthistoricism of the late twentieth century and that derive not from Ledoux but from two other, earlier studies of instaurational moments: that of Alberti and that of Viollet-le-Duc. In both cases, Damisch is concerned with structure—not exactly the material structure of a building, although this too, but structure in the sense of thought. Architectural thinking is here carried out through the idea of structure and turns on the Albertian problem of "column" and "wall."

Interrogating the idea of "structure" in Alberti's treatise, by way of distinguishing between the idea of *continuity* signified by the word in Vitruvian and Roman usage and that of *discontinuity*—of the assemblage of discrete elements—implied by the more modern usage after Viollet-le-Duc, Damisch confronts the apparent paradox of Alberti's eloge of the column as "the principal ornament of architecture" and his limitations on its use with respect to the wall and its continuity. Similarly, in his article on Viollet-le-Duc's essay "Construction," it is not so much the material structure that Damisch seeks, but precisely the mechanism in thought that would, without rupture, bring theoretical and physical structure together within the same architectural thought.

Damisch, due as much to his interest in "column" as to his interest in "structure," has been called a structuralist. This would be so, certainly, if by "structuralist" one means "an individual engaging in attention to the rational structure of thought, of discourse, and of the relations of one proposition to the next." It would be less true of that Damisch who, in parallel with Lacan and Derrida, and in sympathy with both, interrogates the hidden underpsyche of architectural thought. However, it is also the underneath, that "crypt" of writing investigated by Derrida, that will of itself deny the authority of every statement, every monument to certainty and belief. It is also that underneath, spoken of by Lacan, that remains in the psyche long after the mirror has apparently constituted the self as a whole, structured the world as an imago, formed a supposed whole out of part objects. It is this "whole," this surface unity, that Damisch cannot in the end find satisfactory as an explanation for the perfection of an architectural object, itself in classical theory a stand-in for the human body and its qualities.

Which is why, in a later iteration of his own (hidden) architectural theory, Damisch finds solace in the fact that a building, like a painted image, can be a cloud: formless, yet structured and technologically sound; Viollet-le-Duc welded to Turner, the classical to the modern, transformed in Diller + Scofidio's Blur pavilion for the Swiss Expo 2002 into a shifting, nebulous, *in-forme* architecture—an architecture that, finally, will speak of its own internal contradictions.

Anthony Vidler
New York City
March 2015

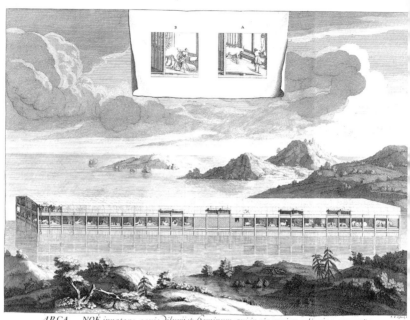

0.1

"Arca Noé." From Bernard Lamy, *De tabernaculo foederis, de sancta civitate Jerusalem, et de templo ejus* (Paris, 1720), facing page 191. Courtesy Avery Architectural & Fine Arts Library, Columbia University.

PROLOGUE: NOAH'S ARK

I

It took Jacques-François Blondel only one and a half pages of the
Encyclopédie to dispatch the article "Architecture" that had been
commissioned by Denis Diderot and Jean Le Rond d'Alembert. In
just three compact and carefully phrased columns, this celebrated
architect, noted for his teaching and publications, began by distinguishing between the different varieties of the art of building
before briefly treating its origins, the invention of the classical
orders by the Greeks, and the long, drawn-out decline of a practice that, having attained its absolute peak of perfection in Rome
under the reign of Augustus, sank into oblivion after the fall of
the Empire. Its slow recovery began at the end of an era described
by the author as "Gothic," when Charlemagne undertook to reestablish ancient architecture—though neither he nor the first
Capetians, whom Blondel credits with "a great liking for that science," were wholly successful. Whether they had intended to react against the taste for heaviness imported from the north by the
Vandals and the Goths or whether the genre declared by Blondel to
be "southern" had been introduced into France by the Arabs, the
fact remains that "the architects of those times created the beauty
of their architectures by means of a delicacy and a profusion of
ornament till then unknown . . . in such a way that architecture,
as it gradually changed its appearance, indulged in the opposite
excess and became too light."[1] According to Blondel, this was less
an interlude than a long period in the wilderness of oblivion; it
was, he concluded, "only in the last two centuries [the sixteenth

and seventeenth] that the architects of France and Italy had exerted themselves to retrieve the original simplicity, beauty, and proportion of ancient architecture; and it is only since then that our edifices have been executed in imitation of, and following the precepts of, the architecture of antiquity."[2]

Antique, ancient (whatever the varieties, variants, or variations may be), but also *Gothic*, and even *modern* (a term Blondel avoids defining, but that was nonetheless already current in his day in architectural discourse): these categories did not only correspond to historical periods that succeeded each other following the thread of a strictly linear and irreversible evolution. For language itself—and not only the French—was not content to pit *modern* against *ancient* unilaterally, as we might be led to believe if we take only a cursory glance at the first edition of the *Dictionnaire de l'Académie françoise dédié au roy*, published in 1694. Indeed, what do we read in the *Encyclopédie* itself in the entry for "modern"? We find that "*modern* is used in matters of taste, not in absolute opposition to what is ancient, but to what was in bad taste: thus *modern architecture* has been used in opposition to *Gothic architecture*, even though *modern* architecture is only beautiful insofar as it approaches the taste of antiquity."[3] For Blondel's part, as he characterizes it, the architecture of the first Capetians could well have been held to be "modern," on several counts, from the moment it opposed the architecture he describes as *Gothic*, a term that contemporaries of the *Encyclopédie* held to be synonymous with "bad taste." But if the only good taste was "antique," then there was no choice but to conclude that a modern architecture could only lay claim to beauty on the express condition of renouncing all novelty that did not overtly revive, in form and even more so in principle, the works of a time "when the arts were brought to their perfection by the fine geniuses of Greece and Rome."[4] Thus, if, chronologically speaking, *antique* were opposed to *modern* in the same way as the *old* to the *new*, then the same reductive division could not be applied in the encyclopedic terms of "good taste." This reveals an initial contradiction in Blondel's definition of architecture; a second lies in his characterization of architecture as a "science."

If science indeed had a place in Blondel's scheme of architectural history, any "progress" achieved was according to a doubly inverted figure: as a decline for which the only remedy was itself regressive (its sole recourse, in the etymological sense, being a return to the antique) or, better, as the resurgence of the antique in the present, and *in the present tense*, following the turn of the Italian and French Renaissance, which would have a much greater impact in the Enlightenment, exceeding the limits of the history of taste, whether good or bad—and this on the eve of a revolution that, though representing a catastrophe in the symbolic order, can hardly be said to have shaken up the reign of the so-called neoclassical aesthetic in official building. With the Restoration assured, the newspapers had ample time to assert that taste in France awaited its own Fourteenth of July; the day would come when, in response to those who agreed with Madame de Staël that the revolution in politics could not fail to have repercussions in the literary realm, Victor Hugo would write that romanticism was the French Revolution made literature. But the great upheaval that came to a provisional end with the fall of Napoleon I in 1814 was not only a matter of taste—nor always of the best taste. No one put it better than Karl Marx when he said that the revolution had to adopt first the costumes of the Roman Republic and then of the Roman Empire for its actors to appear on the new stage of history—in a disguise and speaking a language that was certainly borrowed and better suited than the romantic wardrobe to the task and roles awaiting them.[5] Architecture was no exception to the rule; 150 years later, Bertolt Brecht would still repeat that the proletariat has a right to columns.

Blondel found proof of the perfection the Greeks attained in architecture in "the three orders, Doric, Ionic, Corinthian, that we inherit from them."[6] The Romans would only produce two others, and although these were merely imperfect imitations of the Greek, in Blondel's view they still had their "usefulness." Each of the five orders in fact corresponded to a specific genre of architecture: the rustic, the solid, the intermediate, the delicate, and the composite genres, which express, respectively, the Tuscan, Doric, Ionic, Corinthian, and Composite orders "that together comprise what is most exquisite in architecture."[7] The notion that architecture, like all the arts, has its limits, that it is not open to indefinite progress, and that there would always necessarily be a return to the example of the Greeks and Romans is demonstrated by history, "for we have not been able in France, despite the celebrated opportunities to build over the last century, to compose orders that could come close to the Greeks and Romans; I say *come close*, for many talented architects have tried, such as Bruant, Le Brun, Le Clerc, and so on, without being applauded or imitated by either their contemporaries or their successors."[8] But the orders would not have the importance Blondel gave them if they had been reduced to an accepted convention among the specialists of the art. Born of the necessity that first taught men how to build huts, tents, and cabins, architecture would have doubtless developed when these same men, forced as they were "to buy and sell," and living under common laws, gathered together and managed to make their dwellings "more regular"—the laws of proportion following the conformity to rules and vice versa. If exchange is at the root of societies, then law is at the root of architecture and the regularity that defines it. The ancient authors credited the Egyptians with being the first to raise buildings that were "symmetrical and proportional."[9] As for us, declares Blondel, "we look upon Greece as the cradle of good architecture, either because the rules of the Egyptians have not come down to us, or because what remains of their buildings manifests only a solid and colossal architecture (such as the famous pyramids that have triumphed over time for so many centuries) and that does not affect us in the same way as the monuments we have from ancient Greece."[10]

When Solomon undertook to build the Temple of Jerusalem, it is said that he called on Egyptian artists but that it was God himself who taught him the precepts of good architecture. The fact that Blondel raises this discussion without entering into it is significant. Architecture is a matter of rules—but also of affects. The architecture of pharaonic Egypt does not *affect* us in the same way as that of ancient Greece; it is in the way it affects us that confirms that, like the laws men have given themselves, the rules to which the art of building should conform have their raison d'être. But just as general agreement is not a necessary condition for the existence of natural rights,[11] so too the diversity of historical forms of architecture, their value, their singular charm—perhaps "eternal" charm, as Marx would not hesitate to say of Greek art—and their internal richness to which we gain access through "empathy" is not an argument against the existence of universal norms, which all good architecture ought to respect. The very transgressions of such norms (symmetry, for example) merely bear this out. That one can and should refer to antique architecture as the model of all architecture worthy of the name shows that this art is not controlled by any given society any more completely than by the period in which it is practiced and that architecture is in search of a standard that would allow its productions to be judged on the scale and in the suprahistorical dimension of allegedly "natural" rights. That this model is borrowed from history and corresponds to a precisely dated and localized architecture (that of ancient Greece) changes nothing. This apparent contradiction is merely a consequence of the constraints imposed on an art that (as Viollet-le-Duc would again assert a century after Blondel) obeys eternal principles, independent of the forms that express or betray them.[12]

In Blondel's view, the entire merit of architecture consists of "the justness of the proportions and the correctness of the drawing."[13] For the proportions to be considered "correct" or "false" in the same capacity as symmetry, however, we must call on criteria other than those suggested by history—first and foremost starting with mathematical criteria. This would seem to justify applying the label *science* to architecture, as well as the various attempts (to which Blondel himself refers) to treat the art of architecture as a purely demonstrative form, *more geometrico*. The article "Proportion" in the *Encyclopédie* does not go quite so far. In relation to architecture, it keeps to Vitruvius's definition of symmetry, understood as "the relationship [*rapport*], the suitability [*convenance*] of the whole and of the parts among themselves in works of taste."[14] Proportion consists in "the correctness [*justesse*] of the members of each part of a building, and the relationship of the parts to the whole; as, for example, the measurements of a column in relation to the *ordonnance* of the building."[15] But it is also "the different sizes of the architectural members and forms according to how they are meant to appear from their viewing point."[16] We are thus referred back to the division of optics known as "perspective" and, by the same token, to geometry. This is an old problem, which had already held the attention of the Greeks and the Neoplatonists: Can the art of architecture, as the closest of them all to the Idea and that which, more than any other art, presents *le cose alla virtù* (to adopt the expression used by Daniele Barbaro in his edition of Vitruvius prefaced by Palladio[17]), be allowed to deceive itself by all manner of refinements, corrections, and "temperaments" designed to redress errors in meaning by means that are themselves illusionist? Even Plato seems to have taken sides, so quick was he to condemn the artifices of art, starting with trompe l'oeil, which he sees as not far from a kind of "witchcraft."[18] Plato, though, would not have dreamed of accusing architects of not seeking uniformity and harmony for their own sake; he condemns them only in relation to vision, as though the mind could only benefit from the struggle of appearance against illusions and of illusion against appearances.[19]

It may have been an old question, but it was still relevant in the age of reason (just as it would become relevant again at the beginning of the twentieth century and through to Erwin Panofsky's work on perspective and its "temperaments").[20] This is attested by the fact that, in a text as brief as the article "Architecture," Blondel insists on defining what he calls *architecture in perspective*: "We call architecture in perspective that architecture whose parts are of diverse proportions and diminished by distance so as to make the general disposition [*ordonnance*] seem bigger and taller than it is in reality, as we see in the famous Vatican staircase, built under the Pontificate of Alexander VII from drawings by the Cavalier Bernini." Proportions are a matter of measurement, but also every bit as much a matter of perspective—and thus doubly a matter of science.

Another term should also be taken into consideration in addition to *proportion*: that of *composition*. Of the three kinds of the art of building that Blondel distinguishes—civil architecture, military architecture, and naval architecture—the first, which he defines as "the art of *composing* and *constructing* buildings, for the convenience [*commodité*] and different purposes of life, such as sacred buildings, royal palaces, and private houses, as well as bridges, public squares, theaters, triumphal arches, etc.," is the exclusive subject of the article "Architecture."[21] Composition here is what distinguishes architecture from the simple art of building—in other words, from *construction* as it is practiced in military or naval architecture—though it is no less an integral part of civil architecture. Yet the article "Composition" in the

Encyclopédie, which is concerned with composition in painting as well as composition in the rhetorical sense of the term understood as "the order and connection that an orator should apply in the parts of a speech,"[22] says not a word about composition in architecture.

The art of building is scarcely better served when it comes to construction, which is somewhat surprising in a work that presents itself as a dictionary of the sciences, arts, and crafts. Grammatical construction is the subject of an article of over twenty pages, but that is because it relates to the arrangement of words within discourse, and discourse is based on grammatical construction, as is the *Encyclopédie* itself. Construction in geometry is not overlooked, since it corresponds to "operations that must be performed to execute the solution to a problem," as well as to lines drawn "either to arrive at the solution to a problem, or to demonstrate some proposition."[23] When it comes to architecture, by contrast, the article says nothing about the various attempts (which Blondel mentions only in passing) to confer upon architecture an appearance of scientificity: that of an art, if not demonstrated *more geometrico*, at the very least "reasoned," as much as the *Encyclopédie* could be and as Viollet-le-Duc's *Dictionnaire de l'architecture française* would be. Blondel's article is limited to defining construction as "the art of building in relation to matter,"[24] without amplification, save for references to the articles "Carpentry," "Masonry," "Joinery," and so on.

However well ordered, the article "Architecture" responded poorly to what might have been expected from the *Encyclopédie* on the subject, considering the space given to that art (or science?) in the historic project of the Enlightenment. The editors seem to have been aware of this: the *Supplément*, published in 1777, contains two articles that expand the articles "Architect" and "Architecture" with material taken explicitly from Johann Georg Sulzer's *General Theory of the Fine Arts*. Both articles are equally flat but, significantly, insist on the social connotations of the art of building and on its potential effects in the cultural realm.

Perhaps we should look for the causes of Blondel's brevity in the constraints imposed on the contributors by alphabetical order. The article "Architecture" appears even before the article "Art," which was written by Diderot and intended to serve as a prospectus for booksellers. The fact that the entries in which it would have been possible to take a fresh look at the question of architecture—starting with the article "Composition"—were not used to remedy the problem seems to indicate that neither the author nor the editors felt the need to do so. This, however, should not stop us from taking a closer look, given the surprising fact that nothing is said about civil or military construction in the article "Construction," whereas more than six pages are devoted to the third kind of the art of building: *naval architecture*.

II

The relative brevity of the article "Architecture" is all the more surprising if we compare it with the length of another *Encyclopédie* entry that precedes it: the article "Ark" (*Arche*), produced by the abbé Edme-François Mallet, one of Diderot and d'Alembert's principal collaborators. As the *Discours préliminaire*, or preface, notes, the abbé Mallet was the author of all the articles on ancient and modern history, as well as the articles "Eloquence," "Literature," "Poetry," and (as is only right) "Theology." When it appeared in the *Supplément*, the article "Ark" required just a few typographical corrections and the addition of a certain number of titles to an already copious bibliography. Even in the body of the *Encyclopédie*, it takes up four full pages, or eight columns—close to three times the space reserved for the article "Architecture." It is clearly not unrelated to architecture, whether in terms of the meaning of *arched*, which is naturally joined to the idea of an "ark," or to Blondel's taxonomy. The ark of Genesis—that "kind of boat" or "vast floating building" constructed by Noah to protect the various species of animals that God ordered him to take in from the Flood—in effect falls under the heading of the third branch of the art of building that Blondel describes as "naval," the purpose of which is "the construction of vessels, galleys, and all floating buildings in general, as well as bridges, breakwaters, jetties, rope makers, warehouses, etc., erected along the seashore or at its edges."[25] The space given to this same naval architecture in the article "Construction" corroborates the hypothesis whereby "Ark" and "Architecture" cannot be considered separately in the general economy of the *Encyclopédie*. If we find the classical definition of the art in "Architecture," along with a list of its merits, the rules it obeys, and a brief summary of its history, then the article "Ark" that immediately precedes it in the first volume of the work introduces considerations of another order, which take a singularly "modern" turn. Once articulated, the goal of the construction of the ark—nothing less than ensuring the survival of the main species of animals, besides the aquatic animals not imperiled by the rising waters—as well as the design, development, and maintenance, if not management, of such a "floating building" would not have failed to pose a number of problems, both technical and logistical, and their discussion takes up almost the whole article. Although we cannot ignore either the background or the patristics of the article, the fact remains that the abbé Mallet seems to have been less concerned with proving the tale's authenticity than with exploring what we might call the functional implications of the story of Noah and his ark—an initial foray into what would later be called functionalist thought in architecture.

The abbé Mallet begins by reviewing the information supplied by the text of Genesis and the various hypotheses issued by the church fathers and modern critics regarding the time of construction of the ark, the materials used, and its dimensions. This is, first and foremost, a matter of *scale*. If we accept, as tradition has it, that the first men were much taller and stronger than those of today, we can allow that Noah and his three sons, to believe Mallet, would have been up to the job of building a vessel that required the felling of a great number of trees, whether cedars, cypresses, or any other species denoted by the Hebrew word *gopher*. But the same cannot be said for the dimensions of the ark indicated in Genesis (6:15): three hundred cubits for the length, fifty for the breadth, thirty for the height. This seems disproportionate to the quantity of creatures and provisions that were to find a place onboard, and it has raised, as the abbé Mallet concedes, many doubts about the veracity of the biblical text. On this point, the scalar argument suggesting that the cubit, which is a human measure, has varied over the course of the centuries in proportion to the height of human beings is weak. It matters little, asserts Mallet, whether the building's dimensions increase or decrease, so long as they do so relative to the measurements of the people and the animals the ark was supposed to house. Church Fathers Origen and St. Augustine, among others, claimed that the cubit referred to was the geometrical cubit used by the Egyptians, which would make the ark 1,700 feet long—longer than the biggest ocean liners of the twentieth century—dimensions a contemporary of the *Encyclopédie* could not have accepted. Hence the efforts of a number of scholars, from Father Athanasius Kircher to Isaac Newton, to show that if a cubit were around fifty centimeters, the ark would have been big enough to accommodate not only Noah's family and the animals in their charge but also a sufficient quantity of provisions and fresh water.

The functions assigned to the ark are clearly set out in Genesis: beyond the eight members of Noah's family, the vessel was to contain one pair of each of the species reputed to be impure, and seven of the species reputed to be pure, as well as provisions for a year, "which at first glance would seem impossible, but if we work out the calculation, we find that the number of animals was not as great as we had at first imagined."[26] Mallet in fact claims to know of only just over a hundred (from 100 to 130) species of quadrupeds, and as many birds, on top of which must be added, if we hold to the letter of the Scriptures, every creeping thing of the earth—but not the forty aquatic species that were apparently not targeted by the divine malediction and announcement of "the end of all flesh." John Wilkins, the bishop of Chester, felt that only seventy-two species of quadrupeds needed to be preserved. By Mallet's own admission, evaluating the ark's capacity is an extremely difficult thing to do, considering how incomplete were the lists of animals then in existence, especially for the still unexplored regions of the world, and thus how impossible it was to determine the dimensions of the vessel "relative to its use" any more accurately than is done in the Scriptures.

When it comes to the provisions necessary for such an enterprise, the calculation seems a bit easier, even though the parameters are relatively complex. In the case of carnivores, each one would consume a certain quantity of meat that could be measured in numbers of livestock required, but the sheep needed to feed the carnivores would in turn consume a quantity of hay that would decrease as the livestock dwindled. Bishop Wilkins supposed that all the carnivores together could be calculated as equivalent to twenty-seven wolves, plus the space required for their food (which he calculated to be 1,825 sheep). The herbivores, which he estimated as equivalent to 208 oxen, would seem to need 109,500 cubits of hay. Butteo's estimate went higher, with the carnivores as the equivalent of eighty wolves, which needed to be fed ten sheep a day, a total of 3,650 sheep in the course of a year. With the number of animals destined to serve as feed diminishing every day, we should be able to count on a fixed number of 1,820 beasts in order to calculate the amount of hay needed to maintain them, which would support 1,900 sheep and 120 oxen. If seven sheep eat as much fodder as one ox, for a year's supply there would have to be 146,000 cubits of fodder.

These estimations might cause some amusement, as might the discussions about the ark's form, its internal layout, and the administration and management of the whole, which today would be called maintenance. If we are to believe the text of Genesis, it was to God himself that Noah was indebted for the vessel's specifications: The ark was to be made of wood and reeds (though the Hebrew word *qanim*, as we will see, is open to debate) and coated with pitch inside and out; it was to be three hundred cubits long, fifty wide, and thirty high, to be covered with a roof, and to comprise three floors. Even the position of the door was subject to divine instruction, which provided that it be placed at the side. In the eighteenth century, several critics fretted anxiously over this. If we understand the ark to have been a rectangular parallelepiped, then the door would have been better off placed on one of the smaller sides than on one of the longer sides, where it would have risked compromising the balance of the whole and spoiling the symmetry (not to mention that the ark would then have had something like a facade, which hardly seems right for what was ultimately just a great big barge). But if this were the case, then the vessel would have been heavier at one end and would have risked not listing to starboard but sinking at the front or back (if indeed these could be distinguished from one another).

As for the different levels provided in the divine program, commentators generally agree to reserve the top floor of the ark for the patriarch's family, who would have found themselves with a lot of room, even though they had to share it with the birds and find a place for the household utensils, digging tools, fabrics, grains, and seeds (not to mention a kitchen and space for taking a walk). The middle floor would have served to store the provisions, while the bottom floor housed the quadrupeds and reptiles (or the other way round). To these three floors mentioned in the Bible, some have been tempted to add a fourth: a kind of bilge for storing the ballast and the excrement, which could not be thrown overboard (thus implying that the ark had no opening other than the above-mentioned door, which would have been hermetically sealed for the duration of the ordeal). This same space could have also served as a hull to hold potable water—the water of the Flood, as abundant as it was, not being enough to desalinate the seawater.

But this does not solve the problem of the vessel's internal layout—a problem great enough to hold Blondel's attention, as indicated by the fact that he went to some trouble over the article "Distribution." "Make yourself an ark out of resinous wood," states the Jerusalem Bible. "Make it with reeds, and line it with pitch inside and out." The Hebrew word *qanim*, "reeds," is merely conjecture here. The word could also be *qinnim*, "nests," to be understood in the sense of "cabins." This would imply that God himself stipulated the division of the living quarter decks into cells (or, as Mallet prefers, "stalls"), the number and size of which remained to be determined; thus, each pair or species of animal is imagined to have had its own stall—yet it would seem that eight people would have had difficulty in the cleaning and provisioning of such a large number of stalls. To this, the abbé Mallet replied that it would have been far more difficult to take care of 380 animals (not counting those much more numerous needed as fodder) if they were all mixed together.

Such a fable is only a fable if we see it as nothing more than a fairytale defying all plausibility, freighted as it may be (as we read further in the Jerusalem Bible) with an eternal lesson about justice and divine mercy, the malice of man, and the salvation granted to the just. If, on the other hand, we take the program assigned to Noah seriously, along with the many problems commentators have raised in its regard, we cannot help but be struck by the fact that the article "Ark" actually offers a rough sketch (or caricature, perhaps not devoid of humor) of an authentically functionalist approach, one that even goes into detail. Whether concerning the building of the ark, its internal layout, or matters of logistics and accommodation (to say nothing of the problems, never alluded to, of security), there is no problem raised by the critics that is not echoed today in the technical specifications or rules imposed on those in the profession of architecture. We might restrict ourselves to two examples of this. The question of the method of loading the ark, its access, is not unconnected, though within a biblical time frame, to concerns that these days preoccupy those in charge of public access whenever a very tall apartment block is slated for a high-density area or one poorly serviced by public transport. Here, we only have to look at the apocalyptic provisions occasioned in their day by the Pan American Building in New York or the John Hancock Center in Chicago. As for the ark's internal layout, and in particular the layout of the floor reserved for the menagerie, the question is exactly the same as for the plan: Whether it should be free or otherwise depends on whether we favor having a number of stalls corresponding to the number of different species or prefer instead to regroup the animals by genuses or families. If we take into account the fact that extra space would have become available as time went by and the vegetable and animal provisions were consumed, the best solution would have been to provide removable bulkheads to allow the occupants of the ark to gradually make themselves more comfortable as the cargo dwindled.

Humanity, Marx said, only asks questions it can solve. Following this, Engels held that the *housing question* could only be solved by a revolution—which deferred not only the solution to the problem but also the right way of formulating it, thus leaving room only for a critique of reformist utopias in anticipation of the revolution to come. The problems posed by the building of the ark and its maintenance were no more than what humanity was able to solve by relying only on its own strengths, as developed at the time, nor any more than what we would be able to solve today. Thus, Bishop Wilkins, and the abbé Mallet with him, concluded:

> *The ark, which has been used as an objection to the truth of the Holy Scriptures, here becomes a proof of that truth, since we may safely assume that in the early ages of the world men versed in the sciences and the arts must have been infinitely more subject to error than we are today. Nonetheless, if today we had to match the capacity of a vessel to the mass of animals and their food, we would fare no better . . . for the human mind tends in such a case to wildly exaggerate objects. What would indubitably have happened with the dimensions of Noah's ark is what happens with the estimation of the number of stars visible to the naked eye; just as we judge that number to be infinite, we would have carried the dimensions of the ark to vast magnitudes and would accordingly have engendered a building infinitely greater than was necessary, sinning more through its excess capacity calculated by the historian than by what those who attack the story claim is its sin of parsimony.*[27]

This development is somewhat surprising, not only for the way it revisits the discussions to find within the doubts raised by the biblical tale proof of that tale's veracity but also for the argument that springs from this demonstration. No one but God could have conceived the measurements of the ark, for this was a matter of *proportion*, both in the singular sense (as Blondel used it) and in the pragmatic, functional sense that Le Corbusier later intended with the example of the ocean liner *France*, built in the 1920s by the Saint-Nazaire shipyards.[28] But if the human mind were not adequate to the task, the reason for this was not to be sought in the mind's inability to manage complexity: the plans and sectional views of the kinds of Noah's arks represented by the heavy vessels of the East India Company, which one can see in the National Maritime Museum at Port-Louis, France, are proof that the ship owners of the day and their engineers already had a pretty good idea—at a scale, once again, of that time. The problem lies above all in the opposite: in the propensity of modern societies to deal with the difficulties they must face *by excess* rather than *by lack* and to imagine solutions, to devise projects, to impose tasks on themselves, and to fuel dreams of an exaggerated scope, beyond all proportion, that are ultimately totalitarian. Whereas man, left to his sorry fate, would have designed a gigantic ark that he could not possibly have floated—such as the craft Robinson Crusoe built in the middle of the forest without first working out how he would transport it to shore—God alone was able to take the proper measure of things. Indeed, he himself had ordered and, so to speak, programmed a universal and devastating catastrophe, though one that contained a safety clause, for it was to be a prelude to the regeneration of the human race. As such, it would find an echo in the project of the Enlightenment.

III

The time is long since past when—after the two worldwide catastrophes of World War I and the Russian Revolution—Le Corbusier could cry: "Everything remains to be done! An immense task! And it is so pressing, so urgent, that the whole world is absorbed in this imperious necessity. Machines will lead to a new order of labor and rest. Whole cities must be built or rebuilt in view of a minimum of comfort, the prolonged lack of which might unsettle the social equilibrium. Society is unstable, cracking under a state of things upended by fifty years of advances that have changed the face of the world more than the six preceding centuries."[29] A gigantic task it was indeed, one worthy of "modernity," one that could not avoid taking on a cosmic dimension. To "an indolent respect for tradition," the architect was to prefer "respect for the forces of nature" (well represented by the idea of the Flood); to "the pettiness of middling conceptions," he would substitute "the majesty of solutions following from a problem well posed and required by this century of great endeavors, which has just taken a giant step forward. The land-dweller's house is the expression of an outdated world of small dimensions."[30]

As far as the instability of the times, it was as if the place made for Noah's Ark in the *Encyclopédie* was dictated by a premonition of a flood of another kind, which the French Revolution came to represent for the European consciousness. The revolution began with the destruction of the Bastille, that monument of (military) architecture and symbol of the ancien régime, whose end it marked at the same time that it heralded, as Jules Michelet would write, the triumph of "what is outside time, outside the future and outside the past, immutable Right." This takes us back to the *Encyclopédie* and the analogy Blondel's text suggests between the rules obeyed by architecture and the principles of natural Right. *Architecture or revolution*—the modernist watchword, posed in the form of an alternative or a dilemma—was to translate as clearly as possible the ambiguity of the relations that the art of building, if not architecture itself, has never ceased to maintain with the prospect of a generalized catastrophe: either architecture looks to stave off such a catastrophe by rendering it useless, or it merely aspires to furnish humanity with the means to survive such a catastrophe without too much damage. In the history of the world, the Flood has not only corresponded to a moment of crisis. The rupture of the seawalls put up by God between what Genesis calls "the waters from under heaven" and "the waters from the great deep" signifies a return, at least momentarily, to original chaos: the time to wipe out all flesh, or at the very least all flesh "wherein is the breath of life" and that found itself on terra firma (Gen. 6:17), to the exclusion not only of the animals that move in the water but also of those that move in the air and managed to find refuge either on the water (in the case of sea birds) or on the ark. The evangelists, followed by the church fathers, would not fail to exploit this typology: the Flood prefigured the Last Days just as the salvation granted to Noah and his family prefigured salvation through the waters of baptism.[31] Water in this context takes on functions that seem paradoxical, or at least contradictory, for it is both through water that the catastrophe occurred and through water that the inhabitants of the ark escaped that catastrophe. The fact that the covenant between God and Noah had recourse to naval architecture takes on symbolic value here. In the Latin translation the same word, *arca* ("chest"), is applied both to the ark of the covenant in which Moses enclosed the tablets of the law and to Noah's Ark, but Hebrew uses two different terms: the word *tebah*, which applies to Noah's great vessel, is found again in the Bible only in relation to the basket made of bulrushes in which the infant Moses is laid when his mother entrusts him to the lifesaving waters of the Nile.[32]

On Imminent Disaster and Means of Mitigating It

Le Corbusier's discourse echoes those of professional revolutionaries, even as it occasionally takes on biblical overtones: "My own duty, my quest, is to try and place the man of today beyond harm, beyond disaster."[33] We are a long way, apparently, from the project that could be said to be a part—but only one part—of the avant-garde: the program of a kind of art that, in the words of André Masson, would "explode reality."[34] But if modernity was associated with awareness of a rupture, of a radical break in the continuity of history, as well as with an idea—the program of a fresh start—then the sometimes all-too-real fantasy of the tabula rasa corresponded to another kind of disaster, in the commonplace sense of the term. To start afresh, it would seem there is no choice but to begin by making a clean sweep, by pulling everything down. The difference between a France devastated by World War I and the Plan Voisin was merely one of modality; there were many architects who deplored the twice-missed opportunity that reconstruction represented for the profession immediately after the two world wars and their processions of ruins. The turn that reconstruction took in Berlin after the fall of the wall says enough about the ambiguity that attaches to the notion of "reconstruction" when it is not mitigated (in the absence of any project in good and due form, like Auguste Perret's program for Le Havre) by thinking that is actively "deconstructive" in the most radical sense of the word: that is, tearing down all presuppositions underpinning the connection architecture tends to maintain with construction in the sense understood by Blondel—namely, the art of building, viewed in its relationship to matter and not just to *disegno*. Bramante's ambitious aedilic endeavors, such as pulling down Old St. Peter's Basilica, and his great aborted projects (at the time of his death, the "new" St. Peter's rose only a few centimeters above the ground) earned him the nickname *maestro ruinante*. The time had not yet come when, a good distance from Ground Zero in Lower Manhattan, metropolises would spring up in a matter of a few years from the deserts of the Middle East, much as they did just after the Flood, based on something like a throw of the dice, which is meant to abolish terror, or outsmart it, yet which leaves open the question of the relationship that the art of building might today maintain with some form of thought.

From the invention of the ruins of Pompeii to the erection of a house in the shape of Noah's Ark[35] based on the plans of Margit Kropholler (an architect of the Amsterdam School), the specter of the final catastrophe has never ceased to haunt the imagination of modernity, just as the specter of decline haunted the classical age. The film industry did not wait for the terrorist attacks of September 11, 2001, to impose the icon of "the disaster movie" (*filme catastrophe*): the towering inferno, of which the image of the *Titanic* standing hull in the air before it sank like a stone is but one variant—the myth of the ocean liner having prevailed for a time over the myth of the ark. But the term *catastrophe* does not only have apocalyptic connotations. It can also be understood in a more *extended* sense, as in the theory of the same name. This remains as valid in matters of architecture as in others, the mathematical theory precisely described as "catastrophe theory" finding in the art of building a privileged domain of application; a building, a built structure, a "construction," however provisional, must first stand up, the way a boat must first float and a plane must fly. ("If we built a plane the way we build a house, it wouldn't fly," Jean Prouvé liked to say.) A matter of arithmetic, you might say, as long as we give ourselves the means to allow for discontinuity and all forms of rupture, fracture, general instability, and disequilibrium.[36] Take a "modern" example, though one that is not without precedent in Gothic or Renaissance architecture (think of the solution Brunelleschi brought to bear on the problem presented by the dome of Florence Cathedral, which took the form of a double brick hull): it turns out that as a tall building goes up it encounters a certain number of "catastrophe points," which can now be precisely pinpointed, each one corresponding to a threshold beyond which a different structural solution is required. Above fifty stories, the traditional system of concrete construction is no longer open to improvement and must give way to tubular structures that are themselves contained within precise limits. We might agree with René Thom that the set of these catastrophe points, or breakpoints, combined with the set of "regular points" that correspond to a continuous, noncatastrophic development, defines the substrate space of the morphology concerned, on the basis of which objects are produced—in this case, buildings. The fact that morphologies, if not morphogenesis (as Thom calls the theory that aims to account not only for the appearance of forms but also for their emergence and disappearance), are back on the agenda of mathematical science today is an indicator of a major epistemological shift. But it is no less significant that architecture itself seeks to make a return as a theoretical object (and as a domain of objects) at a time when the threat of widespread catastrophe has become so commonplace that we cannot continue pretending to wait for the means to vanquish it through the art of building. How could it be risked, when modern architecture's own relationship to catastrophe too often takes the form that Le Corbusier meant when, upon discovering New York, he wrote "a catastrophe, but a beautiful and worthy catastrophe"[37]—though now without an aesthetic effect to redeem the social or ecological mess?

The form of tabula rasa, if not a hole, to which the place known as Ground Zero now corresponds in Lower Manhattan does not invalidate the thesis underlying the organization of articles devoted to architecture in the *Encyclopédie*. The al-Qaeda operatives hit hard and on target (at least technically speaking), so much so that some people have felt the attackers had some knowledge of the catastrophe points affecting very high buildings. But even if the World Trade Center might seem to take after the Tower of Babel more than after Noah's Ark, its destruction was not by natural or divine forces but solely by human malice in its most detestable form. Yet architecture will gain no supplement to its soul, or to its existence, by attempting to anticipate the worst, in whatever form that might take—even the threat of a latent apocalypse.

In their own way, the Tower of Babel and Noah's Ark form a matching pair, even if two distinct and opposed operations are involved. The myth of Babel aims at a kind of advertisement with fundamentally political overtones: any human endeavor attributable to a united community is subject to a limit; past a certain threshold, catastrophe threatens, linked as it is to a change of scale, and that is where the story ends.[38] When it comes to the Flood, by contrast, catastrophe takes its place at the beginning of the tale, which is all that is needed to relativize it; whatever the extent of the disaster, the world order was not fundamentally altered by it, not even the classification of species, each one being reduced to a stock that was meant to find a place in the ark, wherein reigned a peace unknown since the Fall. And if Yahweh did not, in this case, find any remedy for his anger toward humanity other than its extermination, then what some take as his good will leave open the possibility of regeneration based on the branch whose survival the ark ensured for as long as the Flood lasted. After forty days, the retreat of the waters marked the start of a new human colony, where the survivors, after seeing to its unloading, abandoned the masterpiece of naval architecture to which they were indebted for having saved them from the disaster and once more got their bearings on dry land, each reinventing, on their own and all together, a new, if still tribal, way of living in this world. The alphabetical order of the *Encyclopédie* that called for the entry "Ark" to come just a bit before the entry "Architecture" was, in the end, neither fortuitous nor arbitrary. Architecture could only find its place *after* the Flood—or rather, in its stead.

1 AUJOURD'HUI, L'ARCHITECTURE

What can we learn, today, from architecture? Or, better (though this is already another question), what place does this branch of human activity hold in our culture, this activity that has been, for more than two thousand years, in one form or another, for better or for worse, one of the main agents of the transformation of the world and its hominization, all the while putting its stamp deeply on Western thought? At the end of a century that has seen the built realm grow more in a few decades than in its entire history, but that has also experienced unprecedented destruction from war, as well as every kind of misfortune, catastrophe, violence, and ruination, in all of which architecture has itself been implicated, this is certainly no moment to reassert the confidence of the first masters of the modern movement. If some are still concerned with a resolutely architectural way of thinking, still most professionals are turning toward other branches of knowledge for the apparatus they need, reducing it to a simple tool. In this, they have more or less deliberately abandoned the formerly conceptual and philosophical dimension of their practice, without taking account of what history, sociology, political economics, semiology, and through to information technology might owe to architectonic metaphors—the utopia of Le Corbusier's *Vers une architecture.*[1]

The relatively reduced importance given to the art of building in critical and speculative literature is a good indication of its devaluation in the contemporary cultural field. We need only refer to the favorable treatment that our philosophers reserve for painting, or what remains of it, in order to measure the regime change imposed on reflection since the time, not so distant, when Paul Valéry recognized in *construction* an operation analogous to that of language, an act comparable to *knowing* (though who today still reads *Eupalinos*?).[2] Is this, as is often repeated, the fault of modernist ideology, which under its double cover as functionalism and abstraction would have succeeded in stripping the art of building of all semantic value, reducing it to products devoid of meaning? Even if equating architecture to an act of communication is no more self-evident than reducing it to a set of functions, the paradox is that "modern" architecture should become so unbearable to so many people at the very moment when, having broken with the recurring fantasy of an *architecture parlante*, it might seem in practice to have revived the symbolic phase of art: the phase that, in Hegel's terms, best corresponds to its concept. For Hegel, the symbol in some way implied a natural alliance between signifier and signified, in which signification imposes itself as such, avoiding the detour through the sign—with the exception that although, as Hegel states, "whole nations have been able to express their religion and their deepest needs no otherwise than by building, or at least in the main in some constructional way,"[3] the representations evoked by architecture today amount to plays of oppositions that are partly emblematic, such as the opposition between the skyscraper and the suburban house, and the ideas and values displayed by architecture are far from having unanimous support. It is nevertheless not the fault of modernist ideology to have wished that humanity, like the ancient gods, be housed suitably in an environment created by architecture. The disappointment is all the more poignant in the face of the avant-gardes' long-held dream for architecture to participate in the construction of a new world (architecture *and* revolution)—when they were not casting it, in Le Corbusier's terms, as the sole antidote to revolution (architecture *or* revolution). A sign of the times: having run out of inspiration, *Waiting for Godot*'s Estragon cannot find any worse insult than that of "architect!"[4]

At a moment when criticism, lacking an identity, complacently pins on the "postmodern" label and pretends to renew the threads of a history that the modern movement, in its desire for a radical break with the past, chose to ignore, it seems the time is ripe to unravel the complicated skein of relations Western thought has historically maintained with the art of building, or at the very least to test the idea (the suspicion?) that the "crisis" in architecture today might be prompted by causes beyond the economic or ideological. These determinations of a more secret order are connected, beyond the sphere of artistic practices, to the history—if not to the very economy—of thought. Not that philosophers in the past have gone to any great lengths to deal with architecture as such; with a few exceptions—foremost among them Hegel, whose passages on the column rank among the best articulated texts on the subject—reference to the art of building has been essentially of a metaphorical order. In *Discourse on Method*, Descartes sets "buildings which a single architect has planned and executed" against those which "several have attempted to put together by using old walls that have been built for other purposes" and contrasts "those well-ordered places that an engineer has freely planned on an open plain" with ancient cities that start out as simple villages and become, over time, large towns "that are irregularly laid out."[5] Such a development might well have only a rhetorical function, serving to introduce the philosopher's plan to reform, if not the world, then at least his own thoughts, building on a foundation that was uniquely his own. Nonetheless, he shows—just as Plato does in his description of prehistoric Athens in the *Critias*, or of the ideal city of the Magnesians in Book Four of the *Laws*—a remarkable attention to the specific characteristics of the built environment and to its concrete conditions in practice, while at the same time understanding the significance, historical as much as epistemological, of a *topos* through which is revealed (if need be, in the form of a utopia) the truly architectonic dimension of the workings of thought.

This would still mean nothing if, as the philosopher admits, the art of building did not occupy a unique place within the field of productive activities, divine as well as human. The metaphor of God the architect, which in the classical age would take on the appearance of a foundational paradox, was already at work in Plato. The demiurge of the *Timaeus* is set up as the archetype of the architect par excellence: was he not given the task of constructing the world in the image of an ideal model, following the lines of a calculation, that aimed at realizing "a work by its nature the most beautiful and best"?[6] But does not the architecture of mankind itself take part, if to a lesser degree, in that singular form of *mimesis* that owes nothing to imitation (in the sense of the figurative arts[7]) but claims instead to be equal to *mathesis*, if not indistinguishable from it? Whereas the other arts, including music, are essentially reduced to conjecture and to an operation of the senses based on hearing or sight, the art of the builder derives from a higher order of knowledge, one that assumes not only the use of precision instruments but also systematic recourse to number and measure. In the final analysis, the fact remains that *topos* operates with much more force than the work of architecture at the same time as it provides the example, at the level of the project, of the most subtle conjunction between *mimesis* and *mathesis*, corresponding in its effects and in its very regularity, its symmetry, to what Hegel regarded as "a purely external reflection of spirit."[8]

From the perspective of a genetic epistemology, it is certain that a number of familiar notions are propped up, even today, by reference to the art of building. At a higher level, the fact that the eminently technical analyses of a Viollet-le-Duc paved the way for structuralism makes it clear how significant the architectural model has been in our culture through to the present. It is all the more symptomatic that at the moment when the appearance in the built realm of original, if not unforeseen, structures (those qualifying as "self-supporting," reticulated or supported on continuous sheets of concrete) seems to contradict one of the precepts on which is founded not the method or thought of structuralism but its ideology (an ideology that requires structures to be finite in number and envisaged a priori applicable to any domain)—a moment when architectural theory (or what stands in lieu of it) is drawing attention to itself through the massive and often uncontrolled importation of notions borrowed from disciplines that define themselves as following in the footsteps of structuralism—it is at this moment that the architectural paradigm seems to have lost all critical and heuristic force, to be reduced to a simple stylistic figure. Having claimed to discern in culture, with Claude Lévi-Strauss (if not in the unconscious, with Jacques Lacan), "an architecture similar to that of language,"[9] we have come, with Jacques Derrida, to propose the task of philosophy as one of *deconstructing* the web of conceptual oppositions that have made up the most constant armature of Western metaphysics (inside/outside, closed/open, continuous/discontinuous, etc.). Architectural practice may well seem to be out of place in our culture—a defection that goes hand in hand with a far more durable and profound eclipse: that of a settled model of coherence (fundamental if not foundational), an archetype of which would be the work of architecture.

Fates of a Metaphor

Our science has chosen to have no other object than what is defined and established by its operations. It constitutes its knowledge by means of formal or experimental models that display their structure and that can be subjected to any variations and transformations at will. The scientist either conceives them from scratch or borrows their schematics by analogy from another area of research or activity. Yet even if he purports to eliminate all reference to concrete imagination, the devices he resorts to nonetheless correspond (merely by virtue of the fact that they proceed from a *construction*) to a concern for order and balance, perhaps even for harmony, symmetry, or elegance, the architectonic connotation of which can be more or less pronounced. These kinds of models cannot in fact function as such, nor can they have any usefulness, any operational value, unless their economy is rigorous and systematic enough to allow a modification in any one of their parts to be reflected, according to a preconceived sequence, in their overall organization. Similarly, in the twelfth century, the substitution of ribbed vaults for the compact vault led, step by step, and following an implacable logic over the course of the century, to the complete overturning of medieval building structures. Again, an epistemological model cannot take into account all aspects of the phenomenon under consideration; the *parti* to which it responds, like any construction that claims to be "functional," implies a choice among the empirical givens and the elimination of a certain number of parameters (as we see, for example, with Galileo's construction of the experimental model of bodies falling in a vacuum). In the same way, the abstraction of an architectural project assumes that some sort of order has been introduced among the elements of the program, since the architectural form is unable, in any circumstance, to display all the functions to which the building must answer.

Science manipulates things, said Maurice Merleau-Ponty; it has given up trying to *inhabit* them.[10] The world in which man has his place, if not his dwelling, well before he attempts to form a systematic representation of it, is a world the scientist is happy to posit as object x of his operations. No doubt, contemporary science is not worried whether or not its constructions reduplicate the "real" scheme of the universe, of which it strives only to set up a coherent model. It is all the more significant to see it unwittingly close itself up when, for example, it claims to account for the working of the brain in terms borrowed from information technology in a circle analogous to the one established, this time deliberately, by the creators of mathematical physics.

The fate of architectonic metaphors in the philosophy and sciences of nature, from Plato to Leibniz and beyond, is too complex for us to deal with here; we will confine ourselves to the decisive overthrow of the figure of God the architect in modern cosmology. Whereas for Plato human art was reduced to simulating the operation of divine *mimesis*, using instruments of *mathesis*, such was the prestige bestowed upon the work of architecture in the classical age that Johannes Kepler did not hesitate to confirm the image of a creator God, in a kind of retrospective projection, by referring to the art of building: "I need not stress how important a witness my subject is for the act of creation, questioned as it is by philosophers. For here we may behold how God, like a master-builder, has laid the foundation of the world according to order and law, and how He has measured all things so carefully, that we might well judge it is not nature that human art copies, but that God in His very creation was thinking of the way in which man yet unborn would be building one day."[11]

By this, Kepler did not mean to reduce divine thought to human thought or the brilliance of the "divine temple" to the light given out by the architecture of men: "The work of those who wish to understand the Creator through His creatures, God through men, . . . is no more useful than that of those who wish to understand the curved through the straight, and the circle through the square."[12] The metaphor developed in the *Mysterium Cosmographicum*, from the dedication on, in fact revives Plato's argument: the works of so-called Nature were only able to come into existence as the result of a spontaneous, "automatic" cause, whose action would not have been accompanied by thought; they were produced according to reason and carry the mark of a divine science.[13] But the progress of modern science, and even the project formed by Kepler, could not occur without conferring a new status on the figure of an architect God. What the Platonists merely glimpsed—the existence of a harmonic order to the world ("that occult harmony that keeps discordant elements in proper concord," as Philibert de l'Orme had already written at the beginning of the first volume of his *Architecture*[14])—was confirmed by the dynamic approach to celestial phenomena and the search for the causes of the movement of the planets. The quantitative relationships that Kepler set himself the task of revealing are merely so many "signatures" the Creator left on his work.

But there is more: The reversal sketched in the dedication of the *Mysterium* ("We might think that . . .") in fact echoes a movement characteristic of a hypothesis at the same time that it appeals to *mimesis*, in the strict sense of the word, which puts two productive subjects on stage rather than assuming a resemblance between two things produced. If it might seem that God was inspired to create the world by the architecture of a future mankind, this is because science itself can only know anything via some kind of construction. Such a construction—if we keep to the model proposed in this youthful work of Kepler's, which brought him to the attention of the scientific world—is essentially static and designed according to the norms of spatial geometry, based as it was on the five regular polyhedrons. What is interesting, then, is what happens to the architectonic metaphor when Kepler moves from a static to a dynamic vision of cosmic order, carrying his investigations to bear not just on the metric proportions that govern the spatial distribution of the planets but also on the chronological relationships of their movements: "Once the world appears less like a monument built according to an architect's plans than like a ballet danced or a chorus sung according to a composer's score, it is revealed that the divine geometer was also and firstly a holy musician."[15]

There is no antimony here, to the classical mind. Briefly, and speaking figuratively once again—even if the figure is anachronistic and somewhat old-fashioned—I refer to the legend of Amphion, as fashioned by Valéry: "Amphion, man, received the lyre from Apollo. Music was born in his fingers. At the sound of the nascent music, the stones moved and joined, and architecture was created." Architecture, to which the mind is indebted for "the very idea of construction, which is the passage from disorder to order and the use of the arbitrary to attain necessity,"[16] is an operation whose effects are felt without distinction in both synchrony and diachrony, both in the form of a simultaneous ordering of parts and in their sequential arrangement, as is the case with music or speech. According to its legend, architecture emerged from music, but in return, it was in architecture that music reflected itself and became aware of its means. This might lead one to believe that when Kepler's God created the world, he took his model from the future Amphion. Thus, while everything depended on the will of God (this was to be Descartes's thesis), he obviously did not will anything without reason (this was to be Leibniz's thesis), as witnessed by "the artistic structure of the movements" and the astonishing metric and cinematic relationships that make the world "a wonderfully organized work of art."[17]

The world is not mute: it speaks, and even sings, as Valéry's Eupalinos would say of the most exceptional works of human architecture.[18] This implies that we do not treat it only as a system at rest but also in its regular functioning. The reference to art is decisive here, in that there is access to meaning only in the moment of its production, in the action of its enunciation—with the proviso that divine art, which leaves no room for the contingent, the arbitrary, or the conventional, is radically distinct from the art of men, which suffers under these conditions (and this is so, no matter what value certain celestial phenomena, which seem to elude the regular course of things, may have as *signs*). And how could it be otherwise? For "geometry, which before the origin of things was coeternal with the divine mind and is God himself (for what could there be in God which would not be God himself?), supplied God with patterns for the creation of the world, and passed over to Man along with the image of God; and was not in fact taken in through the eyes."[19] In the final analysis, for Kepler, the order of the world was such that the structure that seems to be the condition of meaning itself, through the play of a paradoxical *mimesis*, has a symbolic determination. The revelation expressed in the spectacle of the heavens is accessible to the eye of the mind alone. It does not lend itself to interpretation or to being translated into the terms of human language. The meaning that fills the world can be understood only by one who follows the ways and speaks the language of God, the (sacred) mathematics that is the first principle of things, even as it reveals their necessity.

Doubtless, this shift can most easily be seen in Leibniz. It will lead to a new meaning for the idea of architectonic rationality while at the same time driving an ever more pronounced and problematic rift between the functional constructional order and the semantic order. In his classifications, Leibniz consistently associated architecture with mechanics, astronomy, and strategy—all disciplines in his system, based on a calculation of effects wherein considerations of order were allied (as in Kepler) to those of harmony and finality.[20] Leibniz's lifelong project of a universal characteristic, employing symbols that could be used in invention and evaluation (new notions never proceeding, apparently, except by combining already acquired notions), itself echoed the work long accomplished by architects. Would the architecture of his day not have furnished Leibniz with the model for an *art of inventing* that could in essence be reduced to the combination of preexisting elements: columns, pilasters, entablatures, niches, pediments, and so on? The institution of a *universal* architecture, like that of a universal language, presupposes the elaboration of a preliminary lexicon—if not an alphabet, then an index of signs at once simple and "motivated."[21] These either present some trait or property of the signified (such as the column, in Vitruvian interpretation, made in imitation of the tree trunks that were used as supports in primitive architecture and proportioned according to the canons of the human body) or they are the object of a *real* definition that would articulate—by progressing from a vault or arch as from a circle or a series—the generating principle, the law, of construction.

The dream of a universal language that reflects the innate logic of the human mind has not lost all its authority. The dream of an architecture that would ultimately exclude all idiomatic difference has become a reality, for better or worse, in a world where the same body of construction techniques and functional principles has imposed itself everywhere as the common substance of architectural expression. That substance is, in the end, hardly subtle, and even vulgar. That being the case, it is not surprising that the architectonic metaphor has essentially ceased to inform a thinking that now works on constructions that are infinitely more complex, flexible, and mobile than those built structures on which the model was founded. This holds true except for the models of mathematicians, who remain attached to the notion of an "architecture of mathematics," which appeals less to the economy of a finished building than to the endless extensions, improvements, alterations, and transformations of urban space—to say nothing of the noted innovations in construction, which demonstrate that the repertoire of built structures is in no way immutable or closed, and at the same time bear witness (even in the absence of any explicit reference to the problem of "foundations") to the distance covered in this domain since Descartes's day.[22]

Yet constructional figures continue to circulate (surreptitiously) here and there. For it is true that science, even in its most sophisticated forms, cannot make progress without maintaining a few points of contact if not with common sense then at least with common language. Confining ourselves to the sphere of the "human" sciences and more especially to linguistics—the only one of these that can rightfully lay claim to "exactitude"—we note how after Saussure the linguists of his day made use of the terms *structure* and *construction* to account for word formation and, among other things, the slow "cementing" of elements that ends by agglutination in a synthesis whereby the original units are completely obliterated.[23] This is a notion of structure analogous to the notion we find in Vitruvius, who regularly associates the term *structure* with the continuity of masonry that uses bricks or stones embedded in mortar to ensure its cohesion.[24] But the comparison works at the level of systems themselves when Merleau-Ponty, illustrating the diacritical concept of the sign developed in *A Course in General Linguistics*, defines the unity of a language as a "unity of coexistence" comparable to "that of the elements of a vault that support one another"[25]—the play of metaphor implying, here as there, a design that is no longer merely static but dynamic, the model of which the philosopher might well have found in Viollet-le-Duc.

No doubt, the significance of such metaphors should not be exaggerated, given the context in which they operate. Nonetheless, the notion of *structure*, like that of *system*, owes something (genealogically speaking) to the consideration of constructional, if not architectural, issues. Given developments in structural anthropology, it is not correct to say that these concepts are exclusively linguistic in origin. Pierre Francastel has rightly reminded us of their sources in construction.[26] It is in the art of building that the notion of structure finds not only its etymology but also its natural iconography, and it is through the treatises on architecture—starting with the English translation of Alberti's *De re aedificatoria*—that the word has seen its semantic field gradually broaden. Structure, *struere*, to construct: Émile Littré did not fail to note the filiation that justifies the use of the term in both the technical and epistemological senses. When we say "structure," we actually think *construction*: construction of a house, but also construction of a model. There is no point in trying to make an absolute distinction between the two uses of the word, because it may well be that a building also takes on the value of a model— both for the architects, who work at reproducing or varying the building's layout, and for the theorist, who recognizes it as the product of a construction *raisonnée*.

All considerations of number and harmony aside (though such considerations are undoubtedly not to be excluded ultimately), the architectural work carries at once the idea of an *order*, that of a *necessity*, and a *purpose*: an order that can be read in the composition of the whole, in the distribution of parts, and the combination of elements; a necessity that follows from the laws of solid mechanics and the resistance of materials; and, lastly, a purpose that either derives from an ideal principle or is understood in a strictly utilitarian sense. The one does not exclude the other: Kant defines architecture as "the art of presenting concepts of things which are possible only through art, and the determining ground of whose form is not nature but an arbitrary end," while stressing that what is essential in an architectural work remains its conformity to a certain use.[27] In fact, the distinction between buildings that are designed in principle to pure, technically utilitarian ends and those that take on symbolic or representative functions is not always self-evident. The temple mountains of Angkor Wat, for instance, were inserted into the hydraulic network that ensured the irrigation of rice paddies, thus guaranteeing, in terms of symbolic economy, the regulated operation of the system. Conversely, Walter Gropius and Le Corbusier were able to use the beauty of the great grain silos of North America to justify the project of a strictly functional architecture to no less effect. It is never easy to make a *theory* out of any building—to decide on the nature of the principles that govern the ordering of structures and forms within the framework of any given system: the *calculation* of which Leibniz speaks. How can we define and *characterize* this calculation, and with it the reasoning that obtains in the architecture of mankind, if the technical and functional register never ceases to interfere with the symbolic and even semantic register—notwithstanding the possibility of confusing the "two"?

The Word, the Thing, and the Appeal to the Concept

It is precisely because the work of architecture seems to offer an example of an ordered device—one that allows itself to be applied, simultaneously or alternately, as a system of functions and as a system of signs—that it has managed to maintain a semblance of relevance for thinking informed by the linguistic model. Even Saussure himself, when seeking to illustrate the mechanism of language and the two kinds of relationships on which it relies, syntagmatic and associative (today we would say paradigmatic), compares the linguistic units that compose speech to the parts of a building—notably, to the column.[28] For a column, Doric or otherwise, belongs simultaneously to two orders of coordination: one real (or syntagmatic), corresponding to the axis of combinations, and the other virtual (or paradigmatic), corresponding to the axis of substitutions. Two sets of forms "float" around the column: On the one hand, the column maintains a relationship with the elements that come before or after it in space (the base or stylobate on which it rests, the architrave or arch that it supports), a relationship comparable to that which links the consecutive elements of the spoken sequence within the framework of speech. On the other hand, the column (like any term borrowed from the lexicon of architecture) calls to mind, through a play of mental associations, the group of forms to which it is related: columns of different orders, piers, pillars, and supports of all kinds, and even the wall whose negation it represents.

The comparison between the order of speech and the order of architecture calls for serious critical caution. This is particularly true in light of what Saussure says about the mechanism of language: a mechanism that, if it were entirely rational, we could study on its own and for its own sake, but that in fact amounts to nothing more than a partial correction to a naturally chaotic system.[29] Indeed, we might be tempted to say the opposite of architecture. But if the comparison were to be truly convincing, then it ought to work both ways. We would then inevitably be led (as long as we did not look too closely) to see architecture as a system of signs or—*and this comes down to the same thing*—as a system of functions, even if we admit (with Roland Barthes) that a function is necessarily penetrated by meaning and that the same element, the same *function-sign*, can be put to work, simultaneously or alternately, for its use-value and for its sign-value. A system of functions as such necessarily lends itself to functioning not only as a system of differences but also as a system of groups. The selection of any unit whatsoever will be made according to a double mental opposition, the idea (the function) calling not for some determined form but for an entire latent system through which are obtained the oppositions involved in the constitution of a sign.[30] If the column takes on (or can take on) value as a sign, this is not so much through the relationship that binds it vertically to the elements with which it combines as it is through the distinctive lateral relations it maintains with other forms that represent so many different variations of the notion of a support.

The tradition, therefore, had a few good reasons to consecrate the column as one of the privileged members of architecture (Alberti even recognized it as "the principal ornament in the whole art of building"[31]), regardless of whether the persistent recurrence of this form throughout history could be explained by the universality of the function to which it corresponds or by a determination—at once semantic and formal—that has played out across the diversity of cultures and eras in ways we still do not understand. With respect to this quandary, it would be a good exercise to reread Hegel's commentaries on the column (here we will only focus on those that might serve our purposes, though the entire essay should really be quoted).[32] Born of a form borrowed from the natural world of plants, the column in classical architecture becomes a support for rational and regular forms. With the column, architecture emerges from the purely organic world only to be restricted (as Kant clearly saw) to a partly double finality: on the one hand, to the need to satisfy, and on the other, to autonomy, the *Selbständigkeit*, exercised without any precise aim. As a sign, the column provides proof, in its very appearance, of the labor at stake in it: a labor in which arbitrariness and necessity constantly exchange masks, a labor that plays at will with all of the motivations from which its form emerges. The column has no role but to bear weight. Yet its independence in relation to its context is marked from the outset in its circular section, which clearly demonstrates that it only acts as a support on its own account and that, unlike a square pillar, it does not lend itself to forming a continuous wall through adhesion. Contrary to Alberti's definition, which does not take into account this nevertheless decisive feature, the column cannot be regarded as a fragment of a wall but owes its value as a sign, as well as in plastic terms, to the fact that it is irreducible to the wall.[33] But its independence is further marked by the fact that its beginning and end, its base and capital, can be displayed in and for themselves,

as moments that rightly belong to it alone. Whereas organic formations are endowed with an immanent reason that delimits
their forms from within, "for the column and its shape," Hegel
writes, "architecture has nothing but the mechanical determination of load-bearing and the spatial distance from the ground to
the point where the load to be carried terminates the column. But
the particular aspects implicit in this determinant belong to the
column, and art must bring them out and give shape to them."[34]

This would still be nothing if the work of art did not correspond, at root, to a determination that we would say was logical, since it refers back to what provides the very condition for
the development of architectural thought: "Columns are indeed
load-carrying and they do form a boundary, but they do not enclose anything; on the contrary, they are the precise opposite of
an interior closed on all sides by walls."[35] It would be hard to put
it more accurately or more concisely. But surely we cannot fail to
see that what Hegel is well on the way to defining here is nothing less than a logical system of architecture, the philosophical
resonances of which are obvious. In other words, the operation
of *constructing* has not only structural but also topological implications. If the column plays an essential role in the classical system, this is because it forces the distinction between two
functions that are blurred by the wall, that of an *enclosure* and that
of a *limit*, at the same time as it contradicts the oversimplified
opposition between the inside and the outside as well as between
the two spatial modalities—the "interior" in its finiteness, if not
its enclosure, and the "exterior" in its indefinite openness.

Faced with such a model of *deconstruction*—one that corre-
lates, so to speak, with the labor of construction of which it is an
integral part—we are forced to admit that thought still has something to learn from the art of building. This assumes that thought
lends itself to playing its own game and that, rather than miming
its operations, it takes up residence, inhabits, and allows itself

to be taught by architecture even when architecture abandons what has long passed for its most beautiful ornament. "I don't like to say *columns*," Le Corbusier once said. "The word has been spoiled."[36] Spoiled the word no doubt is, and irrecoverable, irrecuperable, irremediably worn out, as perhaps is its form, which created its semantic function. There remains the thing, together with the appeal that emanates from it—an appeal to the future of the concept and of building itself.

2.1
Leon Battista Alberti, Palazzo Rucellai, Florence,
1447. Photo: Alinari/Art Resource, New York.

2   THE COLUMN, THE WALL

If we are to believe Viollet-le-Duc, the Renaissance, nourished as it was on Vitruvian literature, had nothing but contempt for structure; the classical architect simply supplied the form in the shape of a drawing, and the mason translated it as best he could and as the materials at his disposal allowed, a process that paved the way for all kinds of mistranslations.[1] "Tota res aedificatoria lineamentis et structura constituta est":[2] the first great treatise on architecture of modern times, Alberti's *De re aedificatoria*, takes its point of departure from an explicit distinction between *form* and *matter*, if not between *design* and *structure*. But how are we to understand "form" or "structure" in this instance? When one speaks of structure today, it is in terms of assembly, a combination of discrete elements, and consequently of discontinuity, whereas the definition of form, understood in its unity and essential coherence, implies continuity. We are inclined, since Viollet-le-Duc, to think of structure in terms of frames and articulated, discontinuous systems. Yet the Romans, and Vitruvius above all, would have associated the word *structure* with the continuity of masonry—brick and stones set in mortar to ensure its cohesion.[3]

Was Alberti, then, simply the precursor, still hesitant and sometimes feeling his way, of a classicism that was to become only truly self-aware in the sixteenth century? And was his treatise, in the end, less important theoretically than historically, as Anthony Blunt claimed, with its historical importance largely due to the fact that it contained the first modern exposé of the doctrine of orders and the rule of proportions? Whereas Brunelleschi chose to use the column in a deliberately antique spirit (but with the greatest liberty and with little respect for ancient canons), Alberti developed the principles of a rigorous classicism based on a deeper knowledge of antique monuments. Beyond this, he also had the distinction of having recourse to the orders in order to resolve the compositional problem of multi-story facades—linking and superimposing columns and entablatures in order to organize them in a grid, the clarity of which was to become an element of the best Tuscan tradition. Despite this, we still had to wait for the second half of the sixteenth century to see the principles and rules he formulated enter into architectural practice: the Doric column only made its appearance in 1509, in Bramante's *tempietto*, and Italian architects—to say nothing of those further afield—were to hesitate for a long time before employing the orders in codified form.[4]

Art historians have accounted for the delay between Alberti's first formulation of the classical norms and their systematic use in practice by the need to discriminate between the value of the column as a constructive and a decorative element. Doubtless, the column first had to lose its place as the unique architectonic element (as it was for the Greeks) before it could be accepted as one of the privileged terms of what was to become the language of ornament.[5] The use of orders applied to a wall clearly derived from the Roman tradition, Alberti himself having acknowledged that it was of *Latin*, even *Italic*, rather than Greek, origin. Yet if it is clear that he had intended to create a doctrinal work, what does it mean for the theoretical foundations of a doctrine to be based on Roman models? In fact, the brief and deliberately cursory exposition of the doctrine of the five orders appears only in Book Nine of his treatise; the preceding books were devoted to a critical analysis of the elements of the art of building, as Alberti attempted to put his observations into good order and—as his first French translator, Jean Martin, put it—"to give to each thing the proper reasons concerning the matter."[6] This poses a problem: could Alberti have known enough to press his analysis far enough to expose the contradiction inherent in the classical doctrine and in the use of the classical orders in the context of what is now commonly understood as *wall architecture*?

Rudolf Wittkower was the first to read *De re aedificatoria* without attempting to trace early signs of the classical doctrine, following instead the reasoning that led Alberti to distance himself from the Roman ideal on one essential point: the use of the column as an element of an order applied to a wall.[7]"In the whole art of building the column is the principal ornament," Alberti wrote. "There is nothing to be found in the art of building that deserves more care and expense, or ought to be more graceful, than the column."[8] These formulae seem to be completely in line with the first Florentine Renaissance and with an architecture that Brunelleschi had understood to be defined by the column as well as the dome.[9]

Yet Alberti considered the column from a very different perspective than that of Brunelleschi. He criticized the early Christian basilica for its light wooden roofing supported by rows of slender columns (which were also often reused, introducing an additional factor of "disorder"), which appeared to him to contradict the "dignity" of sacred building and against which he set up the model of a vaulted building, the roof of which was to be supported by thick walls.[10] He advocated the use of the classical orders to animate and break up the continuous surfaces (*parois*), the uniformity of which is tiring to the eye.[11] All these theoretical assertions, formulated before their execution in his projects for the Palazzo Rucellai in Florence (in 1447) and Sant'Andrea in Mantua (in 1470), testify to a change of direction that would prove decisive for the evolution of architecture in the classical and/or the baroque period. Whatever Bruneslleschi's taste in the treatment of surfaces, the projection of an articulated structural scheme on a neutral wall (*paroi*)—following the principles of early Christian architecture—in which the column in combination with the arch plays the leading role, seems to contradict the very principle of wall architecture associated with Alberti's name. Does this mean that Alberti's definition of the column necessarily implies abandoning the system outlined by Brunelleschi, one which Alberti himself was pleased to celebrate for its novelty, and the study of which—as much as that of the monuments of antiquity—strengthened his doctrine?

If we accept Wittkower's interpretation of the passages in *De re aedificatoria* devoted to the problem of the column, then it would seem that we have to accept that Alberti thought of architecture in terms of a continuous structure, in the Roman sense, and that he held the column to be an essentially decorative element and, as such, subordinate to the wall. His definition equating an order of columns with a wall that is pierced and open in several places[12] seems to be a misinterpretation of the Greek system, in which the column is presented as a formal unit independent of, and diametrically opposed to, the wall. However, it is in fact situated in a direct line of descent that can be traced to architecture of the twelfth-century Tuscan Proto-Renaissance and the Late Imperial period, whose arcaded street facades and engaged columns provided Alberti with his model.[13]

Despite this apparently surprising definition, Alberti may have understood the true significance of the column and of the Hellenic orders better than any other architect of his time. Certainly, if the column is reduced to being a part of the wall, it is difficult to see how its cylindrical form could be justified. Yet if we consider not the engaged column but the freestanding, independent column, we find that, in accordance with an architectonic principle that he twice formulated in his treatise forbidding the discontinuity of superimposed members, Alberti rejects the idea of a square arch—which would itself be cut out, so to speak, from the mass of the wall—resting on a cylindrical support. Although he accepts the column as being a support for a horizontal architrave, Alberti nevertheless requires (except in the case of small-scale buildings) an arch to be regularly combined with a pier, whether or not engaged to half columns (as would Viollet-le-Duc). Otherwise, the "building" (*construction*)—as he puts it in a singularly "modern" way, thereby setting off a train of formulations that would turn out to be particularly productive—would be "false."[14] But in this strict distinction between the functions of the column and those of the pier, and in restricting the specifically architectonic value of the column by associating it with the entablature, does not Alberti show himself to be as much Greek as Roman? Hence Wittkower's conclusion: if the emphasis placed on the wall is essentially Roman, then the limits placed on the use of the column are tied to the logic of the Greek system.[15]

What, then, is a *wall*? What is the logic that defines and characterizes it? Beyond this, what is the logic that might be imposed on the building as a whole? It is clear that if there is a contradiction between column and wall, it arises at a level of coherence distinct from the strictly constructional, one related to the plastic properties that are irreducible to the simple mechanics of solids. But if the principles of combinatorial order that come into play at this level take on a logical value, are they in fact necessary, bound up as they are with the very nature of the wall (if there is such a thing as "nature" in this case)? In the absence of a portico set some distance from the wall, why would the pilaster be better suited to the wall than would the engaged column? And why should a wall present a rigorously flat surface purged of all accident? Then again, what is the origin of the Renaissance and baroque taste for facades with diamond-pointed rustication? Is a facing with cyclopean rustication and huge, rough-hewn blocks any closer to the "essence" of the wall than the smooth, whitish surfaces characteristic of Brunelleschi's art? Brunelleschi could treat the inner walls of his basilicas like so many planes of projection, inscribed by the main lines of a space at once perspectival and architectonic; what was important for his design was that these walls be stripped of all material appearance so they could function as the imaginary support for the constructive and ordering activity of the mind.[16] Yet, as the cyclopean facade of the Pitti Palace reminds us, there is nothing immaterial about the wall, and it is hard to see how a uniform roughcast would be better adapted to the nature or essence of the wall than would a treatment perhaps rougher but more revealing of the wall's underlying structure.

More to the point, it seems as though an exaggerated respect for the planar quality of the surfaces implies a questioning of the wall itself, if not its negation. This is a paradoxical outcome to say the least, but one that we need to assess carefully if we want to understand the different modalities of wall treatments in their dialectical succession and of the use of the classical orders exemplified in the architecture of the sixteenth and seventeenth centuries. In fact, it is not enough to characterize the architecture of Michelangelo or Palladio by pointing to the emancipation of the elements of the order and to the supposedly "tragic" contradiction between the decorative frame and the surfaces it defines. For—as we see on the lower floor of the vestibule of the Laurentian Library, where the coupled columns are set back from the plane of the wall, recessed in niches opened up in its thickness, and defined by thin perpendicular pilasters, or in the application of giant orders to the facades of Vicenza or Venice— the insertion of foreign bodies into the wall does not hold only negative consequences. The conflict between members and surfaces, their interpenetration, even their exchange of roles and functions, and the whole play of inversions and permutations, as well as of calculated ambiguities that could be characterized as baroque (or even as mannerist),[17] only brings out more clearly the respective qualities of the wall and the elements of the order. On the contrary, the (partly imaginary) synthesis of frame and wall achieved by Brunelleschi, and after him by Alberti, implies the deliberate negation of the wall, whether considered in its materiality or in its continuity. Here, the emphasis placed on the *plane* of the wall in some way entails, to speak in phenomenological terms, its "neutralization"—its reduction to the status of an imaginary screen, a simple support for a plan—in the same way as Alberti's metaphor of the window in his discussion of painting is meant to correspond to the nullification of the picture plane that once ensured its transparency.

Take the wall of Santo Spirito Church in Florence as it can be seen today, after the transformations that Manetti (under Alberti's influence) contributed to Brunelleschi's initial project. With its contradictory surface of columns and niches enclosing an illusory mass—a mass that is more like an empty shell—such a wall is in no way a natural given. The structure in which historians believe they see the system's point of departure, far from being definable as a reality, is in this case the outcome of a cultural work that follows no deductive logic but rather reveals the largely regulatory, and consequently a posteriori, nature of a system like Alberti's. In the final analysis, the difficulties arising from any attempt to reduce a given architectonic system to an elementary structure—whether of wall or partition, intersecting ribs or classical orders—depends on the fact that the structures revealed by analysis are not so much objective or technical as they are logical and perhaps semantic; in fact, it is impossible to treat any architectonic element while disregarding the *value* it assumes in the context of the system. Whether Roman, Carolingian, Brunelleschi's, Alberti's, or even the wall that modern architecture is supposed to have eliminated completely, the wall is in no way a stable and unequivocal idea—and still less a simple structure that imposes its norms on the total system. Rather, it is the system itself that assigns the wall its place in the hierarchy of constitutive elements, thus endowing it with its logical value, constructing it, and setting it up where appropriate as a generative structure. In accordance with the classical order (from which the column cannot strictly speaking be deduced), the wall appears as the support for a certain number of functions, essential or discretionary, from which the systems are selected: one system stressing the load-bearing function of the wall, another its function as a screen, another the outer skin, and yet another (as we will see with Alberti) its inner articulations.

The wall, then, is not an objective idea. In fact, a wall is only a wall when it is *instituted* as such, and this institution acquires a logical and structural value depending on whether the structure operates as a generative, or merely subordinate, element of a system. That is to say, a rational inquiry into the wall cannot proceed on the assumption that it is a natural and unequivocal reality, for the oppositional, if not contradictory, relationships are inherent in the structure as such, even when the architect claims to celebrate the unity and coherence of the partitioning (*paries*). This is particularly evident in the case of Renaissance architecture (which we can indeed define as wall architecture), but only if the structure in question is understood as the site of an articulation that, even if it occasionally takes a conflictual turn, is no less essential or irreducible. This is why the architects of Alberti's generation, who considered the niches and engaged columns of Brunelleschi's Santo Spirito to contradict the principle of the continuous wall, developed in their turn a simulacrum of the wall and established in the same gesture the wall (though a contested one, a wall called into question as such) as a fundamental structure of the new architecture—as if its affirmation only had meaning in this instance with regard to its possible negation. This is the contradiction that will haunt architecture throughout the so-called mannerist period and into the age known as the baroque. Architects would strive to overcome it by superimposing a grid over the surface—or at least the elements of a false articulated framework—a combination of the classical order and the wall (and no longer just their simple opposition). In this way, the classical system, which is the basis of both mannerist and baroque experiments, was endowed with a paradoxical dimension of *truth*—albeit a truth corresponding to the fundamental intention of the system. It was Goethe who observed that despite the contradiction involved with combining columns with walls, there was something "divine" in Palladio's plans, "something comparable to the power of a great poet who, out of truth and falsehood, creates a third term whose borrowed existence enchants us."[18] Yet here one should guard against using Palladio's example to draw an overly strict division between reality and appearance, truth and lying. No longer conceived in terms of the Roman system, Goethe's "third term" in no way depends on the category of the mask; for if a mask exists, the column order and the wall can each in turn function as a mask, as a false structure overlaid on the real.

The fact remains that if the wall is seen as an institution, it is not only as a three-dimensional structure with the potential, when appropriately treated, to be used in various contexts. Even where the wall cannot be reduced to a simple simulacrum (the most frequent case), it appears as the result of a constructional operation and of an already institutionalized technique, which in turn entails a series of structural consequences that have an effect on the system as a whole. This is why, when dealing with the logic of the wall and with the problem of wall architecture, we cannot simply dismiss in a few lines Alberti's long exposition of technical developments in building and the elements composing the *paries*, that ever-privileged structure to which he devotes the first three books of his treatise. Alberti even goes so far as to use the two terms *structura* and *paries* interchangeably to designate the same reality, one that is in no way reducible to the "wall" (*mur*) in the strict sense of the term. Of the three components of the art of building that constitute the material edifice—the wall, the roof, and the openings—the *paries* comprise every vertical structure supporting a covering (in the same way that the *tectum* designates not only the roof but also any type of "covering," whether floor, ceiling, vault, etc.).[19] To translate *structura* and even *paries* as "wall" (*mur*) in fact prevents us from following Alberti's reasoning to the end and from measuring the scope of a reflection aimed at nothing less than inscribing in the wall itself the structural determinations obeyed by a system that is based, from Brunelleschi's day, on a double movement of assertion and negation of the wall (*paroi*), seen in its continuity and its regularity.[20]

To ask whether Alberti, given the position of the wall in his problematic, was more Roman than Greek is to forget that this first great Renaissance theorist was above all a man of his times and thus keen to interrogate the past and interpret its remains, but within the terms of a culture that was not without its ties to the trecento nor solely committed to dealing with the ancients and the reestablishment of the civilization of antiquity[21]—a culture completely bound up, in its humanist project, with a mental apparatus and a set of professional traditions that surface most clearly (and with good reason) in the technical domain. Is architectural practice, then, as Alberti defines it, the reflection of Roman modes of construction? Does it thus owe nothing to the legacy of the Middle Ages? The question is posed on the very ground that served as a base for Alberti's own thinking, as he showed himself (at least initially) to be more concerned with *construction* than with *form giving*.[22] After all, it was not only a wish to distinguish himself from Vitruvius that compelled

Alberti to give his treatise a title in which construction explicitly prevails over architectural aims. In *De re aedificatoria*, problems of a mechanical and technical nature are no less important than considerations of harmony and number, fashion and ordering (considerations often overemphasized by academic criticism). Nothing in Alberti's analyses, apart from a few debatable references, allows us either to link his concept of the wall to the traditions of Roman masonry or, less still, to oppose the principle of the solid, homogenous wall to the Gothic (or even contemporary) model of a load-bearing skeleton that may be completed with a simple infill.[23] It remains for us to inquire how, following the example of *De re aedificatoria*, the difference between two types of architecture—one according the wall a primary place among the elements of the art of building, the other relegating it to a subordinate position—operates not on the level of constructional necessities but in terms of their interpretation according to the perspectives of the Albertian system.

It is a mistake, writes Alberti in Book Seven (which is devoted to the "ornamentation of sacred buildings"), to believe that the thickness of the wall adds to the majesty of a temple. Is not Hadrian's Pantheon made up of a *solid skeleton* into which intervals are hollowed out with niches and openings—thus considerably reducing load and cost while the building gained in elegance?[24] Whatever attitude toward the monuments of antiquity is revealed by this interpretation (the Pantheon is one of the rare Roman examples referenced in *De re aedificatoria*), we see that when Alberti defines the *paries* as structure he is not thinking solely of masonry (unlike Vitruvius) any more than he sees the wall as a homogenous and continuous mass. And if he distinguishes between the different kinds of *structure*, in the Vitruvian sense of the term, then this is done to comprise the three modes of facing stone—ordinary (*ordinaria*), reticulated (*rheticulata*), and "uncertain" (*incerta*), or as Jean Martin translates it, *rustique*, made up of unhewn stones—which in turn correspond to the three parts of the wall: the base (*podium*), the middle (*procinctus*), and the upper (*corona*).[25] To this initial distinction between the successive (or should we say superimposed?) parts of the outer walling should be added the differentiation between the inner infill (*media muro infarcinatio*) and the outer revetment (*cortex*)—that is, between the inner cement and the outer skin, or "crust"—which vary depending on the type of wall under consideration.[26] But the distinction between the vertical and horizontal layers making up the *paries* does not exhaust its structural features. The parts of the wall that belong to the skeleton must also be defined: the corners and buttresses; the pillars, or "columns," inserted in the wall (which function like bones supporting the covering);[27] and the infill parts between the bearing elements.[28] Are we then to suppose that the prevalence, at the time Alberti was writing his treatise, of the "bony model" of structure, which he conceives as the solid armature of the building, proves that he was still in the grip of the Gothic building tradition or that, on the contrary, the subsequent progressive elimination of the column from his built work illustrates a shift toward a wall architecture, rigorously conceived and deduced?

There is nothing to indicate that Alberti, in the moment of writing his theory, hoped to save on the cost of the wall by preferring a discontinuous skeleton. Rather, his entire effort seems to have been directed toward defining a mode of construction in which the skeleton could not be distinguished from the *paries* and in which the relationship between the column and the wall was expressed in mechanical (rather than decorative or plastic) terms. In such a system, the column could not be opposed to the wall any more than it could be simply coupled to it. The column constituted the system's principal element, and the wall was raised in proportion to it—no higher, wider, or thicker than the rule (*ratio*) or the mode (*modus*) required.[29] In articulating the wall in this way, Alberti resolved both technical and economic problems by conceiving of a structural arrangement that assured the stability of both the walls and the "covering, or roof." Anyone who took no heed of expense might just as well build the whole building as a "continuous column."[30] But that would be both wasteful and incongruous. A masonry skeleton infilled with smaller mortar-bound fragments—whose division, Alberti notes, parallels that of the social body—would guarantee stability.[31] When the *paries* is defined as a structure that supports a roof, the concept becomes much broader in scope than a wall (*mur*) in the strict sense of the term. Once again, if Alberti is to be believed, the order is nothing but a wall pierced in several places by openings.[32]

In such a system, the column does indeed appear to be a *reinforced* part of the wall. As if recognizing the paradox involved in such an assertion, Alberti insists that "it may not be wrong to describe [the column] as a certain, solid, and continuous section of wall, which has been raised perpendicularly from the ground, up high, for the purpose of bearing the roof,"[33] given that the disposition of columns and the spaces between them is related to the load. As for the openings and passages let into the wall, Alberti further notes that the ancients were careful to pierce only the weakest sections of a wall that had little or no load-bearing function, and then as far as possible from the corners and the points where columns rose, while keeping great sections of the wall *complete and unbroken.*[34] In fact, it seems that Alberti intended to take a critical attitude toward the ancient models, recognizing the value of a mode of construction that, unlike the Roman system, allows for a greater number of openings—by which he meant not only doors, porticos, and windows, but also niches and recesses that, *without piercing the whole thickness of the wall*, add to its elegance and lightness.[35] This is to say nothing of the fact that an opening, far from being detrimental to the stability and strength of the wall, may indeed contribute to it, provided it is treated in accordance with Alberti's principle, with the jambs taking on "the character of columns"[36] that, covered by a lintel in the form of an architrave or arch, are themselves counted among the bones of the skeleton: "For I call an arch nothing but a curved beam, and what is a beam but a column laid crossways?"[37]

In this way, step by step, the building as a whole is conceived as skeleton and infill. All that has just been said about the wall is equally valid, mutatis mutandis, for the coverings; the beams, in turn, are nothing but columns laid transversally and the arches themselves but bent beams.[38] Better still, where the roof spans a vast surface it should be articulated and compartmented following the same principles as the wall.[39] Alberti, to repeat, did not appreciate bare surfaces without relief: if a wall is too long, columns should be used to ornament the wall over its full height and should be spaced far enough apart to let the eye rest and to make the length of the wall appear less offensive;[40] if it is too thin, either a new section should be added to the old to make a single wall, or, "to save expense," it could be reinforced by means of "bones" (i.e., pilasters or columns).[41] Should a wall be too high, a second story of columns (or preferably pilasters) may be added with little expense, on top of the ground-floor columns, to guarantee the firmness of the wall and to imbue it with an incomparable majesty[42]—horizontal and vertical partitioning simultaneously satisfying both the requirements of stability and the imperative of "dignity."

There is no formalism in this. What Alberti was defining, in theory, was neither more nor less than a structural model that, by submitting the classical orders to the law of the *paries*, made explicit their constructional function. This was in essence the system of architecture Viollet-le-Duc would praise Philibert de l'Orme for having defended in an age when, as he claimed, architects professed the greatest scorn for masonry and were only interested in "marvels" (*mirelifiques*)—ornaments without rhyme or reason.[43] But did he not think that even in Italy, the architecture of Bramante and Palladio had itself responded to this trend, which in no way excluded—no more at the Vatican or in Vicenza than in the Tuileries—a spectacular handling of the orders? Certainly, the pilasters of Valmarana Palace, built of bricks like the wall itself, are no less dependent on the wall than were the ringed columns of de l'Orme's Tuileries facade, of which Viollet-le-Duc approved for its correspondence with projections in the wall's foundations. What would he have said about the arcades in the courtyard of Saint Damasus inside the Vatican, where Bramante demonstrated the principle of superimposed orders and their potential for developing walls that were extremely light and virtually transparent?

Long before Choisy and today's engineers, Alberti recognized that despite its monolithic appearance the wall of Hadrian's Pantheon was itself reinforced by means of a network of superimposed brick arches embedded in the mass of the masonry, with the wall presenting itself as a *rational* system in which the loads were progressively distributed and concentrated on eight enormous pylons corresponding to the nonvoided parts, as revealed by the floor plan. Yet there is a big difference between this model and Alberti's interpretation, from which he draws conclusions as to the constructive use of the classical orders. For the Albertian skeleton is not necessarily, or even principally, made up of solid elements embedded in masonry. In fact it consists of a *reinforcement* of the wall, a reinforcement that can be external to it so that the applied order contributes to the stability of the whole while also fulfilling its own specific function, which is to support the bony rib elements of the roof. For whoever wishes *to build at little expense* (a constant concern for Alberti's contemporaries, as for those of de l'Orme and Jean Martin), such a dressing of the wall provides a particularly refined principle of construction, so long as care is taken to link the external orders to the internal ones by long stone ribs running crossways through the entire thickness of the *paries*.[44] Thus, by a structural inversion for which we are now prepared (and whose modernity we do not need to stress), this would ideally ensure the cohesion of the double network of bones into which the wall is set.

As the most solid part of the wall, the column, "and all that relates to it," is indeed "the noblest" of the wall's elements, in both its form and its functions, and even in its very display.[45] Nevertheless, if the column, in the strict sense of a standing shaft, can be regarded metonymically as representative of a much more general class—indeed, Alberti did not hesitate to assimilate pilasters with square columns (*columnae quadrangulae*), beams and inferior purlins with recumbent columns, and even arches with curved columns, and so on—this is at the cost of an ambiguity that he did not care to resolve. As a fragment of the wall, and a structure's noblest element, the column nonetheless possesses an identity, if not an autonomy, that is particularly marked in the case of monolithic columns hewn from a single block. As remarkable for its technical quality as for the beauty of its proportions, the column also appears metaphorically as the model par excellence of the bone of the skeleton: a discrete structural element, itself articulated (if considered as a whole with its base and its capital) and suited as such to being combined with other elements of a similar nature so as to constitute the solid framework of a building. When Alberti defines the column as the principal ornament of architecture, does he mean to ignore its structural properties in order to concentrate solely on its appearance, its decorative value? In fact, it does not seem as though he saw the relationship between structure and decoration in terms of an entrenched opposition. Books Seven, Eight, and Nine of his treatise, although dedicated to the ornaments of sacred buildings and public or private constructions, deal in detail not only with the decoration of those buildings but also with their general arrangements, plans, main parts, and the different elements in use. The fact is that any single structure is likely to contribute to the ornament of the whole: the column to that of the temple, the temple to that of the city, and the city to that of the state. A building has no finer ornament than its columns. But what would a town be if it were stripped of its buildings, and even of its inhabitants, who by their number ultimately represent its finest ornament and (we would have to agree) its most essential?[46]

Brunelleschi placed the Florentine Renaissance under the sign of the column as much as of the cupola. The paradox of the "austere" style generally associated with the Counter-Reformation—(which could claim Alberti among the initiators a century before the promulgation of the edicts of the Council of Trent)—is that it tended to economize on this incomparable ornament—if not eliminating the column completely from architecture, then at least restricting its use to functions and strictly defined parts of a building that often had more to do with furniture (altars, etc.) than with masonry. As we have seen, a similar concern for economy was present in the writings of Alberti, who seems always torn between his desire to see architecture held to a tasteful modesty and his idea of the representative value that attaches to its works, particularly to sacred buildings. The systematic and rationalizing effort of *De re aedificatoria* is thereby all the more significant: educated as he was in the linguistic disciplines, Alberti conceived of a logical procedure that would govern any handling of forms in accordance with their *definition*,[47] a definition that each generation was obliged to formulate for itself. Indeed, in the case of the column, the structuralist approach of the present essay parallels the concern that motivated Alberti to justify the use of this architectonic member from a standpoint that was not merely archeological, or picturesque, to use the strict sense of the term, since, as Alberti states in *Della pittura*, architecture borrowed its ornaments—starting with the column—from painting.[48] Yet the reciprocal is also true: it was obviously not for strictly logical reasons that the column, so brilliantly celebrated by Brunelleschi, was eliminated from the architectural vocabulary of the following generation, only to return with familiar connotations in the sixteenth and seventeenth centuries.

Alberti's rejection of the column as the principal element of architecture in his own architectural practice does not imply that, as an architect, he broke with the concepts he defended as a theorist, including in particular the definition of the wall that we find in *De re aedificatoria*. Alberti admired certain old masters for knowing how to erect vaults in such a way that the columns could be removed without compromising the stability of the structure as a whole. If such artifice amazed him, however, it was not because he regarded the column as merely a decorative element; the presence of a regular row of flat pilasters over the facade of the Palazzo Rucellai (where those pilasters combine with cornices to form a veritable tracery thrown like a net over a wall treated with flat rustication), as well as over the facades of Sant'Andrea and San Sebastiano,[49]indicates that he never abandoned the principle of the articulated wall. It matters little in the end whether or not the order has a constructional value, for even if the column may be eliminated *as a form*, the articulation of the wall following the lines of a skeleton is maintained.

So it was in no way the so-called logic of the wall that led to the exclusion of the column, but the very opposite. The elimination of that eminently plastic element seems to have allowed Alberti to consider the wall as a support for words (orders, triumphal arches, etc.) that could be inscribed in ways that would no longer be structural but spring instead from a very different order of determinations: that of the graphic, of the drawing, known otherwise as "drawn architecture" (*l'architecture dessinée*) that would become the support of academic instruction.

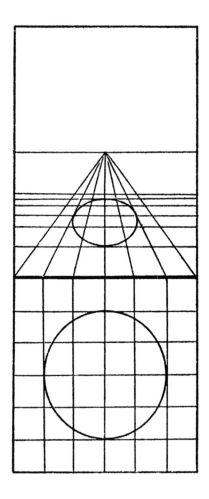

3.1
Diagram of a circle drawn in perspective. From John
Spencer, "Notes to Book Two" (1435), in *On Painting*,
by Leon Battista Alberti (New Haven: Yale University
Press, 1956).

3 COMPOSING WITH PAINTING

Alberti opens Book Two of *Della pittura* with a eulogy to painting that, despite its slightly surprising emphasis, fulfills a precise purpose: justifying the pains he has already inflicted on his reader as well as those to which he will soon subject him. In effect, Alberti is preparing to take up his analysis of the device of perspective at the point where he left off at the end of Book One. Once the squared pavement that serves as the ground in the representation has been constructed, it must be given the appearance of a stage on which the *istoria*, the ultimate goal of painting, might take place. This operation implies going from a two-dimensional device (the base plane of a chessboard) to a three-dimensional device (the stage or scene as a plane of support but also of volume). By the end of Book One—a volume *tutto mathematico*, "entirely mathematical"—the reader is convinced that the construction of the scene in perspective is not without difficulties, as Alberti announces as early as the prologue to the "vulgar" Italian version of his treatise.[1] Before going any further, however, Alberti deems it necessary to pause and attempt to persuade the painter—his reader—that the effort asked of him is justified. Is not painting something divine? Should the painter who can give the appearance of life to the beings he represents not himself be held as a god? For Alberti, however, the painter's power does not stop there. Not content to confer a semblance of presence on the absent, and even on the dead, Alberti holds that painting is the mistress and principal ornament of all things:[2]

mistress, if it is true that all the arts model themselves on painting; ornament, in that there is no art that painting cannot touch up or perfect.

Indeed, so great is painting's inherent power to transform, to transmute, if not to metamorphose, that it can be said to be "the flower of all the arts" (*fiore d'ogni arte*). It adds to the pleasures of the soul, as well as to the beauty of things, and is able to render precious the basest of metals, such as lead, and even more so the most precious, such as gold. But what are we to make of the assertion that if all the arts in some way model themselves on painting, this holds true even for the art of the architect? "If I am not mistaken," Alberti writes, the architect takes from the painter "architraves, capitals, bases, columns and pediments, and all the other fine features of buildings."[3] It is one thing for Alberti in *De re aedificatoria* (which he wrote nearly twenty years after *Della pittura*) to present the column as the principal, if not the primary, ornament of architecture,[4] but the assertion that architecture is indebted to painting for this "ornament" might come as a surprise. We can understand why commentators have routinely preferred to pass over it in silence rather than having to reconsider, in this unexpected light, the whole question of ornament, and of ornament as *addition*,[5] indissociable as such from the notion of composition as defined, explicitly or not, in Alberti's text.

The word *composition* does not appear in *De re aedificatoria*. If we really want to find a notion, or group of notions, in Alberti's conceptual apparatus that could play a role analogous to the one the classical tradition assigned to the idea of composition, we must call on the notion of *concinnitas*—the proper relation (*convenance*) between the parts—and on the three principles that govern it: number (*numerus*), proportion (*finitio*), and especially the location or relative position of parts (*collocatio*). As Françoise Choay clearly understood, the notion of *concinnitas*, which the

Renaissance took from Cicero, corresponds in Alberti's essay to the organizing principle that requires the different parts of a living organism to be harmoniously subordinate to the law of the whole. But whereas *concinnitas* goes hand in hand with a kind of inherent beauty based on "that reasoned harmony of all the parts within a body, so that nothing may be added, taken away, or altered, but for the worse,"[6] ornament corresponds to a form of auxiliary, or complementary, beauty. Resembling painting in this respect, ornament is of the order of added value. Yet there is an obvious difference between a complement and a supplement: a complement corresponds to a possibility, even a necessity, inscribed in the object itself, which would remain incomplete without it; a supplement remains external to the object to which it is added, just as the sign remains external to the object for which it stands in.[7]

To discover what Alberti meant by "composition," we must return to *Della pittura* while bearing in mind that his proposition that architecture is indebted to painting for its principal ornaments comes just before he defines the three parts that comprise painting: circumscription, composition, and the reception of light. Of these three, which Alberti says he took from nature,[8] only the first two hold our attention here, for reasons that will become clear. Circumscription (*circumscriptio*) corresponds in painting to the delineation of the contours of objects by means of the outline;[9] composition (*compositio*) governs the articulation in the painted work of the elements thereby defined.[10] All of the painter's fame and talent rests in the articulation, or composition, of bodies, for *istoria* itself[11] consists of nothing but the articulation, or composition, of the bodies and their parts in the form of surfaces, which are brought together in projection on a plane according to the model of the visual pyramid and the intersecting plane, or *intersegazione*. On the plane of the painting, the surfaces that *compose* members and bodies should then fit together like the pieces of a jigsaw puzzle or, better still, like a piece of marquetry work.

The relationship between the notions of *compositio* and *concinnitas* is thus established. Both refer to the way in which the parts of the same object, the same body, the same organism respond and adjust to each other. Is not the function of the architect himself to project and realize—through the distribution of weights and the gathering together and conjugation of bodies—buildings that fulfill the needs of mankind in the most dignified way,[12] with the parts of a building having to be in harmony with each other just like the limbs of an animal?[13] Yet whereas a body, a living being, finds its place in a three-dimensional space, the notion of composition (as well as that of *decomposition*, as advanced by Peter Eisenman[14]) makes sense only if it is brought back to the two dimensions of the plane of projection or inscription. Hence the analogy Alberti made between an apprenticeship in painting and one in writing, at least as it concerns the alphabet:

> I would like to see young people who are learning the art of painting today do what I see practiced by teachers of writing. They first teach all the signs of the alphabet, which the Ancients called elements, separately; and then how to put syllables together, and then whole words. Our students should follow this method with painting. First they should learn how to draw the outlines of surfaces, as the first elements of painting, so to speak, then the way in which surfaces are joined together, and after that the individual forms of all the members; and they should commit to memory all the differences that can exist in those members, for they are neither few nor insignificant.[15]

I consider it significant that Alberti resorts to this same paradigm of writing when he comes to describe the different orders of columns in *De re aedificatoria*. The contoured profiles (*modé-natures*) that ensure the connection between (or mark the articulation of) the different parts, or members, of architecture indeed allow themselves to be decomposed, if not spelled out, into a certain number of elements, each one of which presents, as a projection on a plane, a characteristic profile that refers back to the graphic model of writing. This is the case with the lintel or the fillet, the projection of which corresponds to the outline of the letter L, as well as with the "neck" or concave moldings, placed beneath, that are shaped in the fashion of a C or an S.[16] Thus, by way of this operation of projection (or of transcription), ornaments are reduced to a succession of elements that combine on the plane in a strictly linear fashion, just like letters on a page.

As if to further underscore this connection between the agency of the ornament and that of the letter, Alberti points out that *modénatures* can be decorated with sculptures in the form of shells, scrolls, or even letters of the alphabet. If ornament does indeed present itself as being of the order of the supplement, this is because it refers back, in its economy and its own logic, to the dimension of writing—the writing that an entire tradition (at the heart of which Alberti thus finds his place) has placed precisely under the title of the supplement—what Derrida proposed to call the "graphic" of the supplement, the better to reveal the constitutive, foundational relationship that such a supplement maintains with the order of the brushstroke, the outline, the line.[17] Ornament, then, would be added to the built object in the same way that writing is supposedly added to speech as its image. (In his translation of *De re aedificatoria*, James Leoni went so far as to compare it to the quarter-round ivy that runs along a building's members and attaches itself to them.[18]) Ornament adds to (or attaches itself to) the built thing as a sign, if not as a mask, that passes itself off as the built thing itself, which from then on is posited as absent and will have no other presence than the one conferred on it by ornament—in much the same way as painting can give presence to the absent and the dead in effigy.

The same goes for the column. Whether Doric, Ionic, or Corinthian, the column as ornament takes on functions quite different from the purely mechanical and static functions assigned to it as an element in a vertical skeleton in the constructional apparatus.[19] It assumes the value of a sign within a system that works, as the Saussurian metaphor would have it, according to the double dimension—syntagmatic and paradigmatic—of language, with the syntagmatic relationship resting on the effective presence of several elements in a real series and the paradigmatic relationship referring to terms given in absentia in a virtual series (e.g., in the classical orders).[20] Yet Alberti's reference to alphabetical writing signals that from the very beginning ornament is not a matter of syntax or semantics; it proceeds as supplement from an order of concatenation that has nothing grammatical about it—an order that is strictly graphic, if not orthographic—and springs as such from a power of prior articulation that is, ontologically speaking, the power of speech.

If we now return to the apparently paradoxical proposition that first caught our attention, we see that the idea that architecture drew its principal ornaments from painting is neither rhetorical nor conjectural and that its significance is not limited to the field in which a treatise on painting might belong. If architecture (architecture, that is, not building) pertains to the order of the supplement, it is not (however much we might be tempted to agree with Schelling) as the metaphor of the art of building. Architecture is bound to painting, and painting to architecture, by a bond that is equally fundamental to both disciplines (or practices). This is indicated by the fact that the notion of composition has been able to migrate (or spread) from one domain of expertise to the other. It has often seemed astonishing that, whereas Vitruvius deals with perspective under the heading of *scenographia*, *De re aedificatoria* leaves no room for perspective, save implicitly, and then only to exclude it—that very same perspective to which, in *Della pittura*, Alberti devotes the arguments we have discussed. But this is because the *perspectiva artificialis* was the business of painters, even if it was an architect—the same Brunelleschi to whom Alberti dedicated the Italian version of his treatise on painting—who invented it. No doubt the perspective of painters (the *prospectiva pingendi*, as Piero della Francesca was to call it) acquires a specifically constructional dimension to the extent that all perspective is ultimately architectural, the very architecture of representation essentially deriving from the representation of architecture.[21] We cannot claim, however, that the *res aedificatoria*, architecture as built object, must necessarily find a way of externalizing, asserting, and expressing itself in graphic terms through the detour of a construction (in the geometrical sense of the term) that assumes the perspectival scene as its precondition.

If we accept Rudolf Wittkower's hypothesis, it was in response to a properly architectural (and not merely constructional) requirement that Brunelleschi was led to invent perspective. Keen to prove that the metrical coherence of a building was not altered by the distance from which it was viewed, Brunelleschi needed to demonstrate that the apparent diminishing of objects in space obeyed a regular and constant *ratio*. The consequence was that a building's proportions could only be judged in perspective and with reference to an ideal plane of projection—the difference between architecture and painting thus being merely a matter of the medium, not the essence.[22] But to use the term *medium* might again be going too far. For what I have called "the Brunelleschi demonstration" might seem as though it were reviving what Edmund Husserl would regard as the inaugural act of geometry: the reduction of visible bodies to "limit-forms"—that is, to a set of surfaces with clearly drawn edges—such that one no longer knows, and no longer can know, anything about a volume except what is said by the planes on which, in a sense, it projects itself (the *plane* in this case being as important as the *projection*).[23]

Alberti, who is perfectly explicit on this point, offers an entirely different view: "The difference between the drawings of the painter and those of the architect is this: the former takes pains to emphasize the relief of objects in paintings with shading and diminishing lines and angles; the architect rejects shading, but takes his projections from the ground plan and, without altering the lines and by maintaining the true angles, reveals the extent and shape of each elevation and side—he is one who desires his work to be judged not by deceptive appearances but according to certain calculated standards."[24] This statement responds to the definition of *disegno* with which *De re aedificatoria* opens: "All the intent and purpose of lineaments lies in finding the correct, infallible way of joining and fitting together those lines and angles which define and enclose the surfaces of the building,"[25] and thus obviating any need for shading (the "reception of light") or scenography.

Is this to say that there is no architecture, nor should there be, at this stage, unless by the relay of paper? The fact that, according to Vasari, Brunelleschi was able to construct his "views of architecture" in perspective from a building's plan and elevation says enough about the value and constructional significance of these two modes of graphic representation, which constituted a primordial frame of reference for perspectival construction and at the same time provided the information necessary for its establishment. Similarly for Alberti, there is no ornament (or composition, in the sense we have defined) except in relation to the two dimensions of the plan, whether a ground plan, an elevation, a section, or even a perspective view. Yet if architecture is right to claim a kind of beauty that is something other than natural and, so to speak, organic, it no less owes this beauty to painting, that "flower of all the arts," and of architecture itself. It is painting that provides architecture with the means of articulating—of *composing*—in the two dimensions of the plane of projection the surfaces that might be seen (or "read," as the metaphor of writing would have it) in the three dimensions of an imaginary space that perspective teaches us to build, but also in the three dimensions of the built object, given that the "wall architecture" attributed to Alberti only conceives of the column as a type of pilaster that corresponds to its projection on the wall, a process whose operation only painting can describe. At this stage, it is most definitely from painting that architecture borrows its ornaments, starting with the first and principal among them. Indeed, it is true that there is no ornament unless it is designed, developed, and worked in the two dimensions of the plane that carries it; and painting, when it chooses to be itself, necessarily participates in the décor and thus is naturally decorative.

Without architecture, as Serlio said, there is no perspective. Yet without perspective, there is no (or no longer) architecture. An affair of the trace, composition refuses to be separated from the delineation with which it ultimately merges, for the outline represents nothing other than the line of demarcation, of separation, the hinge between two surfaces. But it is also an affair of concatenation, of spacing, distribution, *collocatio*. After all, does the principal ornament of towns not lie in their geographical situation, in their implantation, their trace, as much as in the relative distribution of buildings, insofar as they allow themselves to be translated into graphic, even pictorial, terms?[26] Architecture is indebted to painting for its ornaments—but it must first compose with, come to terms with, and make an alliance with painting, as painting must do with architecture, to achieve by this detour the projective dimension to which it aspires: the dimension that refers back, following a henceforth acknowledged play of oppositions, to the order of the *project*.

4 PERRAULT'S COLONNADE AND THE FUNCTIONS OF THE CLASSICAL ORDER

On May 14, 1667, Jean-Baptiste Colbert presented Louis XIV with two drawings for the east facade of the Palais du Louvre, after Louis Le Vau, Charles Le Brun, and Claude Perrault—the members of the committee charged with finalizing the project—had been unable to agree on a single *parti*. Of the two drawings submitted to him, the king would retain the first, the one "adorned with an order of columns forming a peristyle or gallery above the first floor," over the other, which according to Perrault was "simpler and more unified, without an order of columns."[1]

I do not wish to intervene here in a discussion of the problems of attribution posed by the Louvre Colonnade. I am content to introduce a few thoughts that seem to me to clarify its significance and to briefly demonstrate that the choice offered to Louis XIV was neither gratuitous nor arbitrary and that his decision would not have been simply a matter of taste. If the selection may appear to illustrate the king's penchant for pomp, grandeur, and a certain form of ostentation, it corresponds more profoundly, as we see in its antecedents and implications, to a form of logic that since the mid-sixteenth century never ceased to play a determining role in the historical development of the Louvre and in the avatars of what has been called the *grand dessein*.

If we claim to be able to determine what the significance of the colonnade might have been over the course of the classical age, then we must accept a priori (and without this being a simple tautology) that a building such as the Louvre had to be

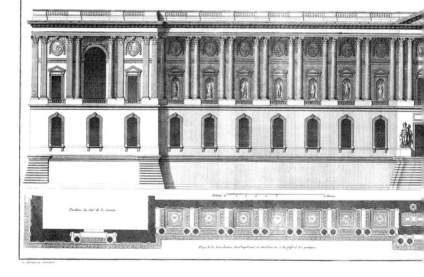

4.1
Engraving of the east facade of the Louvre. From
Jean Mariette, *L'architecture Françoise* (Paris, 1738).
Courtesy Avery Architectural & Fine Arts Library,
Columbia University.

& le ministere de Jean Baptiste Colbert, sur les desseins de Claude Perrault de l'academie royale des sciences.

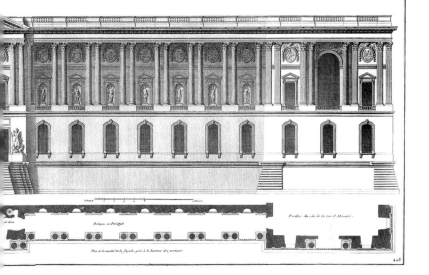

Echelle de

Portique, ou Peristyle.

Pavillon du côté de la rue S.ᵗ Honoré.

Plan de la moitié de la façade, pris à la hauteur des portiques.

448

77

organized in a way that could, as a whole and in its parts, *signify* something. We thus need to define what the building constituted as an ordered whole as well as what classical architecture itself was as a *signifying* order. We know that, as Michel Foucault brilliantly reminded us, the notion of *order*, associated with that of *measure*, occupied a central place in classical thought.[2] And it is not merely playing with words to insist that the architecture of the century of Descartes and Leibniz was itself based not only on knowledge and the institution of the principles of the classical Order (with a capital *O*)—understood, following Perrault's definition, as furnishing a rule for the correct proportioning of columns and their ornaments and for figuring the elements appropriate to them[3]—but also on a much more general notion of order defined by Vicenzo Scamozzi, in extremely vague terms, as "a certain kind of excellence that greatly increases the good grace and beauty of edifices sacred and profane."[4] Other authors such as Roland Fréart de Chambray assimilated the idea of order to *ordonnance*, by which they meant both *ordinatio* and *dispositio* in the sense those two terms have in Vitruvius—namely, *ordinatio* meaning that which determines the relative size of the different parts that compose a building and *disposition* (or as Perrault also calls it, *distribution*) meaning that which determines the placement, sequence, and connection of those same parts according to their characteristics.[5] Thus, when speaking of order, we should beware of an ambiguity that in the eyes of a disciple of classicism could mean the order of a facade, a building, or even an urban ensemble, without any application of the classical orders. Yet from the moment that the elements (in the archeological sense of the term) make their appearance, a certain number of observations emerge that give rise to the thought that the implementation of elements did not simply obey considerations of measure and harmony but also responded to a strictly formal order based on a network of structural relationships, the most visible of which are topological in nature. (This occurs even if we confine ourselves to considering the way these elements are used, how they are divided up over a facade, and especially their relative distribution, *according to their characteristics*, across the different facades and parts of the same building.) In this context, I want to demonstrate (all too briefly and with the single example of the Louvre Colonnade) that the distribution of the elements of the classical order across the different parts of the building demonstrates the existence of a veritable topology of the classical order, one which has never been given explicit form in theory but which must nonetheless be considered as one of the formal components that constitute the classical system as a signifying system.

An initial formal sequence that can be to put into play in terms of opposition, distribution, correlation, and substitution is formed by the sequence of the three external facades of the Cour Carrée: the north facade, on the rue de Rivoli, which is devoid of all decoration and simply pierced with windows and which Perrault apparently completed according to Lemercier's original scheme; the east facade, which corresponds to the colonnade; and lastly the south facade, which in its current state presents a colossal order of pilasters extending over two stories of windows, supporting an entablature and a balustrade, and resting on the same high base that serves as the base for the colonnade. These three facades are well known to every passerby. The important thing is to see that they form a system and that, beyond the order of rules referenced by the members of the academy when discussing the projects submitted to them, what emerges is a form of structural regulation, the effect of which seems to have been experienced over the course of execution and which tended to establish a systematic and coherent play of oppositions between the principle of the bare wall, that of a colossal order of

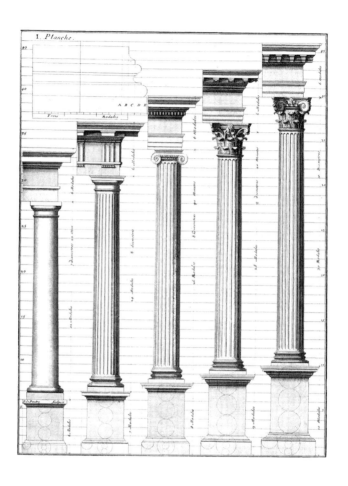

4.2
Claude Perrault, *Ordonnance des cinq espèces de
colonnes selon la méthode des anciens* (Paris, 1683),
plate 1. Courtesy Avery Architectural & Fine Arts
Library, Columbia University.

pilasters, and that of an open colonnade in the form of a peristyle or gallery.

As a number of historians attest, when work on the lengthening of the colonnade caused the south facade to be set back fifteen meters from the corner of the east facade, Perrault was led to bring it back into alignment. Yet the same demand for regularity, in keeping with the canons of classical taste, would have no effect when it came to the north facade, whose nonalignment was not corrected. If, as a working hypothesis, we ignore the functional demands that could lead to the doubling of the south wing and the correlative widening of the colonnade's corner pavilions (namely, Colbert's decision to shift the king's apartments, originally planned for the east wing, to the wing with a view of the Seine[6]), then we see that, from a strictly formal point of view, the scheme for the facade set up by Perrault in front of the one built by Le Vau from 1660 to 1663 came down to the substitution of a facade composed of two main buildings pierced simply by windows, without any other decoration, and joined together by a central pavilion with a colossal order of columns—a type of facade that was far more regular and imposing and in which the pilaster reigns undividedly. Even if Perrault meant to embellish the central part of this same south facade with columns, as the plan published by Blondel indicates,[7] the fact that such a plan was not pursued underlines the constraining power of the formal order that causes the three facades to constitute a ternary play of opposition (bare wall to open colonnade to colossal order of pilasters) wherein each facade assumes a differential value.

In addition to this primary register of opposition, there is a second, subtler, perhaps more significant one that escapes immediate observation: the relationship between the internal and external facades and foremost between the open column opposite Saint-Germain-l'Auxerrois and the facade on the courtyard to its rear. It would be interesting, from this point of view, to study the series of plans, both French and Italian, that were proposed for finishing the eastern part of the Louvre. Most of these turned on a simple opposition either to emphasize or to overcome, if not to conceal, this part of the building. Thus, in 1661, Antoine-Léonor Houdin proposed to put up an east facade comprising a gallery with a colonnade detached from the wall, leaving the inner facade to be finished, it seems, following Lemercier's scheme for the internal north facade. Conversely, Le Vau's plan of 1663 suggests placing an open gallery with a colonnade into the courtyard at the rear of the east wing, while the external facade was to be embellished with an order of engaged columns. Bernini, in his first project of June 1664, established a double-story portico around the entire perimeter of the courtyard and joined together on the outside the corner pavilions of the north and south wings by a curvilinear facade decorated with a colossal order of columns over two stories high and pierced by loggias—the opposition between the internal and external facades here overcome with the building opened up as much inward as outward. Whether or not they planned to endow the internal courtyard with galleries or porticos, most of the architects concurred in the adornment of the external facade, which in principle faced the city, with an order of columns or even a colonnade forming a peristyle or gallery (to use Perrault's terms). This consensus seems to correspond, on a formal level, to a profound mutation of, if not a rupture with, the principles defined by Pierre Lescot—principles to which, up until Colbert was appointed superintendent of buildings, the Louvre architects seemed inclined to show themselves faithful.

Lescot's Louvre in fact corresponded to a simple given: the elements of the order, whether columns or pilasters, were reserved for the internal facades on the courtyard, whereas the external facades were only pierced with windows, the wall being left bare. But if the orders do not appear, not even simply set into the wall, on the external facades—neither the one facing the Seine nor the one facing the densely populated neighborhood that had sprung up between the Louvre and the Tuileries—this is perhaps because the use of the components of the order, and particularly of the column that constitutes its main element, corresponds in principle to the aim of opening up and communicating with the outside world, an aim manifest in the case of a portico or of loggias but blind, or at least more discreet, in the case of orders set in the wall. In Lescot's initial project, the *corps de logis* with which we are familiar (and which now corresponds to the south half of the west wing of the Cour Carrée) was to be framed on two sides by porticos lower than the facade itself, with the courtyard opening to the outside world, following the classical scheme adopted by Serlio for Cardinal de Ferrare's Hôtel at Fontainebleau. Lescot's use of the elements of the order responded to a given that was ambiguous yet typically French, in that the internal facade was intended to be partly visible from the outside. This ambiguity would be removed by the option of a quadrangular palace with corner pavilions and four identical main buildings opening onto an internal courtyard, which (compared to the initial plan) shows an evident desire for retreat and isolation, if not for defense, with regard to the urban setting.

A portion of the gallery overlooking the water was to have been ornamented at the end of the sixteenth century with a colossal order of pilasters, whereas Philibert de l'Orme's Tuileries responded to yet another given—that of a loggia with columns opening onto the gardens and, we should note, decorated with pilasters at the back, as though the architect had intended even here to set up an opposition that of course has its logic. If we bear this in mind while considering in the abstract the play of oppositions between the different facades and the parts of the complex then formed by the Louvre and the Tuileries, then those oppositions seem to be organized according to a formal model that is certainly incoherent, sloppy, and badly articulated. But this model is in fact not far from a model that is affirmed, in far more rigorous and systematic guises, in various Italian palaces, whether the Farnese Palace in Rome or the Palazzo Te in Mantua: external facades devoid of all decoration (or embellished with only slightly projecting pilasters), internal facades decorated with columns engaged in the wall or forming a peristyle, and facades with loggias or galleries that open onto a walled garden cut off from the urban environment.

We might feel that the project for a uniform east facade devoid of any order of columns—the one Louis XIV set aside—better satisfied the rules of a topological distribution of the elements of the classical order, which we have just defined. But opening a peristyle (or a colonnaded gallery) onto what was supposed to be the palace's external facade would have marked a decisive break with that formal model. Thus, the alternative proposal left the king with a decision that in retrospect appears to have been a matter of government, if not of state. Yet are we really to think that putting up an order of columns detached from the wall along this same facade (with the side pavilions, which projected slightly, decorated according to a similarly logical transformation—not with the customary columns but with pilasters) would have ended the slow process that was to transform the Louvre castle (not to say fortress), set as it was both on the city wall and on the river (as Alberti recommends, for reasons of security), into a palace largely open to the city? This would be to forget that, as Alberti would say, if every tyrant is partially a prince, every prince is himself partially a tyrant; thus, every castle should be partially a palace, and every palace partially a castle.[8] The fortress of the prince should not resemble a prison, but neither should his palace be open to all winds and in no state to withstand the onslaught of the crowd, which Alberti, quoting Euripides, claims is always full of evil intentions.[9] Memories of the Fronde had not yet been erased in the period when they were arguing over the completion of the king's *grand dessein*, as evidenced by Colbert's objections to Bernini's projects: with the royal apartments located in the east wing, the sovereign would have been less protected against a seditious movement, since the open loggias and the columns generously distributed throughout the galleries and vestibules would have provided numerous points of access and hiding places for those plotting a coup.[10] We cannot be sure that in selecting the plan for the facade with the peristyle or gallery the sovereign wished to disregard such concerns any more than he would have broken with a formal apparatus of which the colonnade, in principle, represented not so much a negation as a reversal.

We might recall that as early as 1668 Colbert envisaged transferring the king's apartments to the south wing of the palace, overlooking the Seine. But the very term *peristyle*—which Perrault, as a translator of Vitruvius, used to designate the colonnade—gives pause for thought. What did this word mean for him? In a note in his edition of the *Ten Books on Architecture*, Perrault spells it out very clearly: the essence of peristyles is that they have columns inside and walls outside—not columns outside and walls inside, as seen in monopteral and peripteral temples and in porticos at the rear of theaters.[11] This means that the project retained by the king, which comprised an order of columns forming either a peristyle *or* a gallery, was perhaps itself an alternative proposition: either the facade actually opened to the city and could then be described as a "peristyle," with the columns outside and the wall inside, or, as in Lescot's earlier project, it faced a courtyard, with the columns inside and the wall outside. Here, we should remember that the initial idea for a colonnade, in Léonor Houdin's project, specifically allowed for a closed *place* in front of this same colonnade—or, to put it more clearly, a kind of courtyard that would have been bordered to the north and south by porticos connecting the palace to another circular *place*,

4.3
Claude Perrault, *Ordonnance des cinq espèce de colonnes selon la méthode des anciens* (Paris, 1683), plate 3. Courtesy Avery Architectural & Fine Arts Library, Columbia University.

4.4
Claude Perrault, *Ordonnance des cinq espèce de colonnes selon la méthode des anciens* (Paris, 1683), plate 6. Courtesy Avery Architectural & Fine Arts Library, Columbia University.

also closed, on the Châtelet site. We might further recall that projects for creating a monumental *place* in front of the colonnade and its facing buildings proliferated throughout the entire eighteenth century, right up to the nineteenth, as if in an effort to *close up* the opening inscribed in the very ordering of the Louvre's east facade—to blind, contradict, or negate it by opposing it with another, complementary facade of identical ordering.[12]

Thus, it seems as if, over more than two centuries, the *grand desseins* of kings had undergone a gradual expansion simply because the plan to open the palace up to the city, though intensely desired, was endlessly deferred, postponed, and ultimately rejected. Through a sort of deliberate misinterpretation (accentuated by the 1964 excavation—certainly spectacular, but at the very least questionable—of the moat at the foot of the colonnade), the colonnade took on the characteristic of a paradoxically decorative element, which may not have been present in the minds of its creators—Perrault in particular. This is due first to the colonnade's position (it faces the city without any transition) and second to the digging of the moat, which restored its fortified aspect. It would thus be an error to consider and analyze this facade separately from its context; the contradiction (or at least the paradox) it implies owes less to Perrault than to the program imposed on him, or even to the king himself. Just as the *grand dessein* was at the point of achieving its definitive form and logical conclusion—and of the Louvre being transformed from a castle to a real palace open to the city—Louis XIV effectively turned his back on Paris, first by taking up residence in the wing overlooking the Seine and then by moving to Versailles. Indeed, during construction Perrault decided to seal up the open windows behind the colonnade and replace them with niches for statues,[13] as though he intended to signify that opening the palace up to the city could only be a sham or feint. The formidable deployment of columns in front of the blind wall hence confers a provocative value on the facade and at the same time amounts to an admission of failure to which we are no longer sensitive today.

At the beginning of this chapter, I declined to enter into disputes over attribution. But considering what I have said as to the way in which formal determinism would have weighed on the entire historical development of the Louvre, as well as the rhetorical character of the work of those architects attempting to elevate the classical order into a signifying system, it seems that we should see Perrault (who, like Lescot before him, was not a professional builder but a scholar and thinker of language—and *fine* language at that) not as the inventor of the Louvre Colonnade but as one who was able to conceive of its most coherent and expressive idea. It is nonetheless true that after having closed the rear wall of the colonnade Perrault soon after envisaged opening a suite of galleries onto the courtyard,[14] which reveals the extent to which this great thinker would have been aware of the logical implication of his architectural *parti* and of the problems posed by the opening up of the prince's palace, both for itself and for the outside world. With Claude Perrault, the clearest concept of the order and its functions is affirmed for the first time, no longer picturesque or symbolic, but systematic and appropriately significant.

The foregoing analysis is admittedly not without its relationships to that type of contemporary description in the study of systems—more precisely, signifying systems—with respect to which architecture presents itself as a particularly complex and interesting model. This is why, in conclusion, I would like to cite from the preface written by Perrault to introduce his translation of Vitruvius, in which he makes reference to language, to writing, and even to clothing. This text seems to me in effect to justify my proposition here, as well as those of the classical architects, concerning the way one can superimpose on the order of utilitarian functions (to which the built work must respond) another order, one that is arbitrary and conventional—a procedure that, like any code, language, or system of signs, will be imposed *by institution* and, as such, will have authority: "It is certain that rules are so essential in all things that, if Nature refuses them to some things—as she has done with language, with the letters involved in writing, with clothing, and with all that depends on chance, will, and habituation—the institution of man must furnish them, and for this we agree upon a certain authority that takes the place of positive reason."[15]

5.1
The ideal cathedral. From Eugène-Emmanuel Viollet-
le-Duc, "Cathedrale," in *Dictionnaire raisonné de
l'architecture française du XIe au XVIe siècle* (Paris,
1854–1868), 2:324. Courtesy Avery Architectural &
Fine Arts Library, Columbia University.

5 THE SPACE BETWEEN: A STRUCTURALIST APPROACH TO THE *DICTIONNAIRE*: VIOLLET-LE-DUC AS A FORERUNNER OF STRUCTURALISM

Posterity has not been kind to Viollet-le-Duc. Today, his name is associated with an incorrect conception of the restoration of historic monuments, which (notwithstanding its alignment with the romantic imagination and the picturesque) has not lost all its influence in our own century, so enamored with objectivity. It cannot be too often repeated that these at best unfortunate restorations are the price that must be paid to see the church of St. Mary Magdalene of Vézelay and a good number of other medieval buildings still standing. In retrospect, one might wish that Viollet-le-Duc's successors and disciples, instead of trying to improve on his fantasies and phantasms, had kept to the letter of his doctrine as expressed in the article "Restoration" in the *Dictionnaire raisonné de l'architecture française du XIe au XVIe siècle*. In these pages, one will find nothing to justify the absolutely caricatural interpretation of his theories, but rather an appeal to the modesty, honesty, and scruples of the architect; the least one can say about it is that it has lost none of its relevance.[1]

I am not concerned here with presenting or defending the works of Viollet-le-Duc, architect of the Commission des monuments historiques. This immense oeuvre, which still today presents a certain image of the medieval past, was not the work of a single man but an entire generation, and Viollet-le-Duc himself did not regard it as an end in itself. In his *Entretiens sur l'architecture*, he makes it clear that he saw the work of restoration and preservation of ancient monuments as a substitute for the activities of architectural creation, which were denied to him in an age that could not provide the necessary technical and educational facilities. The reasoning behind Viollet-le-Duc's archeological inclination is articulated by Victor Hugo in *Notre-Dame de Paris*: in a century when the decadence of architecture seemed irreversible—and pending a hypothetical renewal of this "royal art"—there seemed to be no more exalted task for the young artist than that of conserving ancient monuments, and first in line those of that "Gothic" Middle Age, so decried by the École and the undying lesson of which Viollet-le-Duc would soon proclaim.[2]

The Gothic quarrel opened up amid the battle cries of the romantic movement and continued throughout the nineteenth century. It was not simply a question of taste but of principles and, at the same time (as is so often the case), of institutions and distinct interests. Firmly held in the hands of those whom Hugo savagely dubbed "maçons en habit vert," official education held itself to be the guardian of an academic order that owed more to Roman archeologists and decorators than to the French tradition. For in this French tradition—the high point of which was named by Viollet-le-Duc as the "Renaissance of the thirteenth century"—the École saw only darkness, unreason, and pathological disorder. In their efforts to restore and bring to light the monuments of the French Middle Ages, Prosper Mérimée's circle and those who worked in the service of the Commission des monuments historiques (which then had the profile of an avant-garde institution) were working against an established order that paralyzed all creative initiative. Viollet-le-Duc himself, in composing the volumes of his dictionary, proposed nothing less than to forge a theoretical instrument that would allow him to definitively discredit an anachronous education system that allowed no place for the reasoned study of the monuments of the past or for the knowledge of its constructional principles. If Gothic architecture had any didactic value for Viollet-le-Duc, it was not so much in the echoes it raised in the imagination of the time as it was a model one would be content to imitate: whereas the École taught copying, Viollet-le-Duc intended to explain, to analyze, to reason. No other architecture than that of the twelfth and thirteenth centuries, in its rigorously deductive and logically ordered character, appeared to him better suited to this intellectual exercise, which he expected would open the way for a new architecture, one—let us say the word—resolutely *modern* in the sense understood by his century.

Held up as a kind of bible by two or three generations of archeologists, and under the title the "Raisonné" by Frank Lloyd Wright and his generation in the wake of the Great Chicago Fire, the *Dictionnaire raisonné* became the object of a number of violent attacks and critical analyses in the years that followed World War I. These relentless critiques sought to destroy Viollet-le-Duc's ambition to penetrate what he believed to be the true logic of the art of building while at the same time providing the means for a systematic analysis of its works. In the very pages where Viollet-le-Duc believed he had developed the logical consequences of objective principles, Pol Abraham found the mark of a genius inclined to dream (if not in an architectural delirium), but hindered by an ideology in which vitalism and organicism conflicted with naturalism, and geological metaphors with anthropomorphism.[3] In a well-known article, Henri Focillon dismisses this ostensibly "scientific" and technical criticism, which opposed Viollet-le-Duc's more or less reasoned approach with nothing more imaginative than a new form of descriptive archeology.[4] Nevertheless, one must recognize that Viollet-le-Duc's theoretical work lost much of the authority and intellectual prestige that it enjoyed at the beginning of the twentieth century. Today, we are led to see the *Dictionnaire* as a historical document that demands to be treated as such—in terms of taste ("taste," that is, as it was then, eclectic and itself reasoned) more than thought— and not as the irreplaceable instrument of initiation into the problems of medieval architecture (or indeed, architecture in general) recognized by Focillon. But perhaps it is less important to defend the *Dictionnaire* against unimaginative criticism that lacks any real theoretical and speculative substance than it is to propose another reading: one deliberately presentist and, if possible, attuned to the constructive cast of mind that makes the work invaluable.

Viollet-le-Duc's contemporaries and close friends were astonished that he should twice choose to present his archeological theories in dictionary form. They found his theories fascinating for their breadth and resonance, but felt that their coherence and logical rigor would not be adequately served by a series of fragmentary articles scattered among several volumes, prey to the arbitrary demands of alphabetical order. Mérimée himself (to whom Viollet-le-Duc owed his career and, perhaps more than this, a certain idea of tradition, of monumental inscription of the past in the present, and of the perpetually renewed process by which each epoch invents its own past and the task of conserving, its establishment equal to that of its *restoration*) made no secret of his reservations: the content was rich, the information considerable, but the *Dictionnaire* was not a book. Less still was it a fresco, a continuous panorama of the development of French architecture or of the evolution of medieval furniture that one had the right to expect of such an eminent connoisseur (whose qualities as a writer had earned the first literary claims for a genre of writing normally regarded as strictly functional).

But if Viollet-le-Duc had chosen to distribute the content of his discourse according to the discontinuous rhythm of dictionary articles, it was not because he had taken the easy way out or because he lacked a systematic mind. To the contrary, the preface of the *Dictionnaire* informs us of his desire to profit from the dispersion of the large number of terms in his lexicon: "This form [of a dictionary] . . . seemed to us, precisely because of the multiplicity of given examples, to be more favorable to studies, better made to understand the complicated but rigorously deduced parts of the elements that enter into the composition of our monuments of the Middle Ages, since we are obliged, so to speak, to dissect them separately while describing the functions and transformations of these different parts."[5] Again, this choice of form was not simply the result of a desire to educate. It also had (and has) an epistemological value that we can recognize today: the very *discontinuity* that is the principle of a work that wants to be reasoned is the mark of a system that is the most well linked, closely woven, and content rich that architectural thought has ever conceived.

The *Dictionnaire raisonné* is certainly rational in that its author applied himself to uncovering the raison d'être—the *why* of each part and element—of a medieval building[6] while at the same time defining the principles that govern and determine the arrangement of parts within an organization, at once constructive and concrete, as well as their morphological evolution within a single system or from one system to another (e.g., from the system of antiquity to that of the Middle Ages). It is in the very composition of this dictionary, in its overall plan—the choice of entries, the relative length of articles, the endless references from one rubric to another, the multiple cross-checks, and even the inevitable repetitions in such an undertaking—that reveals a properly structuralist conception of the relationship between the architectural whole and its component parts. (If I refer to the concept of *structure* here, it is chiefly because this word is to be found in all but a few of Viollet-le-Duc's entries.[7]) But this is not simply a question of vocabulary or fashion. If one looks for something other than straightforward information or comments on certain points of detail, and if one takes care to read the dictionary as it should be read, paying constant attention to the relation of the parts to the whole and of the whole to the parts, then this "reasoned" dictionary (as, in another age and from another viewpoint, Diderot and d'Alembert intended their *Encyclopédie, ou, Dictionnaire raisonné des sciences, des arts, et des métiers* to be) will not fail to appear as the singularly precocious manifesto—at least in outline—of the method, ideology, and structural thought as it has since been elaborated in linguistics and anthropology.

In truth, the idea of looking at a building as a more or less coherent and coordinated whole was not new in Viollet-le-Duc's time. And it is not unhelpful here to recall, through the lens of what Michel Foucault has called "archaeology," that the idea of organized form, and even that of structure, owes more than a little to the theory and practice of architecture. The etymology of *structure* (from *struere*, to construct) alone would not justify this affiliation, but the application of the structural method to the study of communication in its broadest sense opened up perspectives and involved us in a series of problems that were anticipated, or at least portended, in the writings of Viollet-le-Duc. It is highly surprising that criticism has not recognized the truly epistemological quality that constitutes the real value of the *Dictionnaire*. For the interest of this work lies not so much in the technical exposition of the genesis and development of the Gothic style—beginning with the ribbed vault and the principle of elasticity—as in the way it discusses, for any building, the relationship of the parts to the whole and the whole to its parts. For example, one has only to compare Viollet-le-Duc's writings on the architecture of ancient Greece to the description of a Doric temple in Jakob Burckhardt's *Der Cicerone* (1855) to understand how foreign to him (whatever other opinions may have been expressed[8]) was the type of organicism, a premature Bergsonism, that flourished in the writings of his contemporaries. The *Dictionnaire* contains very few descriptions that appeal, through empathy, to the so-called vital élan of a building considered as an animate organism. When he discusses a specific architectural member, Viollet-le-Duc is always aware of the totality into which it is inserted, the system to which it refers. But the very idea of a system, far from seeming to provide an explanatory principle, rather presupposes in spirit the decomposition of the whole constructed into its constituent parts and in turn of each of these elements into their component parts. In such a perspective, *synthesis*, as the permanent horizon of the analytical process, is neither privileged nor given any logical priority. On the contrary, synthesis is only justified, only meaningful, from the moment when analysis succeeds in reading the whole in the parts and in deciphering in the elements themselves the principles that regulate the general organization of the building; it is from this that the style of the monument, its system, derives.

One of the clearest tenets of structuralism as it has gained success in the field of the human sciences is the possibility of using a single element to reconstitute a system—or at least the broad lines of its structural agency—and the modalities under which this element enters into composition with other constituent unities and defines itself with respect to them. This principle is particularly productive when applied to the study of architecture: in discursive terms, an architectural element has value—signification—not in itself but only in terms of its assigned place in the system, which designates the ensemble of relations, positive or negative, of association or of exclusion, that it sustains with the other elements of the system. Like the elements of a verbal chain, the elements employed by architecture have only differential value—or, in linguistic terms, *diacritical* function. When Viollet-le-Duc chose to shed light on the logical principles that ensured the unity and coherence of the medieval system in considering each element in turn, defining them as so many bundles of relations in composing a reasoned dictionary, he was constructing a work of a truly structural nature. If he describes the transformations of the pillar in the Gothic period, it is in order to assert that this element "expresses more clearly than any other architectural feature . . . the experiments and efforts of architects and represents the logical outcome of principles conceived at a moment when art was becoming increasingly secular."[9] Yet the pillar is hardly one of the generative elements of the rigorously deduced Gothic system, which, according to Viollet-le-Duc, was planned entirely "from above," starting with the arches. If the morphological evolution of this subordinate member of Gothic architecture can serve to illuminate the development of the system itself, then it is by negation or reflection. For architectural syntax, contrary to the wishes of academic teaching, cannot be reduced to the combination of conventional forms of constant and equal value; rather, it implies a hierarchical organization of constituent units, of which some are subordinate and some privileged—a necessarily unstable hierarchy constantly subject to revision, if not revolution. Thus, in the Gothic system the setting out of the arches determines the distribution of the points of support at ground level, as well as their section and profile, whereas the Greek system, which is planned "from below," starts with the supports—first and foremost with the column.

It is through this principle of subordination that we are able to appreciate in logical terms (and no longer as merely descriptive and picturesque) the relative positions of different elements within a larger context as well as the way these elements combine to constitute the architectural organism as such. This principle is found at the level of the different members of architecture of which the constituent parts are in their turn regulated according to a hierarchical order that allows us to define them as terms of a structural unit. Although partial and not possessed of its own rationale, this structural unit carries the mark of the system from which it derives, inscribed in its structure, if not in its form, at the same time as it in turn serves as the context for even smaller units. The articulation of the column, for example, with base and capital apparently subordinate to shaft, illustrates the structural principles of a system based on vertical supports and horizontal transoms. Thus, it is clear that the morphological evolution of any element whatsoever reflects the evolution of the system itself. This can be seen in the development of supports in Gothic architecture, from the circular pillar with base and capital, which introduced an element of rupture (or at least of discontinuity) into the first buildings of that style, to the composite pillar, which in section reflects, without solution of continuity, the springing of the arches and the prominent members of the vaulting, as seen very early on at the Church of Saint-Urbain in Troyes.[10] In the case of Gothic architecture, this evolution is evident in the increasingly strong emphasis that architects placed on the vault and on the ribbed tracery that supported it.

This is to say that, unlike the signs of language, the elements of architecture are not arbitrary in form and appearance because they depend on the totality in which they are inscribed. If the Gothic—that is, the medieval system—has taken on the force of style, then it is precisely in the sense of a system that finds its expression in the most immediate register of morphology. In short, to characterize Viollet-le-Duc's structural thinking as expressed in the ten volumes of the *Dictionnaire*, one could say that his desire to think through the phenomenon of architecture in terms of *systems* corresponded to his constant concern with showing how the simplest modification of any element or structural unit of a building cannot fail to affect the other parts of the structure in conformity with the system's own logic (so long as it does not involve a major rupture in the ordering of the whole, which would lead to a more or less fundamental modification of the system itself—perhaps even, in the end, to the projection of new structural systems).

It is not difficult to detect the language of modern structuralism in Viollet-le-Duc's work; the *Dictionnaire* is full of references to elements, functions, systems, logic, structural equilibrium, reasoning, and deductions, which are rarely without consequences or, sometimes, a few contradictions. Certainly, Viollet-le-Duc draws from the language of naturalists, but he uses it to endow the imperious demands of rationalism, in which he recognized the true mark of Gothic architecture, with strikingly effective imagery that would persuade his readers of the merits of a system that aimed (at least in its ideals) to construct lost buildings from the fragments, vestiges, and *traces* left for the archeologist.[11] But what did he have in mind when he discussed the logic and the general principles that apply (or should apply, according to him) to all architecture in any time and in any place? Or when he claimed that certain contradictions mire all architects who, despite their claims to the contrary, leave the problem of structural organization, the very art of building, to tradition or to their own caprice? And if these general principles owed nothing to history or convention, by what authority did they impose themselves in forms and styles that transcend the permutations of time and place? To these questions the *Dictionnaire* supplies a series of responses that, although inconclusive, may help us to distinguish more clearly some of the difficulties that from the outset have been at the center of the problematic of structuralism.

The first of these difficulties, and the only one that will occupy us here, relates to the status that should be assigned to so-called structural logic and to the degree of objectivity of the *models* constructed by linguists, anthropologists, and historians in order to reveal the structure—the system of connections and variables underlying the phenomena they seek to explain.

Does this logic reside in the things, the facts themselves, or in the mind that knows them and seeks to discover their agency and function? And again, in the case of systems that might be considered under the rubric of signification (among which architecture is obviously included), what weight should be given, in their elaboration and their very functioning, to the different states of the conscious and unconscious mind? Viollet-le-Duc was convinced that the "ideal," "complete," and "finished" model he proposed for the Gothic cathedral was *something that no architect had envisaged* at any moment in history;[12] if it had a place in the *Dictionnaire*, it was precisely because as a model it was an entirely graphic and conceptual instrument suitable for shedding light on the structural relationship that joins the many realizations of the Gothic age, the common ground they shared, and the common problematic beneath their individual experiments. The Gothic architects' task far exceeded them, yet they worked without any models (save for the buildings they erected) and without any precise notion of the end toward which they directed their efforts. Nothing indicates that they were ever compelled—or even had the chance—to give theoretical or programmatic form to their enterprise. Yet the concrete nature of the logic that pervades their work, endowing it simultaneously with meaning and an appearance of finality, is evident on every page of the *Dictionnaire*.

Viollet-le-Duc was not content to describe the external workings of buildings, or to provide a systematic explanation of the way in which architectural members are composed and articulated, simply for the sake of formulating a series of principles whose validity is judged by the light they shed onto the objects considered. If he denounced academic teaching, it was because it stopped at the appearance of buildings, at their superficial envelope, and enunciated only the basic rules of monumental composition while ignoring the real logic on which the art of building is based. The method of the *Dictionnaire* responds to that of the École in that it starts with the visible elements of architecture. But it is distinguished immediately by its refusal to recognize the conventional terms of a combinatory game whose rules were founded partly on tradition and partly on an ensemble of transcendent principles, such as the rules of harmony, proportion, and symmetry. The movement though which Viollet-le-Duc cleansed the theory of architecture of the idealism that underlay academic prattle is one that he understood would constitute the architectural phenomenon as an object of science. The "beauty" of a building cannot be measured solely by the quality of its envelope; if the word *beauty* has any meaning (and it must if we are to speak of architecture and not merely of construction), then it implies the idea of a truth, of the close relationship of the form to a reality foreign to the domain of the Beautiful per se—that is, to the reality of received ideas, a reality of a properly structural order. Viollet-le-Duc judged that the primary articulations were first and foremost those of worked stone, assembled wood, and metal—this before the arrival of concrete, which called for a reflection on the continuity of forms and lines as opposed to the discontinuity of elements.

If architecture cannot be purely and simply reduced to construction, and if there are constructions that embody nothing architectural—as well as architectures that cannot in all rigor be called "constructed"[13]—then architecture as understood by Viollet-le-Duc nonetheless finds its primary reason in constructed reality, in the masonry itself, or, to take the word in the sense given by architectural theory since Vitruvius, in *structure* itself. The logic that governs the treatment of forms and their combinations in fact overlies an order of the concrete, or material, relations of structural mechanics. Before appearing as elements of a combination, a pillar, an arch, or a vault must satisfy, in their disposition, organization, and dimensions, a set of conditions formulated in terms of weights, resultant pressures, and so on.

These conditions, these mechanical facts and the constructional principles that follow from them, will vary from a system based on right angles and straight lines to one based on a monolithic principle (such as the Greek system) to a system of passive blocks of solid masonry (such as the Romans') to one based on the interplay of buttresses, active equilibrium, and structural elasticity (principles by which, according to Viollet-le-Duc, the Gothic style could be recognized). Each architectonic style is articulated according to a set of constructional principles—a structural system constituting a specific logical framework that analysis must bring to light.

The composition of the *Dictionnaire* and the doctrine expounded by Viollet-le-Duc in the *Entretiens sur l'architecture* are based on structural *realism*, in the strongest sense of the word. It is on the basis of this logic, inscribed in the stone itself, that Viollet-le-Duc attempted to account for the phenomenal appearance of the buildings he studied. And it was this logic that provided him with criteria for a type of architectural criticism he hoped would spring from an extremely exacting desire for sincerity and honesty in form—qualities that not all architectural periods have known. Surely, by this he meant that the outer envelope, the "form of the art," was simply the result of the precise use of building materials according to their intrinsic qualities and to the fulfillment of the architect's given needs.[14] An architectural style that possesses its rigor, its own "truth," lies in the extent to which the hidden order of relationships responsible for the structural equilibrium of the architectonic whole is manifest, right down to the smallest structural details. Viollet-le-Duc despised "masked architectures," and the architects who would paste on orders borrowed from unrelated structures like so much sumptuous and ridiculous plunder.

This is to say that, from Viollet-le-Duc's point of view, the descriptive approach could under no circumstance prevail over

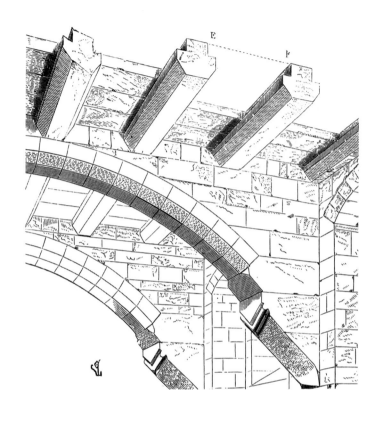

5.2

Construction detail. From Eugène Emmanuel Viollet-le-Duc, "Construction," in *Dictionnaire raisonné de l'architecture française du XIe au XVIe siècle* (Paris, 1854–1868), 4:234. Courtesy Avery Architectural & Fine Arts Library, Columbia University.

structural analysis; it could only lead us indirectly to the "essential being" of a building wherein the architectural form flows out of the constructed reality, just as a logical consequence flows from a premise. But by distinguishing between being and appearance, between phenomena and noumena, did Viollet-le-Duc not reintroduce into architectural theory in a new form something of that transcending illusion he denounced in the teaching of the École? If form has no function or use other than the revelation of structure and if the theory of form only assumed a scientific basis in the nineteenth century, then what is the nature of that so-called medieval rationalism and the almost deductive rigor with which twelfth- and thirteenth-century builders conceived a new monumental style based on unprecedented constructional theories? More fundamentally, what can we make of the *Dictionnaire*'s interpretation of the development of medieval architecture, its approach to Gothic forms, if Viollet-le-Duc's suppositions concerning the equilibrium and stability of ogival structures are called into question? Must we give up on the systematic aim that comprises the interest of his enterprise, renounce structural analysis, and refuse to give a rational basis to that description of the perceived facts, a rational basis that would bring together, at the level of phenomena, the two main paths of modern anthropology—structural ideology and phenomenological description?

The concept of a *model* seems to provide a particularly apt instrument for bringing about such a reconciliation, on the condition that one accepts the basic principle of the structural method—namely, that the notion of structure is related not to empirical reality but to analytical models constructed afterward.[15] This principle, to which phenomenological description can very well adapt, assumes a special significance in architecture insofar as a building that lends itself to structural analysis is also one able to function as a model for thought. Although Viollet-le-Duc's structural realism does not exactly recognize this,

his article on construction is nevertheless designed to convince us that a given structure, far from being a natural thing, has an essentially "rational" character, which the architect may on occasion choose to reveal. Take but one example, which will not lead us far from the analyses of the *Dictionnaire*: the originality of the Gothic style lies, as Viollet-le-Duc correctly perceived, in the fact that the visible skeleton, the tracery of the ribbing and projecting members that is thrown over the masonry like a net, immediately suggests to the observer an ideal construction that certainly does not correspond to the constructional reality in all its aspects but is rather its translation as an image. Pol Abraham, the most acerbic critic of Viollet-le-Duc's theories, himself admitted this when, having denied the load-bearing functions of the banded ribs beneath the vaults, he allowed that these ribs provided the builders with a useful geometrical method for drawing the lines of the penetration and intersection of the surfaces.[16] To this we can add, with Focillon, that their tracery presents an approximate but reasoned image of the mechanical arrangements and, at the same time, a concrete outline of the system of forces and critical areas of Gothic buildings as the architects of the period could represent them.[17] If the eye perceives the ogival framework as a structure, it is not simply because it reveals a hidden constructive order but also because this visible framework has been deliberately conceived as a model—a model at once constructed and constructive, intended not for the observers alone but primarily for the builders themselves. Thus, the structural analysis and the phenomenological description are bound endlessly to corroborate one another.

It should be possible to read the *Dictionnaire raisonné* today and to consent, for example, to the chain of deductions that winds through the article "Construction," choosing to relate the structural reasoning not directly to the constructed reality but to the models proposed by art or elaborated by the theoretician. Although these models are approximations, their imprecision cannot be seen as a problem if it is true that even in the "exact" sciences the perfection of any theoretical model is conditioned by a work of interpretation, abstraction, simplification, and even distortion, as well as the reduction, if not the bracketing, of certain constituent dimensions of phenomena. Indeed, as the great engineers attest, structural analysis in its narrowest sense (that is, mathematics applied to the study of mechanical systems) in fact rests on models that give only an imperfect account of the real behavior of material structures.[18] And this is what the *Dictionnaire* should tell us, as should any criticism of Viollet-le-Duc's structural ideology: namely, that this margin of imprecision, if it is constructive, is a basic principle of both art and science, and that there can be no greater devotion to the aesthetic object than the work of preserving it in artistic discourse, and even introducing it there deliberately. This is another way of saying that the "truth" of a building is to be found not in the bricks and mortar, any more than in the outer form, but in the space between, the space that separates them and by which they become complementary—the space where style is born, the gap between things, which is intimated in the absence of a logical link between the two propositions that open the article on construction: "Construction is the means; architecture the result."[19] For a means, unless it is taken for an end, cannot produce results unless it is used for a particular destination; architecture, then, is only a result and does not contain its own determination. Perhaps it is there between those two small propositions, separated by an ambiguous semicolon, that we should seek the secret of the still-relevant impact of the *Dictionnaire* and its educational value. From this gap between architecture and construction, between a form and a substance that cannot exist separately, the working of stone, steel, or cement can simultaneously assume a structural value, invite meaning, and accede to what is conventionally called "style."

6.1
Plan and axonometric details of engaged column
bases in the church of Saint-Nazaire, Carcassonne.
From Eugène-Emmanuel Viollet-le-Duc, "Base," in
*Dictionnaire raisonné de l'architecture française
du XIe au XVIe siècle* (Paris, 1854–1868), 2:158.
Courtesy Avery Architectural & Fine Arts Library,
Columbia University.

6 FROM STRUCTURALISM BACK TO FUNCTIONALISM

"COLUMN: n. A stone cylinder placed on a base or a pedestal, supporting an architrave or an arch."[1] Viollet-le-Duc's definition of a column in his *Dictionnaire raisonné de l'architecture française du XIe au XVe siècle* calls for a certain number of remarks, the pertinence of which will not necessarily be limited to French architecture from the eleventh to the sixteenth century. As far as archeology goes, the column actually counts among those members of architecture whose seeming universality calls out for its nature both in space and in time to be questioned. This is to say nothing of the fetishism evidenced by its recurrence at certain moments in the Western tradition, in more or less time-honored though occasionally aberrant forms—the same fetishism exhibited in its most direct form in the Middle Ages, in the practice of the *reuse* of antique columns sometimes transported over considerable distances.

Viollet-le-Duc's concise definition has the merit of clearly stating the facts of the issue posed in structural terms. At the outset, however, he emphasizes the potential ambiguity of the subject: a column is indeed a stone cylinder, but it is not only that. This cylinder takes on a value and a figure as a "column" only once it is linked with two other members of architecture: the *base* on which it rests and the *capital* with which it is crowned. As for the *shaft*, the *Dictionnaire* defines it as "the part of the column included between the base and the capital."[2] In other words, the column was established at the outset as a complete and articulated form, deriving from the joining of several differentiated and complementary elements, and should thus be considered in its relationship with other members of architecture—in this instance, the lintel and the arch.

Seen in this way, the definition of the column may be understood as characteristic of the guiding intention of the *Dictionnaire* and of the constant transition from observation to explanation, description to argument, and history to theory that makes for its originality. As its title suggests, the *Dictionnaire* is indeed *raisonné*, and in the most deliberate and insistent fashion. Considering each element, each member, of architecture one by one in its concrete historical evolution as revealed by archeology, Viollet-le-Duc focuses on uncovering their raisons d'être, demonstrating the *why* behind each and bringing to light the logic that might regulate its use and govern its morphological and functional evolution. And it is exactly so with the column, which should not be seen simply as a conventional form deriving from the conjunction of aleatory, or merely decorative, elements. This member of architecture has a determined use value.

The sequence *base, shaft, capital* does not, however, have a raison d'être in itself. To understand the succession, connection, and combination of these three terms within a unitary form, we must refer to the function of the vertical fulcrum that has devolved to the column in the structural system. Viollet-le-Duc's definition of the column accomplishes this while also making perfect sense of what we might call the hierarchical arrangement of that which functions as a completely separate structural element. In the end, a column can be reduced to a skittle stood perpendicularly to the ground in order to support a vertical load. This implies that the shaft constitutes the centerpiece, whereas the base and capital play only secondary roles. The footing marks the passage, or transition, between the vertical axis of the support and the horizontal foundation of the edifice (an apparently

unnecessary function, judged by the Doric order). The capital itself emerges as the obligatory complement to the shaft, whether
the projection of the capital reduces the span of the lintel and
thus prevents the rupture of the horizontal block supported by
the column or its flared form provides a cantilevered equilibrium, ensuring the seating of a lintel that is wider than the shaft's
diameter or of the springing of an arch whose section at the level
of springing is greater than the section of the load-bearing cylinder below it.

Taking into account the function it fulfils in the context of any
given building system and the fact that such a system obeys either the principle of the lintel or that of the arch, we must accept
that the form derived from joining a shaft, a base, and a capital is
in no way arbitrary or conventional. Rather, this joining presents
itself as a structural unit whose constitutive elements demand to
be viewed in their functional articulation, with each part presenting a perfect "solidity"*both in appearance and in reality*.[3] This
role of balancing appearance and reality, being and seeming, in
the genesis of the ideology of modernity scarcely needs to be recalled. But the subordination of the various elements of the column and their component parts to *reason*, to the *why* that governs
their organization as a form, is again illustrated by the fact that
certain parts do not rightly belong to any particular element, and
their function as a "hinge" never appears more clearly than when
it gives rise to a shift in articulation. Consider, for example, the
astragal, the molding that separates the capital from the shaft. It
could be part of the shaft, as in Romanesque architecture, wherever the shaft bulges or tapers, or it could be part of the capital,
as when, for reasons of economy, the shaft takes the form of a
perfect cylinder, as was the case with Gothic architecture from
the thirteenth century on.[4]

The same is true of the *abacus*, which after long constituting an independent slab designed to support the springers of an

arch was over time absorbed into the same course as the capital before disappearing as an identifiable element when the capital was reduced to a simple ring at the junction of the arch and the pier.[5] The constitutive elements of the column are to a certain extent optional and interchangeable; their number is not a fixed imperative, and their enumeration alone does not define the column as such. Yet the characteristic articulation of the parts within a unitary sequence and in keeping with their function seems to be the fundamental rule of the column. Thus, strictly speaking, the column should be defined first as a *structure*, then as a *form*, in that the concept of structure implies the idea of organization or design, not a simple juxtaposition of differentiated elements to be viewed in their functional and, in the final analysis, constructional connection.

Viollet-le-Duc saw the development of the capital as a sure indication of the process of scaling down the supports, the isolated fulcrums, in the scheme of the composite pier, which was designed as the pure and simple extension of the springing of vaults that characterized the evolution of Gothic architecture at the point of its maturity (if he is to be believed). In his article "Capital," we learn that in the twelfth century Île-de-France, the capital appeared as "an *intelligent* extension of the shaft," and so took its supporting functions *seriously.*[6] (Note the shift of attributing to the building, or at least to a particular part of it, some of the intelligence and seriousness that Viollet-le-Duc sees in the builders—a kind of inverted empathy.) The form of the capital is determined in the Gothic system by that of the springer, which corresponds to the springing of the vaults, any modification of which will necessarily affect that of the pier, which thus could not maintain its circular cross section. If we consider the column as a structural unit, one that puts into play a series of discrete elements (the transformations of which have consequences for the functional equilibrium of the whole), then the decline in the role assigned to the abacus and the evolution of the Gothic capital—which was itself gradually reduced to a simple band of foliage and ultimately eliminated—are signs that, even if the column played a seminal role in the original system, in the end it would lose its place, for its characteristic mode of articulation openly contradicted the structural principles of Gothic architecture in its final and, logically speaking, consummate form.

Such an assertion sheds light on the problems posed by the deployment of a given structural or functional unit in a context that is itself specified by name, as well as on the relationship that unites the column as a singular form with the other "units" that the art of building puts in play. Having defined the column as an articulated whole to which the role of vertical fulcrum has been devolved, Viollet-le-Duc hastens to insist that the form is not amenable to an indefinite number of combinations and that, strictly speaking, it can be linked to only two other well-defined members of architecture: the lintel and the arch. And so his analysis focuses at the outset on already structured elements, functional units identifiable as such. But it follows immediately that, though the column can be defined as a singular form, a discrete unit, in its internal articulation, it obeys a principle (if not a law) that endows it with use-value together with relatively limited constructional valences. A column cannot be utilized gratuitously, nor can it be used in any context whatever or separated from its function; its structure permits change only within very strict limits, beyond which the column as such does not exist.

This raises another question: should we exclude from the category of "column" any architectonic member that corresponds to the *Dictionnaire* definition on all points but one—namely, that it supports not *one* but *several* arches? This question is neither superficial nor sophisticated; to confirm this, one need only read the pages devoted to the question, and the distinction between being and appearance arises once again. Indeed, the structure and perhaps even more so the form of the column is not entirely suitable for supporting oblique pressures without the risk of leaning. You might say that all that is needed to reestablish equilibrium is for the thrust of an arch to be countered by the thrust of an opposing arch, the column supporting not one but several arches that buttress each other. But the vertical force resulting from the oblique pressures would be so great that the column would have to be displaced by a much bigger pier whose *scale* (not "proportions") would be such that we could no longer call it a column. Thus, despite the *Dictionnaire*'s ostensibly descriptive and historical definition of the column, there remains a basic incompatibility between the column and the arch, as well as between the column and the vault. It is no coincidence, moreover, that the article on scale gives us the clearest statement of a contradiction that is obviously not just functional: "Since the lintel is no longer acceptable, the fulcrum is no longer a column; it is a pier."[7] By 1220, "French architects, had ceased using the monocylindrical column for bearing vaults and sought continuously thereafter to transform the column into a support for the projecting members of the vault, and thus into a vertical beam for those members."[8] The process came to an end, even before the close of the century, in a building whose precocity has often astounded archeologists: the Church of Saint-Urbain in Troyes. Since then, the pillar has presented a section that corresponds "logically" to the cluster of arches that descend and without interruption or rupture (*solution de continuité*) from the top of the vaults to the ground.

Many of the theoretical problems I have just evoked echo those encountered by structuralism as it was developed more than a century ago in the human sciences, beginning with linguistics and anthropology—and in constant opposition to functionalism, which, as the term indicates, puts function ahead of all other determinations. When, in the preface to a selection of extracts from the *Dictionnaire*,[9] I tried to demonstrate why Viollet-le-Duc should be considered one of the initiators of structuralism, I was accused of having yielded to the seductions of a peculiarly Parisian vogue—but in fact there was no retrospective projection involved. For we cannot ignore the fact that structuralism was not invented in 1950s Paris and that it already had a long history behind it, beginning long before Claude Lévi-Strauss and Roman Jakobson, or even Ferdinand de Saussure. In this context, Pierre Francastel deserves credit for recalling the constructional ancestry of the concept of structure. In the case of Viollet-le-Duc, the work of Philippe Boudon and Philippe Deshayes on the "Raisonné" (as Frank Lloyd Wright called the *Dictionnaire*) confirms the thesis I put forward, to the great displeasure of some.[10] Today, if we are to believe the rumor, structuralism has gone out of fashion—something that can only be a cause for rejoicing—yet I am all the more comfortable insisting on what I said before, even if it means once again displeasing those who do not appreciate seeing art history risk involvement with thought. This is not to say that Viollet-le-Duc could not have known Saussure's name, which was also the name of Horace-Bénédict de Saussure, great-grandfather of the author of *Course in General Linguistics*, who in the eighteenth century made a famous ascent of Mont Blanc, a feat recounted in his *Voyages dans les Alpes*. Following the Lausanne exhibition on Viollet-le-Duc in 1979, the exhibition at the Grand Palais in 1980 reminded us of Viollet-le-Duc's keen interest in the architectonics of the alpine massif, an interest that was obviously connected to his intense passion for architecture in all its forms, including the natural. This passion was equaled only by Saussure's drive to confront language in terms that Lévi-Strauss would make use of when he identified an architecture of culture similar to the architecture of language: "Language can be said to be a condition of culture because the material out of which language is built is of the same type as the material out of which the whole culture is built: logical relations, oppositions, correlations, and the like. Language, from this point of view, may appear as laying a kind of foundation for the more complex structures which correspond to the different aspects of culture."[11]

I wish to conclude with a comment on theory and its evolution, its ebbs and flows. In the domain of anthropology, the structuralist hypothesis came in part from reflections on the contradictions of functionalism. Viollet-le-Duc himself emphasizes the idea of function throughout his work, and yet the idea is never unequivocally defined, either in the *Dictionnaire* or in the *Entretiens*. *Function* at times refers to the constructional value or utilitarian purpose assigned to a particular architectural member or form and at others is used to characterize the relative arrangement of architectonic elements within the same constructional organism. Indeed, it seems that, by placing more and more emphasis on the "needs" answered by the work of architecture, Viollet-le-Duc, in *Entretiens*, took a step back from the theoretical argument of the *Dictionnaire*. Whereas the latter sees architecture as subject not to static *states* but to an uninterrupted series of transitions, the former exhibits a more strictly functionalist turn, whereby the role of historical creativity is displaced by a so-called common stock of eternal principles held independent of the forms that express or betray them. In matters of architecture, Viollet-le-Duc concluded, we can no longer *invent* but merely "submit known elements to analysis, combine them, appropriate them."[12]

The example of the column is provided once more in *Entretiens* and thus attests to the relative decline in a doctrine that, having failed to preserve the full epistemological scope of the concept of *function*, would end in a form of utilitarian empiricism that clearly contradicts the structuralist intention of the *Dictionnaire*. Indeed, Viollet-le-Duc of *Entretiens* does not hesitate to conclude that if the Doric column has no base, this is because a base would get in the way of the passing public and insult visitors' feet.[13] Yet his theoretical retreat is most obvious when he treats the form of the shaft. The *Dictionnaire* article "Scale" in fact develops a notion that would interest advocates of a "nonstandard" architecture: the notion of a *pier articulated at the base*. The idea of giving a pyramidal or conical form to a pier that supports even, symmetrical forces cannot be conceived by a true architect, for any builder (as Viollet-le-Duc asserts) knows that all one needs is an upright pillar that allows for the anticipation of errors in the calculation of forces, insofar as it can pivot on its base to return the resultant of the stresses to the vertical. Yet what do we read in *Entretiens*? "No one will allow that a column, a vertical fulcrum, can be more spindly at its base than at the top."[14] A question, one could say, of empathy. Philosophers are well aware that no matter how opposed rationalism and empiricism may be in principle, they are not averse to swapping roles occasionally. It is only all the more remarkable to see our inveterate rationalist, in an appeal to common sense, take up the example David Hume used a century earlier to illustrate the idea that the rules of architecture have their basis in sensory experience. As Hume wrote, those rules require "that the top of a pillar should be more slender than its base, and that, because such a figure conveys to us the idea of security, which is pleasant; whereas the contrary form gives us the apprehension of danger, which is uneasy."[15]

7.1
Claude-Nicolas Ledoux, Country House for a Man
of Letters (Abbé Delille), perspective view. From
*L'architecture considerée sous le rapport de l'art,
des moeurs et de la législation* (Paris, 1804), plate
69. Courtesy Avery Architectural & Fine Arts Library,
Columbia University.

7 LEDOUX WITH KANT

TRANSLATED BY ERIN WILLIAMS

Publishing delays sometimes have a beneficial effect in that they bring a semblance of justification to the exercise of writing a preface—by definition a risky undertaking. For if the publication, as well as the purchase of a book, always entails an element of risk (which cannot be measured in financial terms alone), then a preface—whether it is the work of the author or of a third party—is supposed to offer both publisher and reader a sort of guarantee or insurance. The reverse is also true: to say that a text calls for a preface is implicitly to admit that it is not enough in itself, that it will only have its effect with appropriate clarification—that the reader, unless alerted in advance, will have no chance of recognizing its importance, will not know how to read it without the appropriate eyeglasses. This presents the distinct possibility of abuse, as when the preface begins to take on the role of an advertisement or instruction manual.

It is different in the case of a historical text and when dealing with a republication or a new translation. French readers discovered the work of Emil Kaufmann in reverse, so to speak: beginning with what appeared his crowning achievement, the great book *Architecture in the Age of Reason* (1955), and only then becoming familiar with *Three Revolutionary Architects: Boullée, Ledoux, Lequeu* (1952), finally arriving at the book published in Vienna in 1933, whose title alone signals Kaufmann's entire intellectual program—*Von Ledoux bis Le Corbusier*. This book has neither the fullness of the two others nor their weight of scholarship, but it contains the seed of an idea that Kaufmann would take up tirelessly throughout his life as he deepened and developed all of its ramifications. It is a book with the appearance of a broadside or pamphlet, and one can see from both its title and date of publication that it was topical enough. At the moment when Nazism was triumphant in Munich and Berlin, strongly supported by a mass of academic rubbish, it was proof of great intellectual courage for a Viennese to attempt to demonstrate the existence of a fundamental continuity between so-called neoclassical architecture and the architecture already denounced by the totalitarian ideology as "international"—all the more so in that Kaufmann pressed his insolence to the point of including under the banner of two French architects a certain number of German architects, beginning with Karl Friedrich Schinkel, that the new order claimed as an integral part of its heritage. (Not to mention the sangfroid Kaufmann demonstrated, in the face of this blackmail and even more in the face of the political hysteria of the avant-gardes, as he celebrated the aspiration to autonomy of a practice that was potentially as profoundly socialized as that of architecture.)

This book was then born of its time. Is this to say that it is only of retrospective interest, as a historical document? While everyone is proclaiming the failure of the modern movement and denouncing its "objective" connections with a technocratic order that ended up adopting it as its own, what resonance can this thin volume and its thesis expect to find without being shored up by a large documentary apparatus? But if (as Jorge-Luis Borges would have it) a preface is no more than a form of lateral criticism, there is no reason the reader should expect to be warned against the book it introduces. To alert the reader to the resistances that the text might elicit is, on the other hand, one of the rights generally granted to one who writes a preface. In this case, since there is a preface, why would this one not take advantage of the gap in time to invite the reader to find in it a way of seeing a little more clearly? Resistance always indicates conflict, and it does no good to ignore it. It is, then, up to us to ensure that this translation too is born of its time, our own, caught as we are in the meandering ways of a discourse that has not yet broken with modernity—and for reasons that the reading of this book should help us to unravel. Despite its brevity, it has lost none of its edge.

One could say that this is certainly the least to be expected of such a book: does its central thesis not suggest that a radical break interrupted the course of architectural production in the era of the French Revolution, a break that would form the distant origin of the modern movement? That the work of Ledoux could be presented as the paradigm of this break assumes that the old and the new are brought together within it in such a way that the rupture is only more evident. Yet it is to this that the most recent discourse on modernity is opposed: a discourse that, far from being one of a "break," works on the contrary to retie threads, to reinscribe in the continuity of a history a practice from which for too long it had the pretention of freeing itself. The paradox that engages us in reading Kaufmann lies in the fact that he himself attempted to give this phenomenon a historical explanation and that, in a single stroke, he restored to the modern movement both a past and a historical dimension. Indeed, to maintain that the break from which modern architecture in principle proceeds goes back to the end of the eighteenth century implies that this architecture does not begin with Le Corbusier and that behind it lies an entire history—including, as we will see, its claim to the tabula rasa.

Kaufmann's thesis, which saw Le Corbusier as the true heir of Claude-Nicolas Ledoux and Schinkel, was bound to scandalize the champions of a showy neoclassicism à la Albert Speer, as well as those on the other side who felt that, after all, the proletariat also had a right to the column. (Question: Does the proletariat therefore have a right to entasis? Can the proletarian column adapt itself to inflation?) Indeed, we often forget that the critique of functionalism did not originate yesterday. Among the Marxists, as well as in Frankfurt with Theodor Adorno, there were a few good minds who denounced what they considered, as Brecht put it, "the last word of bourgeois architecture."[1] The last word, but not the first. One can imagine that those who appealed to the revolutionary ideal might have judged unsuitable the proposition according to which the program of the *Sachlichkeit* would have found its formulation in the period of the "great revolution" (French and bourgeois) of 1789. But Kaufmann's demonstration was no less shocking with respect to the habitual assumptions of art history. This book, devoted as it seems to be to the investigation of the sources of the modern movement, does not obey the law of the genre. If one agrees with Kaufmann's thesis, declared as early as 1928,[2] that Ledoux was a figure who signified a "personalized break point" in history, then one must admit that he is also an end point for any historical tracing of the modern movement. The question, then, would not be so much to search for *whence he came* (even if it is always permissible to support rather than oppose one's predecessors—as in the case of Ledoux in relation to Jacques-François Blondel—it is still a form of owing them something) but rather to know, in Kaufmann's terms, *where he went* and to attempt to understand Ledoux not on the basis of his own antecedents but through the path he opened up. It must be noted that Kaufmann only described the beginning of this path— as if, once he had demonstrated the direction in which Ledoux's work pointed, and how it became explicit in the teaching of J. N. L. Durand and Louis-Ambroise Dubut, a route would be traced that could no longer be mistaken.

Such language is, however, not that of Kaufmann but of Kant, in the preface to the second edition of the *Critique of Pure Reason*. In this preface, Kant makes reference to that other intellectual revolution that concerns the beginnings of geometry, its "origin": the demonstration of the isosceles triangle inasmuch as it derives from an a priori construction, the author of which was named Thales, "or any other name."[3] This is the Kant to whom Kaufmann's text refers from the very first page. Does this mean that from the moment that architecture affirms its "autonomy" it accedes to a new and superior mode of historicity and that its development can be seen, from the logical point of view, as parallel to that of science? Does it mean that this fantasy (if it is one) constitutes one of the impulses behind an architectural ideology that purports to be "rationalist," as evinced by its constant return in Kaufmann's work? Certainly, Kaufmann affirms that if Ledoux's work has value as a symptom and demands to be interpreted as such, he did not for all that create modern architecture by himself; it would have been born "even if he had never existed."[4] But such a proposition does not in the least undercut the paradigmatic reading that Kaufmann proposed of Ledoux's work in 1933, for it was less important for him to write a "page of history" than to construct a *model* to show clearly, beyond all deceptive surface effects, the profound continuity of development that leads from Ledoux to Le Corbusier—a continuity that in effect has meaning only by assigning a *revolution* as its origin, pinning it to the name of Ledoux, or any other name.

Indeed, Ledoux, in his marked preference for the most simple and regular geometric configurations—the cube, the pyramid, the cylinder, the sphere—moves in this same direction, as if he had meant in this moment of origin to reconnect with "the first experience," as Edmund Husserl would say, from which geometry was born. This first experience held that due to technical ability, the Greeks succeeded in detaching certain "pure" forms from their bodily attachments. The Greeks pushed forms to their point of perfection, according to specifications suitable for the instruction of the geometric mind: surfaces ever more polished (whether flat or turned "in revolution"), edges ever more smooth, lines ever more straight and even, angles ever more sharp, points ever more precise, and so on.[5] The same process of autonomization of form is translated, with respect to the elements of architecture, by the rejection of all anthropomorphism, of organic metaphors, and, in general, of *imitation*, beginning with imitation of the monuments of the past. In all things, one should *return to the principle*: if a column, considered according to its function, is nothing more than a post put up to support a load (and Viollet-le-Duc would say nothing less), then there is no more sense in trying to calculate its proportions according to those of the human body than in pretending to stretch it as one would a muscle—a simple cylinder will do the job.

If architecture is no more than the expression of a constructive logic, then its reason for being should be sought in the act of building. In these terms, from the moment it obeyed an external determination, architecture would be no longer autonomous but rather the object of empirical knowledge, technical and experimental, whatever the contributions of calculation. Yet architectonic thought, even if it aspires to autonomy, does not operate in the register of speculative reason. Its aim is not knowledge in itself; it has a task to accomplish, a work to realize, a world to construct. As a matter of principle, it is only so inasmuch as pure practical reason is, in Kant's terms, immediately legislative: that is, it is only autonomous to the extent that the will is conceived as independent of empirical conditions and, consequently, as pure will determined by the sole form of the law called *moral law*. It is certain that Ledoux did not read Kant, but we know how much he owed to Jean-Jacques Rousseau and how *The Social Contract* informed his doctrine of autonomy. If the relationship between

Ledoux and Kant is based on anything, it is from the point of view of a common derivation. "Return to the principle, consult nature: everywhere man is isolated":[6] the formula of Ledoux's *L'architecture* echoes the problem posed by Rousseau: to discover a form—that of the contract—through which "each is united to all, yet nevertheless obeying only himself and remaining as free as before."[7]

For architecture, then, the claim of autonomy has in the first place a moral connotation. One has only to read Loos (in which ornament is associated with a form of crime) or Le Corbusier ("truth" is opposed to lies, as the purity of "whitewash" is to the false appearances of décor) to be persuaded of this; the rigor and the purity to which the modern movement aspired were those of the moral law. Indeed, the relationship of Ledoux, creator of the Saline de Chaux, to Le Corbusier, the apostle of the wall "lait de chaux" (whitewash), is salty enough—if I can say it—in the register of the signifier, especially if one recalls that Le Corbusier was himself born in La Chaux-de-Fonds. If it is in fact necessary to think of Ledoux *with* Rousseau, if not *with* Kant, it is to the extent that this other relationship allows one to understand how the rejection of rules handed down by tradition could for him be joined with the affirmation of a legality that is equally imperative, precisely because it is unconditional. Baroque architecture was heteronomous inasmuch as it obeyed an external exterior determination—that of "suitability" (*convenance*), which called for the elements composing a building to be combined, superimposed, and melded together in the unity of a single ensemble, following the rules of an *order* entirely of the facade, which was itself an image of social hierarchy. According to Kaufmann's explanation, the new principle of autonomy would, on the contrary, manifest itself in the egalitarian system of "pavilions," which assumes that the elements—for example, the different "blocks" or *unités* (of habitation or otherwise)—retain their independence, freedom, and autonomy. The rationale determining the pavilions' placement and distribution would only then appear in full clarity on the level of the plan. In this sense, the rejection of the facade, which the twentieth century would recognize as one of the traits of architectural modernity, appeared from the beginning of the nineteenth century as the corollary of the affirmation of a universal and abstract legality. This legality was to be affirmed in the teachings of Durand, taking the form of a regular orthogonal grid inscribed within a square, which both regulated the mechanics of the composition and informed every ensemble, as it would continue to do in the work of Mies van der Rohe: the grid as architectonic will and representation.

This double function reserved for the grid, both regulatory and generative, testifies a posteriori to the universal pretensions of autonomous architecture. In the first place, the grid is presented in Durand as the mechanism for a change in scale. Kaufmann saw clearly that with Ledoux architecture had attained a new dimension, that of the masses (*grand nombre*). The idea of autonomy is only meaningful in relationship to that of equality, implying that all men have the right to architecture ("Taste, in its combinations with art, recognizes no difference between the poor or the rich," writes Ledoux) and that, in return, architecture ought to be concerned with all of their needs ("Is there anything that the artist can disdain? Pluto's baths, the merchant's warehouse, the farmer's barn must all carry his imprint").[8] The project for an ideal city is thus no longer limited to a perspectival view meant to produce an essentially picturesque effect; it is intended to respond in detail to all the functions of a town in the manufacturing era: "[In my town] I have placed every kind [*genre*] of building required by the social order. There you will see important factories . . . give birth to populous assemblies. A town will rise up to encircle and crown them. . . . For the first time one will see the magnificence of the palace and that of the alehouse on the same level."[9] Indeed, Ledoux treats the question of housing in terms that anticipate the solutions of the Phalanstery, the garden city, or the "apartment block with communal kitchen."[10] Without going this far, Kaufmann insists that one can see in Ledoux's concerns the beginning of a *mechanization* of the dwelling. In fact, it seems as though Kaufmann felt closer to Brecht than to Le Corbusier,[11] in the sense that the idea of a "machine for living" seemed to contradict the very idea of autonomy. As Adorno would later say, in these "modern habitations . . . the nostalgia for independent existence, defunct in any case, is sent packing."[12]

But the adoption of the grid has still other repercussions, which one might call epistemological. Whereas the classical doctrine associated the idea of universal architecture with that of a *characteristic* (to the extent that Leibniz recognized that the classical orders were a model of combination), of a repertoire of signs—signs that brought with them the rules of their combination and connection—the principle of autonomy places the accent less on the elements of architecture than on the rule that determines their distribution in a given space—a rule to which elements are subjected even in their plan. Not that Durand meant to break with the principle of combination: the *Précis d'architecture* supplies the precise nomenclature of the pieces of the game to which architecture is reduced from this point on. Yet the game itself is no longer so much a question of syntax as it is of geometry, a geometry that is flat, elementary, and above all *finite*. Retrospectively, Durand's "system" demonstrates the paradox of an architecture that wanted all the more to be "speaking" (*parlant*), even as it renounced the ordinary means of language. It is as if, once again, autonomy had to be pushed to the point at which architecture no longer borrowed its determination from articulated language, to the point at which it would impose its articulations, structures, and *frameworks* on the symbolic—a definition other than that calculated according to the procedures of discourse.

It was Dubut who showed that the game is not affected in principle by the character of the elements at its disposal. In his *Architecture civile*, he proposed to dress up the same structure with either a "Gothic" or an "Italian" facade: proof, as Le Corbusier would say, following Viollet-le-Duc, that architecture—more than a question of style (in the singular)—is a question of styles (in the plural). From then on, the architecture of the nineteenth century, marked as it was on the surface by the stamp of historicism and eclecticism, was able in its deepest structures to participate in the continuity of a development whose effects would not be revealed until the masks under which architecture had been operating were removed. From this point of view, the neoclassical regression was in fact no more than a symptom of the deterioration of traditional forms, as Kaufmann himself noted. If we continue on the level of a "linguistic" description, we could say that it would take a century to shift from an ornate and "baroque" manner of speaking to a free and natural mode of expression. The shift, then, was from a mode of expression that drew its models from tradition to a mode of expression that some would declare antihistorical, but which in fact would be ordered around a notion of history other than that imposed by a history of art understood as a history of "styles": a notion that, arguable as it may be, demands to be taken into account in and of itself.

In this regard, it may seem that Kaufmann's work itself has the value of a symptom, if not a paradigm, in the way it conjugates the myth of origins with that of the Revolution. In his work on the French Revolution, François Furet has shown how its own history has been conceived with rare exceptions (among which one must cite Tocqueville) as a narrative of origins, the dread of beginnings investing itself precisely in rupture, or the revolutionary "break."[13] If the Revolution of 1789 became a figure of origin in socialist historiography, it is because it appeared as the founding event—the inaugural moment of a history itself revolutionary—released from the determining factors that reduced history before the Revolution to a sort of "prehistory," as Marx termed it. From the moment that it is seen as the origin of a new epoch, as an absolute beginning, a new start from zero, from principle, the Revolution becomes the matrix of a truly human and rational history. If it were not for the fact that Le Corbusier had little sympathy for revolutions, Bolshevik or otherwise, and that he was more concerned with heading them off by the means and processes of architecture, one could understand how Kaufmann might have been tempted to rediscover in the myth of the tabula rasa something of the consciousness ready to shatter the continuity of history that, to believe Walter Benjamin, is the characteristic of the revolutionary classes in the moment of their action. Did not the Plan Voisin, which foresaw the destruction of the greater part of "historic" Paris to make way for a few "autonomous" towers, depend on the same lyrical illusion that prompted the revolutionaries of 1789 to introduce a new calendar and the insurgents of the July Revolution to shoot out the clocks?[14]

But what of Ledoux? Is there not a paradox in regarding him as a revolutionary architect and the paragon of the "break" when, by his own avowal, he only just escaped the guillotine (*la hache nationale*) before welcoming the arrival of the empire with understandable relief? Here, the old debate over the consequences of political and social revolution for the domain of the arts reappears. If Trotsky could not repress the idea that the French language owed some of its "polish" to the sharp instrument named *guillotine*,[15] his contemporaries, ready as they were to recognize the initial extent of the revolutionary event, were much more worried that a similar rupture in the order of things and the continuity of time had remained for so long without effect on literature and art, to the point that it was necessary to await the explosion of romanticism for taste to at last have its own Four-teenth of July (in the sense that, for Victor Hugo, romanticism was the French Revolution turned into literature). For Kaufmann to propose that architecture, with Boullée, Ledoux, and Lequeu, had its own "revolution" (the question remains as to the place that Soufflot should be assigned in this context) was simply to make an analogy between this revolution and the political revolution. Indeed, he later recognized that he was incapable of explaining the change that architecture underwent around 1800, insofar as explanations and reasons of this kind can only be sought in so-called general, if not universal, history.[16] It is surely not an explanation to point to the process of the emancipation of the masses as related to the principle of autonomy. However, we know only too well that, as far as autonomy goes, the French Revolution worked to the contrary, in the direction of an ever more accentuated centralization, the benefits of which Napoleon would reap, to the great satisfaction—must it be repeated?—of Ledoux himself.

Why, then, speak of "revolutionary" architecture? The question, if it occupies us today, in the final analysis bears upon the status that should be attributed to the very notion of *history* itself, in architecture as well as the other arts, and more generally to the work of thought—and with every practice through which man attempts to assure himself of the control of his destiny. The historian is free, according to his own point of view, to deny any and all descriptive and taxonomic relevance to the notions of heteronomy and autonomy.[17] In the present moment, when the history of architecture hesitates between a renewed form of the history of styles and a form of institutional analysis that ignores everything properly architectural, the idea of autonomy, in its philosophical sense, takes on the value of a regulative concept. To think of Ledoux with Kant is to recognize that in the matter of architecture, knowledge is not solely derived from history; better said, in Kant's terms, a knowledge that *subjectively* presents itself as historical, according to the way it was acquired, can participate *objectively* in one form or another of rationality.[18] From this stems the problem of theory—of theory, not of doctrine—in its relationship to history: Does not theory have to specify the object of this history? What determinations belong to it alone?

To think of Ledoux *with* Kant leads one in fact to question what constitutes architecture as an object not only of history but also of thought—a thought that is itself bound by conditions that one will not fear to call formal, if not a priori. Architecture is based on this principle insofar as it is an object of desire, in which the will—as Kant says—finds its determination. But architecture places in this category only empirical principles, in the same way that what constitutes architecture—insofar as it is a thing to construct—is subjected to constraints that attest, even in the constructive order, to the force of the symbolic. Architecture finds its determination both in what constitutes it as an object of desire—or of will, as Kant would say—which in this context only concerns empirical principles, and also in whatever constitutes it as a constructed object, an object itself subjected, like everything in the constructive order, to constraints that attest to the power of the symbolic order. Ledoux did not push the principle of autonomy to the point that Kant would have wished, to the point of viewing dependence on natural law as yet another form of heteronomy. "In all things, return to the principle." This phrase of Ledoux's returns to support the idea that in the field of architecture there are principles that are not the product of history, just as in law there are norms that derive from a law postulated as "natural." It takes no more than this—we have repeated it often enough—to stir up a revolution. But will the fact that revolutions necessarily fail also be made a question of principle?

8.1
Adolf Loos, design for his own tombstone, 1931.
© Albertina, Vienna.

8 L'AUTRE "ICH," L'AUTRICHE—AUSTRIA, OR THE DESIRE FOR THE VOID: TOWARD A TOMB FOR ADOLF LOOS

TRANSLATED BY JOHN SAVAGE

Warum haben die papuas eine Kultur und die deutschen kein?
—Adolf Loos

A city, said Adolf Loos, has the architects it deserves. This remark raises a question: should we credit Imperial Vienna, "Vienna 1900," and later the democratic, republican Vienna that trusted Loos for a time to direct its municipal housing office with producing and giving sustenance to a man who, in his actions as well as his writings, never stopped denouncing the status given to those who aspired to the title of architect in the capital of the *öster reich*, a title that was at best dubious in his eyes? This polemicist is known more today, even in Paris, for the role he played at the beginning of the twentieth century in the campaign against ornament than he is as the author of Tristan Tzara's house behind the Butte Montmartre. If we conclude that Vienna did not "deserve" him, why did this architect (who was one so rarely) not expatriate himself to the America so many of his colleagues had simply refused to visit but that he, in contrast, had traveled to the moment he left school, and his precocious discovery of which was paradoxically to make of him, once back in Europe, a kind of stranger in his own land? Was Vienna really so necessary to him? Why was this true, and to what end?

The Potemkin City

Vienna, for Loos, was first of all a "Potemkin" city: a city that hid its true identity, its nature, its class reality, under the clothing, the rags made for it by its architects, just as Catherine the Great's favorite had erected whole trompe l'oeil villages made of cardboard and cloth on the desert plains of the Ukraine for the visits of the empress.[1] This Austrian Potemkin city razed the belt of its medieval walls only to raise a new ring in its place, made this time of a series of false palaces, rental buildings given the look of the princely residences of the baroque or Renaissance eras: an architecture of the mask, deserved by a capital that sought to preserve aristocratic appearances into the bourgeois age and that assigned its architects the task of dissimulating all social distinctions among its inhabitants, at least in the better neighborhoods, under the camouflage of false broadstone decorated with elements patched together with cement (the problem of working-class areas was only posed later, once Vienna turned "red"). It was a trompe l'oeil architecture that Loos considered "immoral" because it was founded on lies and imitations (the "substitute") and because it was born of a sense of shame. The materials themselves lied, mimicking the signs of a bygone era. The shame did not come from being poor, as Loos writes, but if one was well-to-do, like a bourgeois living on the *ring* amid the banks and luxury hotels, then there was the shame of not being among the wellborn, the shame of having to accept oneself as one is: a bourgeois, a man of one's time, a "modern" man.

Art, Architecture

But modernity itself was still tied to clothing in general—and to the mask. From the beginning, just after the creation of the

8.2
Adolf Loos, Tristan Tzara House, Paris, 1925–1926.
© Albertina, Vienna.

Secession (the Austrian version of art nouveau) with the help of the state and in the prestigious shadow of Otto Wagner, the tone was set by a series of articles on the Jubilee Exhibition of 1898 organized around the themes of clothing (*Kleidung*) and cladding (*Bekleidung*), and by the first work of Loos the architect: the construction of Goldman's men's fashion store in Vienna. A tone, one must say, that was anything but revolutionary, even if Loos had little patience for authority in any form (and did not hesitate to make this plain). The tone was that of an architect who saw himself as modern—that is, of his time. A few years later, anticipating in his own way Karl Mannheim's opposition between ideology and utopia (which was itself ideological), Loos would not hesitate to write that if art, the work of art, has a revolutionary vocation, then the house is conservative (the house, not architecture, because the latter does not only produce houses, but also monuments and tombs, toward which—as we will see—his art ultimately evolves and to which it limits itself). "The work of art is revolutionary; the house is conservative."[2] The work of art is turned toward the future; it opens new paths for humanity, on which the building is of its time and "thinks" in the present tense. In this sense, if the work of art (and the tomb itself, the simple burial mound where class relations dissolve, as well as the "monument," which pushes them to their limits) can have a utopian meaning and function, if it can transcend "the given" and aim to break the bonds of the existing order, then the "house" is on the contrary fully inscribed in the register of ideology, of consolidation, of the confirmation of reality. In contrast with the work of art, whose impact extends, by right, to "the last days of mankind" ("bis in die letzen tage der menschheit"[3]), the house responds to a current need; it is in the service of a present use; it has nothing to do with art; it must please everyone: man loves the house; he hates art. However, it is for this very reason that he cannot adapt to a home conceived for him by an "artist," even a member of the

Secession, short of wearing it like a borrowed piece of clothing. A house, an apartment, lives and transforms itself with whoever lives in it. It must tell a story, that of an individual or a family, not bear witness to the art of he—whether designer, architect, or soon, as Loos predicted, sculptor or painter—who starting from this usurped position is capable of exercising an unbearable tyranny over both members of the building trades and his clients.

The Principle of Inconspicuousness

But why would everyone not live like a king if they had the means (and this despite the fact that, or all the more so because, due to a contradiction that did not escape Loos, kings had lost their sense of splendor and were now living like everyone else—in other words, like bourgeois)? As for clothing, which Loos would always associate with the question of housing, did he not suggest that one can judge the level of a country's culture by the number of inhabitants that used their newly acquired liberty to dress outside of any set hierarchical norm or constraint—even, if they felt like it, like the king himself? Proof of this was found in Anglo-Saxon countries, where "everyone" is well-dressed, as opposed to Germanic countries, where only members of high society are. But what does well-dressed mean, exactly? It is to be dressed in the least garish way possible. Moreover, we must be clear: an Englishman would not go to Peking dressed as a Pekinese, nor to Vienna as a Viennese; that is because in his view he has reached the height of civilization. In its complete, fully developed form, the "principle of inconspicuousness" betrays a radical ethnocentrism. To be well-dressed is to be dressed in such a way that one stands out the least when one is at the central point of culture—that is, according to Loos and at the time he was writing (because a center is always subject to displacement), in London and (at the risk, even in that privileged place, of having to change at every cross street) *in the best society*. "An article of clothing is

8.3
Adolf Loos, Goldman and Salatsch Menswear Store,
Michaelerplatz, Vienna, 1909–1911. © Albertina,
Vienna.

modern when the wearer stands out as little as possible at the center of culture, on a specific occasion, *in the best society*."[4]

Being Outside

It is thus due to its calculated putting into perspective that Loos's discourse, if not his architectural practice, took on a critical function and impact beyond the Viennese context. This was true to the point to which—through the encounter with Tzara as much as by the singularly corrosive tone of his own writings (which, for once, did not escape the attention of "advanced" Parisian circles[5])—an aura of avant-gardism became attached to his name, one that was perhaps dubious, but by the same token very revealing of ideological contradictions whose interplay allowed the encounter of Dadaist negation and the constructive propositions of the modern movement in the pages of *L'Esprit nouveau* as well as at the Weimar Bauhaus. If Loos felt that he was speaking into a void (as suggested by the title of his first collection, *Ins Leere gesprochen*, which was published in Paris before it was in Vienna), it is because in reality his discourse needed a void in order to produce its effects, in order to be produced. It was not enough for Loos to recognize the existence of this void, to mark the difference, the gap between the predominantly Anglo-Saxon state of things that prevailed in the West and the culture (or its absence, the lack of culture; we will see how to understand this) that, according to him, characterized Germanic countries. It was necessary to constitute it as a place, a space from which his statements were generated by an operation that, if we look closely, is the source of all his undertakings, whether in the ideological (literary) sphere or in architecture. An operation, we might say (and Littré wished us to speak in this way, to save an indispensable word from obsolescence), by which the ego is estranged from itself,[6] establishing itself in a position that is outside, if not eccentric, relative to itself, to the point of taking on the discourse of the other. *Das Andere*: once again, the title is explicit. It is the journal that Loos undertook to edit in 1908, inspired by his friend Karl Kraus's *Die Fackel* (The Torch), in order "to introduce Western culture to Austria" (since that was the subtitle of the publication, which lasted only for two issues). If Loos needed Vienna, it was because Vienna, alone among Western capitals, located as it was in the center of Europe "where the world's old axes cross,"[7] made a fiction into reality: that of a circle (the *ring*) that is such a perfect void—in the grammatical sense of the word—that the very question of the "center" had to be asked from a position of exteriority, of alterity.

The Place of the Other

Das andere, the other, the other ego, *l'autre* "ich," Austria, the ego that is other, the *österreich*, the Eastern power, Vienna, soon to be "red" (the Orient is red), a fictional place, a place of fiction and as such open to all sorts of operations on the notions of subject, of identity, of centrality (of point of view), if not of quality: this is Freud, of course, and on a more modest level (but a modesty that had nothing innocent about it), Loos himself. (To say nothing of Musil, who pretended not to give any particular significance to the name of "the" city. It is true that to ask of the complex entity that is the city in which we reside which particular city it is, from the point of view of *The Man without Qualities*, is to be distracted from more important questions.[8] But what other city could Musil have pretended had no name? What other city, if not Vienna, taken as the vaguest of generalizations, as an ellipsis, a grammatical void?)

Modernity and the Role of the Mask

"Certainly the artist is The Other. But that is just why his appearance should match the others. He can only remain solitary if he disappears into the crowd. . . . The more entitled the artist is to be different, the more it is necessary for him to clothe himself in the everyday, like a mime."[9]"Anyone who goes around in a velvet coat today is not an artist but a buffoon or a house painter. We have grown finer, more subtle. The nomadic herdsmen had to distinguish themselves by various colors; modern man uses his clothes as a mask. So immensely strong is his individuality that it can no longer be expressed in articles of clothing."[10]

Modernity implies as its condition, if not as its sign, that the role of the mask be reversed. Indeed, where in archaic societies the mask confers a social identity on its wearer, inscribes him in his place in society, modern man on the contrary uses it to hide his difference, his otherness (just as the artist himself, the other *par excellence*, whose speech always draws on the collective unconscious, but who does not know how to be "modern" as such, both because the unconscious has no history and because in creating a work of art, a work turned toward the future and the end of time, the artist is not of "his" time). Even professional revolutionaries have recourse to this trick, and H. G. Wells was right to say he was wary of Lenin wearing a waistcoat.

This paradox is a matter of class; it should be understood as a paradox that within a class structure leads to an unmasking. The paradox is that, in the Viennese void, the denial of sartorial signification, of clothing as a sign, itself functioned as a sign and was thereby used as such: inconspicuousness (nondifference) became a mark of distinction (of difference). To be honest, it certainly did not bother Loos to be able to write that the greatest tailors of Europe were found in Vienna and that he was their client (it is by the way for one of them that he undertook the Michaelerplatz building). According to Loos, these were real artists and thus, working for a chosen clientele, they avoided all publicity. When the occasion required it, they showed only those clothes that could not easily be copied or imitated. Nothing was more misleading as a result than the "class" of a piece of clothing, in a context in which the aristocracy dressed the way the bourgeoisie should and parvenus wore false fronts and tails. There is never "class" or "style" but for one class, the only one that can be stylish (or have class), where historical epochs never have but one (or several) style(s).

But the tendency of the bourgeois class to confuse its own interests with those of the whole of humanity leads to an unprecedented diffusion, circulation, and exchange of signs (and styles). All clothing is deceiving, and cladding is by definition all the more so as a matter of principle. Even if he is as "smooth" as the Viennese cigarette cases Loos liked so much, a well-dressed and short-haired man should still not be judged by his looks (or his waistcoat): "All that is smooth is not necessarily modern."[11] All of this is another way of saying that in class society, the lack of ornament can still be an ornament; it can assume that function as an absent signifier. In the same way, a steak served plain (without condiments) can take on the value of a sign: a sign of modernity, a sign of "class."

Ornament and Crime

The campaign waged by Loos against ornament (ornament, if not "the fine arts," considered as crime) was one that followed a calculation, a deliberate strategy. But this strategy implied within itself a counterstrategy. In games as in war, and in the game of art as in the struggle among men or the war between the sexes, strategies go in pairs. And if, in theory, a strategy must include in its definition the strategy of the other, this is necessarily otherwise in practice. As in games, strategic struggles, *the strategy of the other is the unconscious*. Loos's trick was precisely that he set himself up (at least fictionally) in the position of the other; he inscribed his discourse, his strategy, in the name of the other. Struggling to introduce Western civilization to Austria was a way of trying to loosen the repression that made a society—a newly

8.4
Adolf Loos, Moller House, Vienna, 1927–1928.
© Albertina, Vienna.

bourgeois city like the Vienna of Loos, Kraus, Musil, but also Freud—refuse to recognize itself in the mirror held up for it by Western cities and to seek in ornament the means to sublimate— in every sense of that word—the most mundane capitalistic drives. A means of sublimation, Loos would say, that represented a veritable crime against the economy, in that it meant a double waste of both raw material and work—that is, in the end, of capital. None of this stopped the Austrian state from supporting the decorative epidemic (of which the Viennese Secession constituted one of the final symptoms) with subsidies while waiting for the hour of the Deutscher Werkbund and the Bauhaus, where one could observe artists working to perpetuate the alliance between art and artisanry that Loos thought went against nature. But that is because the reason of state is never directly modeled on that of capital. If the state works to slow cultural progress, it is because it is founded on the assumption that an uneducated people is easier to govern.

For Loos, cultural evolution followed a simple law, which was synonymous with the progressive removal of ornament from objects of daily use, starting with the foremost among these: the human body. The apparent fascination that the practice of tattooing held for Loos, while normal for a Papuan,[12] had in modern society become (according to Loos) the privilege of known or potential delinquents,[13] as well as a certain aristocracy (e.g., the "dueling marks" then so prized by German students); it is to be considered alongside of the no less *fascinated* status ascribed to "art" in his discourse. If it is true that Loos's comments on the house, conceived of as an object of daily use, contributed to the desacralization of architecture (heretofore reduced to being practiced as art only in cemeteries), this is not true of art, which as we have seen by definition escaped both from common law and the imperatives of modernity (in other words, of capital) and represented in fact—if only under the most revealing category of

Figure 8.5
Adolf Loos, Moller House, Vienna, 1927–1928. View
of hall and stairway. © Albertina, Vienna.

the tomb—the last refuge of the sacred. If art, as the era would have it, originated in decor and if, following the example of body painting or the decoration of a pot, it appears at first as an addition, engraved on a support, on a *preexisting body*, then the surplus that it adds is far, at first, from coming from the "soul."

The simplest, most elementary mark—the cross—was interpreted by Mondrian in a mystical sense before Le Corbusier saw in it minus by minus, the sign of positivity; this mark brings together the masculine and feminine elements in the coitus of vertical and horizontal.[14] This is to say that for Loos there was no art but erotic art, linked in its very principle to basic drives. But if, as Freud teaches us, the progress of civilization demands repression, the denial of these drives, it does not lead to the elimination of any possibility of substitutive satisfactions of the kind that art, in its highest forms, is able to procure. In its highest forms—that is, under the condition that the artist renounce ornamentation—it is that derisory variant of elemental drives that made primitive man smear erotic lines on the walls of his cave, in the way that still today "delinquents" and "degenerates" cover the walls of public lavatories with obscene graffiti: in the way (but this Loos could hardly have written) that the painters of the Secession, starting with Gustav Klimt, covered the ceilings of university buildings and the walls of Vienna's theaters and museums with frescoes in which decorative *overload* was put in the service of an eroticism that, while never drawing on the illusion of "flesh," only better revealed the prestige of the ornament adorning the paint (a purely symbolic prestige, in fact linked to the obliteration of the body). "One can measure the culture of a country by the degree to which its lavatory walls are daubed."[15]

Division of Labor

Ornament, if not art itself in its original, decorative, *applied* form, therefore functions as the repressed, posed as such in Loos's

8.6
Adolf Loos, Kartner Bar, Vienna, 1906–1907. ©
Albertina, Vienna.

discourse. Even better: it is only by starting with this discourse and through its operation that ornament takes over the role of the repressed. It remains to be seen in what form the repressed element surfaces in Loos's own work. In fact, even though he didn't build much (a few private residences and, along with a number of remodelings, the Michaelerplatz building, erected—blasphemy of blasphemies—opposite the monument to the "Power of Austria," by one of the masters of the Secession, Edmund Heller), the very project of an architecture that owes most of its effect, its prestige, to the combination of an honest use of materials and in contrast a totally arbitrary use of form (following the model established in the realm of sound by so-called serial music) was also not above drawing some of its power from the very thing it claimed to exclude. If only Loos had planned the decor (but a decor owing nothing to ornament?) of enough stores, cafés, and private apartments to justify the whole weight of the affirmation according to which the task of the architect should be reduced to enclosing walls around a void, which it would then be up to its inhabitants to *furnish*, with the help of carpenters and upholsterers who do not need to be told what to do by an "artist."

It is here in Loos's text that the postulate comes to light that led him to denounce the efforts of the Werkbund, and later the Bauhaus, to define the conditions of art's intervention in the process of industrial production. For this apostle of the "American way of life" (of everything from eating eggplant to wearing one's hair short) held on, in matters of social organization and cultural hierarchy, to the traditional opposition between art and artisanry, between the work of art and the object of daily use. "God makes the artist; the artist makes the epoch; the epoch makes the artisan; the artisan makes the button." In other words, the artist and the architect himself (all architects dream of being a bit of the artist, and Loos was no exception to the rule) had better things to do than aspire to oversee the production of buttons.

Loos's idea was that every epoch, including the modern era itself, has by definition at its disposal objects that are appropriate to it: furniture, utensils, and so on. If an object or piece of furniture breaks this rule, we can be assured that the fault lies with the untimely intervention of some master of academic or industrial aesthetics. The sketch of a critique of ideology, and still more of design practice, that we can glean from his writings falls heavily under the category of degeneration, of cultural void. "Mankind's history has not yet had to record a period of non-culture. The creation of such a period was reserved for the urban dweller during the second half of the nineteenth century."[16] We are to understand this as a critique of an urban structure that had become one of the sites, one of the instruments of the accumulation of capital, in which neither the artisan nor the architect could be employed *as such*. Loos's revulsion at the idea of taking into account the changing scale of urban development problems (obvious even in his mass housing projects of the twenties) goes hand in hand for him with the idealization of artisanal conditions of production. In this archetypal site of "alienation" that is the large modern city, the architect is never but an uprooted person, just as, in their own way, the abruptly proletarianized peasant masses are. The best he can do is limit himself to specific projects that he attempts to insert unscathed into the urban fabric; a program, as we can see, that is very timely. It is the same one that was behind the Michaelerplatz building, which was scandalous because it made any usurped signs of familiarity, as well as any plagiarism, impossible. In contrast with the baroque palaces, the columns of the ground floor are monolithic and made of real marble.

But what of the artisan? To pretend that left to himself a carpenter could not help but produce furniture that is perfectly adapted to modern housing conditions (if only the architect would let him do as he sees fit), just as a cobbler's shoes are adapted to their use, is to forget that the architect's efforts to make the different members of the building trades conform to his vision (and his interests) are themselves an integral part of the constant process of restructuring the division of labor of which the architect is, in his turn, a victim. The English furniture and Thonet chairs that Loos appreciated so much were not produced by artisans, but by industrial means. The real question, the one Loos stopped himself from asking, is there. He did his best to repress it by dressing himself up in an altogether characteristic "aristocratic" attitude. Are the mechanisms of industrial production so perfectly rational that letting them play out "naturally" allows us to expect the best *qualitative* results? Industry as second nature: that is the implicit message, the unsaid of the liberal ideology of laissez-faire, the actual place from which it is speaking. It pretends to give voice to the other from behind the mask of the first person, but the other cannot establish itself there.

The Law of Cladding

If the profusion of primitive decor is the response, in the traditional interpretation, to the *natural* horror of the void, why would culture—but a culture that is highly sophisticated, urbanized, and antinatural—not play on this void (as others played with velvet) until it could extract from this "horror" and from the desire that is its reverse the basis for new pleasures (*jouissances*)? (This while still giving itself the luxury of simultaneously enjoying the most archaic of products, productions of the *other* whose discourse Loos will not have neglected, but under the condition of clearly noting the place, the unconscious. A Maori sculpture, like a Corinthian embroidery, is part of our culture's unconscious, a culture that is such a *void* that a Thonet chair can itself be listed in the category of *outsider*, if not of the eccentric.)

But if it was true that Loos liked to take as a point of comparison the peasant who builds his own house according to what he needs, without thinking about it, he was far indeed from advocating the return to a "rural" architecture that would become one of the themes of Nazi propaganda. He had learned from experience that an architect cannot help but work against nature. When he wanted to use lake stones to build his first house in Montreux, was he not accused of desecrating the site's majesty? (But that day, as in the case of Michaelerplatz, the police summons gave him the delicious feeling that he was an "artist.") What is left is to use materials in the most honest, the most just possible way. The law of cladding forbids us to give one material the appearance of another, and especially one of higher quality than its own ("false wood"). What is unbearable is not to see the aristocracy dressed as bourgeois, but that the bourgeoisie tries to imitate it down to the smallest signs. We may well all be made of wood from the same forest, but the wood is not all of the same quality. (What, then, would Loos say of the particleboard that industry gives our carpenters to dress up under thin layers of fine wood?) Loos's taste for materials, for the *tactile* aspect of construction and interior design, comes from his need to define the conditions of a new architectural culture within the cultural void of the modern city. A culture no longer founded on ornamenting, but on cladding, which is the basis for all architecture (which, from the start, was never anything but an extension of clothing, in the way we might think of an umbrella). Loos took great pride in having introduced panels of polished marble or pounded copper in interior decor. The look that banks in Zurich, Milan, or New York have now is designed to give the impression that the boundary between ornament and cladding is undetermined and that from one to the other a switch, an inversion of signs is always possible. Is not to clad still to mask, to dissimulate, to mislead, if not—though with the proper "inconspicuousness"— to ornament? In fact, Loos's architecture is, in its own way, an example of the "drama" of modern architecture that Manfredo

Tafuri has characterized best: an architecture reduced to wishing itself pure, a strictly formal exercise, deprived of utopia, useless, but nevertheless preferable to projects that are clad in ideological rags but in fact serve the reigning order.[17]

Tomb

It is here that we find the confirmation, by a new paradox, of Loos's project for the Chicago Tribune of 1922. This project, a skyscraper of more than thirty floors in the form of a Doric column set upon a high cubic pedestal, not only represented (as Tafuri understood) the first manifestation of "pop" culture and the announcement of what were in the end the far more modest "monuments" of Claes Oldenburg.[18] It also corresponds to utopia in its purest form and function, that of the dream which, in order to satisfy desire, knows to play systematically on contradictions. The edifice was to be "the most beautiful and the most characteristic of the world" (as the program of the competition had it). To use the figure of Trajan's column constituted a risk that the sponsors did not know how or did not want to take. There is no way to avoid the funereal significance of such monuments, made as they are to be torn down (and revolutions, as we know, sometimes succeed in doing so).

This project, like the one for Josephine Baker's house (in which a transparent glass cube forming a swimming pool would have constituted the core), allows Loos's obstinate words to assume their full proportions, which are of a totally different scale than the problems architecture seems to struggle with today. Loos affected the belief that one of the principal contributions of the architecture of his time was to teach plumbers and carpenters how to hide a flush toilet under wood-clad paneling. "When we come across a mound in the wood, six feet long and three feet wide, raised to a pyramidal form by means of a spade, we become serious and something in us says: somebody lies buried

8.7
Adolf Loos, Chicago Tribune Tower competition entry,
1922. © Albertina, Vienna.

here. *This is architecture.*"[19] It can still happen today that, entering a bathroom, we notice that the sanitary installation is made in such a way that the evacuating mechanism is hidden from view. Adolf Loos would have wanted no other tomb than that one: a tomb that combined in its arrangement and structure the functions of cladding (the pleasure of tactile appearance) and, hidden away, of evacuation (the desire for the void, in its anal connotation, that characterizes the reign of money). Such a tomb would be in the very image of the pleasures created for everyone, down to the most disinherited, by the modern city, the capital of capital; pleasures that Loos was not, for his part, prepared to renounce. A flush chain in his wooden coffin or his marble (or pounded-metal) catafalque: *Das ist Architektur.*

9 ORNAMENT TO THE EDGE OF INDECENCY

Adolf Loos and the Crusade against Ornament

The quarrel over ornament was not born in 1912, when *Der Sturm* published Adolf Loos's celebrated polemic "Ornament and Crime" ("Ornament und Verbrachen").[1] But the title of his fiery attack shows clearly enough how radical the polemic had become by the beginning of the century. It is this radicality that forces us, even today, to look at this essay—a text all too often misread and misunderstood and one whose virulence historians regularly do their utmost to tone down—not so much to take up the debate where Loos left off as to try to formulate the issue of ornament in terms at once retrospective and critical, historical and theoretical.[2] Written in 1908, when European architecture was just beginning to free itself from the web of art nouveau (and its Viennese variant, the Secession style), Loos's essay immediately took on the appearance of a manifesto and was soon adopted by the adherents of an incipient modern movement. In a 1913 issue of *LesCahiers d'aujourd'hui*, Georges Besson published an abridged translation that, deliberately aiming to shock, cut out the better part of its cultural connotations. It was this translation that *L'Esprit nouveau* republished in 1920 and that served as a pretext for Le Corbusier's appeal for the crusade of whitewash [*lait de chaux*] and Diogenes, for the great purge, the elimination of the superfluous, that by "The Law of Ripolin" would at last sound what he called "the hour of architecture."[3] Of course, the issue of ornament cannot be dismissed with a sudden about-face, no matter how analytical, and it has in no way been settled by the alleged bankruptcy of the modern movement. The question cannot be filed away under the history of taste alone, any more than under the history of styles. For in *style*, Le Corbusier saw only an accidental, superficial, and gratuitous *modality* that, like decoration, must disappear.[4] Nor, moreover, is it an issue that can be limited to the realm of architecture any more than what is called precisely the "applied" arts. To limit the problem to the realm of *art*, in the most general sense, is merely to displace it. If we assume that art cannot actually be reduced to ornament—or, according to Hegel, to "the decor of our life"—the question still remains as to whether the value of art can be considered wholly separate from decorative values and whether all art is not, to some degree, necessarily ornamental.

The Rhetorical Argument

In his book *The Sense of Order*, Ernst Gombrich poses the question of ornament in strictly psychological terms and links it (in highly doubtful fashion) to the avant-garde abstraction of the first half of the twentieth century—considering only Malevich and Mondrian—but concludes that abstraction is distinct from ornament so that it may be associated with Le Corbusier's project of "thinking against a white background." In dealing with this question, Gombrich nonetheless has the merit of tracing it back to its remote sources, which lie in rhetoric.[5] From the beginning of what we call Western metaphysics, ornament was in fact theorized in its relationship to speech, if not to thought. We know that Plato was not loath to use, in the form of the dialogue, some of the Sophists' methods, which he, through Socrates, nonetheless condemns. However, it was Cicero who produced the first doctrine of ornament, which he based on the genre of rhetoric known in Greek as *epideictic*, "because it is made for demonstration, and for pleasure."[6]

Cicero's praise of the simplicity that characterizes the Attic style does not imply that the orator should give up ornamenting his speech with certain of the "flowers" employed by the Sophists. It is less to persuade than to seduce that orators use such devices more often and more overtly; their discourse obeys a different *modality* than one that aims to convince. This modalization is translated into the formal register, into what characterizes an orator's style: They seek parallelism more than correctness; they are full of digressions; they insert anecdotes and are bolder in the metaphorical use of words, which they employ in "the manner of painters with their various colors"; they juxtapose words of equal length or opposite meanings and often end their sentences with the same sounds.[7] All of these features, as we know, can easily be transposed into the codes of painting (to which Cicero explicitly refers) as well as those of music—not to speak of architecture, with which the art of oration shares, at least metaphorically, numerous points. Thus, in *De Oratore*, Cicero speaks of examining and explaining the nature of "the edifice" built by the orator and the manner of its embellishment[8] through the creation of "beautiful vestibules" and "light-filled entrances" in order to plead his case.[9] Even if the literal use of words ought to constitute the ground and foundation of his speech, the orator will not necessarily avoid metaphors, those "species of borrowings thanks to which we take elsewhere what we lack,"[10] any more than he will refuse the help of an architectural mnemonic system that allows him to move, in his imagination, through those spaces of a building into which he has first inserted images that correspond to the different parts of his discourse.[11]

Cicero did not fail to observe that the simplest style can demand much effort, and that the appearance of negligence requires the greatest art: "There are women who are said to be dressed without affectation and it suits them; similarly, the sober style pleases even without ornament (*etiam incompta*): in both

cases elegance has been sought, but not shown. One will therefore set aside any gaudy finery, such as pearls; one will not even
curl one's hair; as for the artificial red and white of make-up, one
will completely reject them; all that will remain are good taste
and cleanliness."[12] The absence of ornament can be, in itself, an
ornament, but on the express condition that it is not flaunted;
an orator should appear more concerned with ideas than with
words. Thus, ornamentation will never be more justified or
richer in effects than where it springs, in some way, from utility: "Columns are made to support temples and porticos; however, they are just as majestic as they are useful. The magnificent
pinnacle of the Capitol, and of other temples, was created not
through a need for elegance but out of necessity itself. In fact, the
means had been sought to make water flow on either side of the
edifice, and the usefulness of the temple's pinnacle quite naturally involved majesty, such that even if the Capitol were placed
in the heavens, where there can be no rain, it seems that, deprived of its pinnacle, it would not have majesty."[13]

Truth and Lies in Ornament: The Metaphor of Dress

We know how much weight the question of roofs, flat or sloping,
has held and continues to hold in the debate over so-called international architecture (to say nothing of the insistent emphasis that those who today define themselves as postmodern place
on entrances, doors, and approaches, thus clearly revealing the
rhetorical nature of their words). However, Gombrich is correct when he writes that beauty and utility, on the one hand, and
makeup and finery, on the other, are two of the commonplaces
borrowed regularly for attacks on ornament, whether on behalf
of the campaign led by the proponents of the severe style against
the fantasies of baroque and rococo decoration or on behalf of
the rationalists' condemnation of the use of historicizing motifs
in metal architecture. The comparison of ornament to makeup,

bodily decoration, and even tattooing served as yet another weapon in Loos's assault at a moment when, as we read in "Ornament and Crime," the tattoo had become a mark of delinquency (we are reminded of Cesare Lombroso's *Palimsesti del carcere*, published just a few years earlier) or a sign of the degeneration of a certain aristocracy.[14]

As for the functionalist argument, we can see that it was to have a particular impact in the field of architecture, where the relationship, if not the opposition, between structure and decoration seems to invite theorization without metaphor, in terms of truth and falsity. That is to say, in terms best expressed in Viollet-le-Duc's question: "Does an architectonic concept include the decoration, or is the decoration summoned by the architect when the composition of the building is finished? In other words, is the decoration an integral part of the building, or is it just a more or less empty dress used to cover the building when the forms have been fixed? The various civilizations that have had an architecture most likely never asked themselves these questions, but proceeded as if they had posed them, which for us comes down to the same thing."[15]

It was from this perspective that Viollet-le-Duc could contrast Greek decoration, which he believed could be reduced to a simple contour of constructive members "with no ambiguity or lie," to Roman decoration, whose classical ordonnance is no more than a borrowed dress with no relationship to the masonry: "For, if there is an architecture in which the decorative mode is out of keeping with the structure, it is certainly that of the [Roman] Empire."[16] Greek rationalism is opposed to Roman eclecticism, just as medieval, and especially Gothic, rationalism is opposed to the eclecticism of the Renaissance, which Auguste Choisy saw, at least in the Italian context, as a simple reform of the system of ornament. According to Choisy, Gothic decoration in Italy—in contrast to France, where tradition impeded the widespread adoption of antique forms—was not concerned with structure and was reduced to an adornment added to the body of the edifice: "When antiquity returned to favor in the fourteenth century, architecture remained essentially unchanged: it went Roman, just as it had once been Gothic—only the dress was altered."[17] Published in 1899, Choisy's *Histoire de l'architecture* may be counted among the first expressions of a modernist ideology—but its impact would be felt even among archeologists. One of the greatest connoisseurs of Hindu art wrote, "Nature allows the Hindu architect to erect the vast rooms of *mandapams* by laying large granite flagstones on monolithic pillars. The construction methods are thus extremely elementary. Only the details of the sculpture are interesting, and the history of the architecture of Southern India can be reduced to the history of ornamentation."[18]

In this way, the metaphor of clothing constitutes, through to Loos, another *topos* of the rationalist critique. Viollet-le-Duc saw in man, as the most complete of all living organisms, *the myth of structure*.[19] As he wrote, this is why the Greeks preferred the *nude*, as much in architecture as in sculpture and painting, which lent their support not to hide but to better reveal the forms; whereas for the Romans, decoration consisted only of *dressing*:

> Greek architecture may be best compared to a man stripped of his clothes, the external parts of whose body are but the consequences of his organic structure, of his wants, of the framework of his bones and the functions of his muscles. . . . Roman architecture, on the other hand, may be compared to a man clothed: there is the man, and there is the dress; the dress may be good or bad, rich or poor in material, well or ill cut, but it forms no part of the body; if well made and handsome it merits examination; if it restrains the man's movements, and its shape has neither reason nor grace it is unworthy of notice.[20]

Yet this metaphor gave rise to contradictory developments as to whether the problems of decoration could be assimilated to those of fashion, where the motifs, all on the surface, are exposed to rapid obsolescence (a crucial theme in the theory of ornament that, as Gombrich has shown, was introduced as early as the beginning of the nineteenth century by Percier and Fontaine[21]), or whether there was a possibility of a "rational [raisonné] clothing" (to use Viollet-le-Duc's word) that would serve as a "true" envelope for the body, precisely revealing its essential forms and registering its inner needs.[22] A dress, then, that is neither a disguise nor a mask: a dress that would primarily have a protective function—though, as Schelling opined, this would not exclude the possibility of a role for the dress in architecture as a metaphor of the body in relation to its construction.

The Avatars of the Mask

The crusade against ornament was, first and foremost, a crusade against masks. This is explicit in Loos, who never ceased to condemn the architecture of trompe l'oeil, or what he called the "Potemkin" city: the fake palaces, all facade and overloaded with showy ornamentation, erected by his colleagues along Vienna's Ringstraße. Planned like the outer boulevards of Paris along the site of ancient ramparts, this ring was designed to strengthen new Vienna's consciousness and to seal, in and through decoration, the union of the Austro-Hungarian Empire with bourgeois society while also effectively reducing the old city to a kind of ghetto. This was an architecture, as I have said, of allure, one that Loos considered immoral because it was based on deceit and imitation ("substitution") and because it was the product of a *false* shame: the falsity of materials, the imitation of the signs of a long-distant past, and the shame of the bourgeois who, denied the privileges of aristocratic birth, was forced to concede his "modernity."[23] But the very notion, the category, of the mask itself is not unambiguous. The mask is not merely a disguise; it can also fulfill a protective function, as with the masks used by certain ethnic groups to dress up the dead, not so much to perpetuate their features as to defend them against the aggressions to which they were exposed in their passage to the beyond (to say nothing of the masks donned by fashionable women, in the classical age, to shelter their faces from the elements and the burning heat of the sun). However, the mask can just as easily ensure the wearer's anonymity. Whereas (according to Loos) members of primitive hordes once got dressed up, first painting themselves in various colors, to distinguish one another, modern man uses his clothes as a mask to hide his difference, his otherness. Individuality, then, is no longer a function of the clothes, and the clothes no longer the sign of any kind of identity.

Loos believed he could contrast clothes (*Kleidung*) with clothing (*Bekleidung*), the *claddings* (*parements*) of marble, wood, or polished metal that give his interior architectures a distinctive period feel. Does this mean that no appearance, no trimming, enters into the cladding and that the cladding (the "pare-*ment*," as Jacques Lacan would say) cannot, in turn, function as a sign, however untruthful? "Everything that is smooth is not modern," Loos's first biographer noted, not without a critical emphasis.[24] The contemporary use of marble cladding as ornament for banks and for those companies whose anonymity lends them all the more prestige is a measure of the alluring power of art, even in its most iconoclastic guise: an art that tends necessarily toward modalization insofar as it is nothing more than a modality of production—and one that cannot help but carry meaning.

The rejection of illusionism, the demand for "truth" (a watchword taken up by various avant-gardes) with which modern art began, is thus partly a matter of taste—but it cannot be reduced to taste, which is why the question of ornament is of interest to theory. "Since iconolatry thrives and spreads as virulently as a cancer, let us be iconoclasts," wrote Le Corbusier in 1925, as the Exposition Internationale des Arts Décoratifs was taking place in Paris.[25] That he could also declare that "modern decorative art is not decorated"[26] is a paradox that would not have escaped him. But did this *impasse* (a word of which Le Corbusier was not frightened) not constitute the aesthetic phenomenon, given that it derives necessarily from the order of communication? Can these positions not be endlessly reversed, from signified to signifier or, to use Choisy's terms, from form to content and from content to form? If Loos set so much store by the principle of cladding, this is because, among other things, it allowed for the concealment of the apparatus of cables and pipes required by those *machines for living* that our houses have become, in keeping with Le Corbusier's express desire. Indeed, for Le Corbusier, tools have their own beauty: "Works of decorative art are tools, beautiful tools."[27] And he was not at all embarrassed to reveal the viscera of the domestic organism—an attitude for which he has been criticized. But even Le Corbusier, who maintained that "art has no business resembling a machine (the error of Constructivism),"[28] could not have foreseen the time when, in the heart of Paris, in a quarter he had hoped to raze to the ground and on the very spot where he dreamed of erecting the towers of his Plan Voisin, the machine's most intimate organs would rise, painted in various colors to distinguish their functions, on the facade of a museum that we still cannot be certain is not "a liar" just the same.[29]

The Hypocrisy of Luxury

Where ornament does not follow directly from construction and is not limited to *emphasizing* it (a word whose ambiguity Le Corbusier considered when rereading *The Decorative Art of Today* thirty years after its publication),[30] it could be, in the view of the "moderns," only arbitrary. It was Auguste Perret, as Le Corbusier recalled, who thought "ornament generally conceals a defect in construction"[31]—but decoration can be a liar in any number of ways.

In his day, Bernard of Clairvaux already had attacked the pomp of Cluny, the gilding of Saint-Denis, and, in Georges Duby's words, "the decoration draped on all sides like the display of a royal treasure."[32] Duby has correctly observed that this was no mere expression of humility, no profession of poverty. After all, the Cistercians spared no expense when it came to building, and their architecture, devoid of all ornament and built with materials of quality, does not fail to seduce us moderns, who have learned—as Loos had hoped—to feel "the beauty of bare stone." In his language and teachings, Saint Bernard never neglected the flourishes of rhetoric. If he did not see the need to adorn the house of God as well, it was because the reform he had in mind was based essentially on a turn inward, a kind of conversion wherein the word alone (the recourse of all iconoclasm) would be the privileged instrument that procured access both to true wealth and to a truth foreign to the visible world.

By the Victorian era, the denunciation of ornament no longer proceeded from any concern for austerity. But if those who posed as reformers also called for a conversion of minds, their crusade bears witness above all to the disarray in which they were plunged, not so much by the vast accumulation of commodities—which, to echo the beginning of *Capital*, heralded the wealth of societies dominated by the capitalist mode of production—as by the industrial progress that led to a general perversion of values. As Marx wrote, the increase in the productivity of labor and the growing mass of material wealth corresponded to a simultaneous decrease in its value.[33] To be sure, Marx did not see the production of luxury articles as a good indication of *material* production, in the technological sense. But the fact is that manufacturing, and then industry, quickly flooded the market with "luxury goods" that borrowed their appearance from a particular kind of ornamentation, a decoration that was merely allure: the allure of *labor*, the machine reproducing the traces of handicraft by which the "artist" is traditionally recognized. There was the allure, too, of materials, for industry never hesitated to borrow whatever it lacked and to employ, always figuratively, the signs by which wealth is recognized—working the fonts, papers, and fabrics as artisans would the most precious materials. (As Le Corbusier himself wrote: "The industrialist thought to himself: 'let us smother our junk with decoration: decoration hides all manner of flaws and blemishes.' Camouflage is sanctified."[34])

If the spirit of reform, as far as ornament is concerned, first showed itself in England, it is because England was exposed to the flood of "junk" very early on. Gombrich has shown that the sort of criticism to which, say, Pugin subjected the "ornamental abominations" coming from the workshops of Birmingham and Sheffield—those shrines of an unwitting bad taste (unlike what would later be the case with kitsch, at least tongue-in-cheek kitsch)—was prompted by the reactionary rejection that fueled Ruskin's campaign against mechanical production in the name of the values of traditional craft. The devaluation of labor linked to the mass production of more or less inexpensive objects went hand in hand with the depreciation of materials. It matters little whether this was the inevitable consequence of the machine's elimination at the execution stage of the qualities of manual labor, as Ruskin thought, or whether it was possible to intervene at the design stage, as believed by the Victorian reformers (and the members of the Deutscher Werkbund). The essential thing is that the profusion of decoration with which industry loaded its products was felt, from the beginning, not only to be an assault on good taste but also an attack on truth.

Does this mean that, unlike common sense, good taste cannot be shared—that in the days when ornament, once reserved for fortune's privileged, was offered to all and sundry, the reformers were working on behalf of an elite who could not quite resign themselves to seeing the signs of their distinction escape? This would be to dismiss the fact that what those reformers said was prompted by a completely opposite determination, because at least some intended not to work against the imperatives of mass production but, on the contrary, to control it and if possible to subject it to the canons of good taste and—why not?—of *refinement*. That is, when they were not striving to reserve the rights of a sector of production they believed should remain the prerogative of the craft industry—as was the case with Ruskin and, curiously, also with Loos. However, it cannot be claimed that Loos's indictment of ornament was not itself clad (that is indeed the word) in ambiguity. Tack is all the more unbearable because it does not try to hide what it is, but the very idea of cladding implies highlighting the peculiar properties of materials, and this assumes that the materials are of some value and could lend themselves, as in the art deco era, to all kinds of fantasies. Now, this is exactly what Le Corbusier would obstinately refuse to admit: "The final retreat for ostentation is in polished marbles with restless patterns of veining, in paneling of rare woods as exotic to us as hummingbirds, in glass pastes, in lacquers copied from *the excesses* of the Mandarins and thence made the starting point for further elaboration. . . . The almost hysterical rush in recent years towards quasi-orgiastic decoration is no more than the final spasm of an already foreseeable death."[35]

"Painting Is the Finest and Most Ancient Ornament of Things"

It is cladding's properties as a *surface* that allow it to function as decoration. The surface is a place of illusion, starting with the perfectly smooth surface of the mirror—but also the surface of the painting, because painting itself, if Alberti is to be believed, is "the best and most ancient ornament of things,"[36] one by which architecture, sculpture, gold and silver work, and all the arts in general are guided: "Whatever beauty is found [in the arts] can be said to be born of painting."[37] This is why, Alberti argues, architecture took from painting its finest ornament, the column,[38] along with architraves, capitals, bases, and pediments—in short, all of the features that make buildings so rich. It is as if, for Alberti, ornament were prompted by the mechanism of borrowing that for Cicero was the province of metaphor. But what meaning does ornament have here? We might observe in passing that commentators have generally avoided tackling this particular passage of *Della Pittura*, but no matter the interpretation, it is a passage that reveals the extent to which the issue of ornament was to be displaced, in the nineteenth century, when metal construction (as Le Corbusier noted) seemed to impose a dissociation between structure and decoration. Indeed, such a dissociation was already noted in Alberti's *De re aedificatoria*, and the beauty associated with ornament is regularly treated there as "attached or additional," fundamentally inessential.[39]What is ornament, other than "a form of auxiliary light and complement to beauty?"[40] But how does that argument work for the column, which, as Cicero liked to say, owes its majesty to its usefulness?

One of the keys to the passage no doubt must be sought in *De re aedificatoria*, in the section stating that the ornaments used by architecture can be parsed into a certain number of parts, each of which has its own profile as a projection: The lintel accordingly has a squared-off projection, like the letter L; the gullet and astragal are placed under it like an S or a C; and so on.[41] If the work of the architect merges into the work of the painter here, this is because the architect borrows from the same paradigm, one that *Della Pittura* explicitly likens to the task of writing and which holds that the field of the visible should be seen as equivalent to what can be written down on a flat plane and reduced through projection to a combination of surfaces, each of which will be defined by its outline and be joined together, in the way letters are assembled on a page to form words and sentences.[42] In other words, the qualities with which classical architecture is generally credited—the consummate art of the molding, the shaping of architectonic members—owes less to the technique of building than to the science of painting, or at least of drafting. The art makes sense only when related to the plane, and the column itself, which is nothing but a wall fragment, can be distinguished from the wall only when it is projected in the form of a pilaster.[43]

The notion that ornament should be considered in its relationship with the plane is something that dawned on the reformers of the nineteenth century, starting with Pugin, who made it a rule to avoid any effect of depth or relief in decoration.[44] That rule is something we rarely see observed in baroque decoration, in which painting does the opposite, playing on all of the effects of trompe l'oeil and even resorting to an illusionistic mode by means of sculpture, if not of architecture. In any case, the idea of decoration, whether employed to negate, respect, exalt, or celebrate it, implies—as Matisse said about his work for the Barnes Foundation—"taking possession of the surface," which can go as far as "correcting architecture."[45]

The Graft

There is nothing anecdotal about the reference to Matisse here, as he was one of those painters who, while keeping their distance from abstraction, always insisted on the essentially "decorative" nature of painting, in opposition to all those who condemned decoration in the name of *expression*. Matisse even said he could only paint portraits "in a decorative manner."[46] For Matisse, decoration and expression were "just the same thing," and how could it have been otherwise?[47] He even went as far as to proclaim *composition* as "the art of arranging in a decorative manner the diverse elements at the painter's command to express his feelings."[48]

A painting must stand on its own, in the density of its paint and the disposition of its elements, no matter its relationship with its support. In terms of the painting and the surfaces it procures in order to take shape and visibility, any opposition between structure and decoration has absolutely no relevance, and we could not salvage such an opposition by arguing for art's decorative origins. Indeed, this hypothesis was key to the resounding success of aesthetic anthropology in the early years of the twentieth century, holding as it did that art as a form was subjugated first to the object, the thing onto which it was grafted. This is one idea among others found in Wilhelm Wundt's *Völkerpsychologie*, which led Marcel Mauss to assert the primacy, based on the use of dyes and makeup, of painting over drawing.[49] One can paint an object or a face, dye it or put makeup on it, but drawing it already presupposes a different kind of transitivity; either the artist draws *on* the object or body, using it as support, or he represents the object or body by copying it onto some other surface. The genealogy that takes us from ornamental art to what Wundt called "ideal art"—that is, "the open art that creates its own object for itself"[50]—implies a real ontological leap for art to free itself from its borrowed body and invent its own support. However, this does not happen without the work of repetition—from dyeing to painting and from painting to drawing to fabric (and to the human body, in which Mauss saw "the most immediately given object for ornament"[51]), as well as from fabric to the wall, from the wall to the panel, and from the panel to the canvas—a repetition that, in each case, is a repetition of the beginning and ready, as such, for every possible twist and turn and return.

It is at this juncture that we must look at the notion of ornament by itself. In confusing ornament and decoration, we overlook the thing that literally forms the *basis* of ornament. Even when it is designed to be worn (as, for example, a jewel, jewelry having constituted one of the starting points for "ideal" art, according to Wundt), ornament retains its independence, as well as a kind of density, which draws its means from the *line*. Gottfried Semper saw the wreathed garland as the archetype of the work of art: the fiber leads to the string and the string to the wreath, if not to the knot, which "is perhaps the oldest technical symbol and . . . the expression for the earliest cosmogonic ideas that sprang up among nations."[52] We may regret, as Joseph Rykwert does, that Semper did not develop this allusion to the knot's symbolism further,[53] especially since it overlaps with the question of the origins of writing and the significance of various kinds of "knot writing," the use of which has continued to the present day.[54] But it cannot be overlooked that all of the arts are based on the quality, at once scriptural and ornamental, of the wreath, the knot, as we see in the art of the steppes, which has overcome its autonomy and is now sustained exclusively by the interlacing of its twigs.

Replacing Ornament

In the West, the transition to "pure" art, art's slow conquest of its "ideal body," was long masked by a proclaimed ideal of the body, and of the body captured in its nakedness, if not in its truth. Certain cultures, such as those of the steppes, went in the opposite direction and accentuated the animal body, with decoration borrowing only secondary elements from the vegetal realm—but this is a specific case, and we cannot, as Wundt tried to, turn it into a general rule.[55] Certain other non-Western civilizations have worshipped the human body, but only by submitting it to quite different canons, as attested by the great statuary of Africa. Meyer Schapiro noted that the nineteenth century, pervaded by a technicism perhaps even more than by a "realist" ideology, was able to appreciate primitive ornament while at the same time condemning the "monstrous" deformations to which the archaic arts submitted the human body.[56] The first chapter of Owen Jones's *The Grammar of Ornament* actually opens with the image of the tattooed head of a Maori woman, in which the author saw a demonstration of the principles of the highest ornamental art: "Every line upon the face is the best adapted to develop the natural features. . . . The ornament of a savage tribe, being the result of a natural instinct, *is necessarily always true to its purpose.*"[57]

Loos would have said the same thing, because he was only too happy to let the modern bourgeois man collect primitive objects while his wife decked herself out in peasant embroidery or exotic castoffs. If he saw *modern* ornament as an aberration, an indication of backwardness or degeneracy, then it was for the opposite reason: because there was no longer anything natural about it. Of course, decoration has always been a matter of luxury and, as such, "useless"; to confine ourselves to criteria that are peculiarly ours (luxury, as Marx said, is the only form of beauty the bourgeois knows), we need only look to the decorative accumulation, to the extravagant ends of food destined to rot on the spot, as Bronisław Malinowski observed while in the Trobriand Islands.[58] But what may be justified within an economy of the gift becomes the unacceptable waste of the labor force in the days of *Capital*.

It is symptomatic that the purism, not to say Puritanism, that was characteristic of Loos as well as of Le Corbusier allows an economic explanation, in both the strict sense and the psychoanalytical sense of the term. Loos held ornament to be "superseded" (*aufgehoben*), as with any technological formation, but equally with sexual drives in the operation of sublimation. The cladding (*Bekleidung*) that hides the fittings in a bathroom does indeed represent a "sublation" of decoration, the way the work of art appeals to the visual drive, "directing some proportion of [our] libido on to higher artistic aims."[59] But in this supersession, this sublation, this *Aufhebung* in the Hegelian sense of the word, what has been superseded is no less preserved in its place than the drainpipes are in the house—however well concealed—or even as the animal of the pleasure principle (*das Lusttier*), which was signaled by Freud and so disturbed Le Corbusier, is in man. If the idea of the beautiful has its roots in sexual excitement, diverted by art from its real aims and thus linked to other objects—first and foremost to the body as a whole—then we can understand that a similar superseding, a sublation, once more takes many twists and turns, displacements and regressions: As a matter of *decency*, decoration (from the Latin *decore*) can be decent to the point of indecency.

10.1
Le Corbusier, La Tourette, Éveux-sur-l'Arbresle, France,
1953–1960. La Tourette as seen from the road
approaching the monastery. Photo: Hubert Damisch.

AGAINST THE SLOPE: LE CORBUSIER'S LA TOURETTE

La Tourette: A Theoretical Object

Why La Tourette? And why La Tourette today? Nearly half a century has passed since Le Corbusier drew up the plans for this Dominican monastery in the foothills of the Lyonnais Mountains overlooking the small town of L'Arbresle, twenty-five kilometers northwest of Lyon, and many things have changed since it was consecrated in 1959. The building was originally intended to house about one hundred young brothers who were to reside there for several years while completing their intellectual training, yet now all pedagogical activity has ceased and fewer than ten or so monks occupy the place. Even the bids to open the institution to the outside world and to offer the resources of the buildings for accommodation and a center for so-called cultural encounters and exchanges seem to have suddenly fizzled out for the time being, and it is not easy to imagine what other new role could be assigned to the buildings. Reyner Banham held as a criterion of architectural excellence the possibility that a building could be used for entirely different purposes than those for which it was originally designed; we are not yet there with La Tourette. However, the daily flood of coaches filled with architecture students of every nationality is enough for us to ask once more: Why La Tourette? And why La Tourette today?

The critics have not really found an answer to this question. On the contrary, they avoid it; they are anxious to assign La Tourette its place in history, as much as within Le Corbusier's oeuvre as to measure its impact at the end of the twentieth century within the short-term perspective of, say, "new brutalism." However, rather than a "historical monument" or "national treasure," La Tourette seems to be simultaneously a milestone and a model, both equally and strangely contemporary and topical in a way that has nothing to do with style. As is the rule in any phenomenological endeavor, we cannot fully measure this idea except by provisionally putting in parentheses—and provisionally not questioning—a number of theses and concepts that keep recurring in architectural history and criticism, including the writings of Le Corbusier himself.

La Tourette is a milestone in the sense that paying attention to such a late work of Le Corbusier may be of help when looking at some recent developments in architecture, and it is a model in the epistemological sense of the term, which lends itself to varied applications in relation to current issues—but first of all, it is an object. More to the point, it is a "theoretical object," a notion that we must construct and whose operation we must also untangle, with one important reservation: among the objects we come to know and eventually put to heuristic or speculative use, the architectural object has a distinctive feature, because in its very being as an object and before any confiscation of a conceptual order, it refers to the idea of "construction" (when it doesn't present itself as proceeding from or inducing some form of "deconstruction"). And this from the very outset, at the project stage, when it is still seen as "to be constructed." This alone makes La Tourette a theoretical object par excellence, a model of its kind, understood not only as an object that gives pause for thought and opens the way to reflection, but also as an object that, when examined more closely, itself secretes theory or at least directs it, feeds it, informs it—in other words, secretly programs it.

There are obviously many kinds of theoretical objects: some belong to a more or less ideal or conceptual order, whatever the

mode of historical inscription might be; others are of an essentially material or technical nature, even if there is a place in them
for something like thought. Both types of objects elude any form
of discursive reduction; in that sense, "art" constitutes a theoretical object inasmuch as history does not have the last word
regarding either its anthropological or speculative implications.
The same goes a fortiori for architecture and its objects: it is not
enough to retrace, however meticulously and in whatever detail,
the history of the project or of the building site in order to en-
compass the entire set of questions posed by La Tourette.[1] On the
other hand, as brilliant and effective as Colin Rowe's analysis of
La Tourette is on a descriptive level, it does not suffice to borrow
from Le Corbusier (himself inspired by Choisy) the concept of
promenade architecturale to exhaust its phenomenology, which is
not limited to visual effects alone—meaning the optical effects of
which the building is host.[2] Objects that we think of as "theoretical" are recognizable in that not content to appeal to history or
to criticism, they question both and may go so far as to escape
the expertise of either. If this happens, it is because such objects
not only belong to theory but rework it, put it to the test, or even
present a challenge to it. So much so—and this is the hypothesis
I am making concerning La Tourette—that space is made within
objects for something resembling thought in such a way that they
seem inhabited, if not haunted, by it. So how do we read this?
What meaning, other than metaphorical, can the verb "to inhabit" (if not the verb "to haunt") have with regard to thought?
What manner of habitat or dwelling can such an object constitute
for thought or offer to it?

 Among the epistemological consequences that arise from the
fact that the architectural object presents itself from the outset as
a built object, or one to be built, the most immediately obvious
touch on the constructive and architectural metaphors as much
as on the functions these may serve in the most diverse realms.

As a theoretical object, the architectural object is doubly so, or is so in a double sense, playing on the difference, or distance, as much as on the seam one is tempted to mark between the so-called built register and the supposedly architectural register. And this in the best-case scenario, and not without proposing a model of articulation between the technical level and the aesthetic level that may go from conflict or, at least, open competition to the subordination of one register to the other, when the relationship between architecture and construction is not taken as itself being of a more or less metaphoric order: either you wholeheartedly share Friedrich Schelling's view that architecture is a metaphor of construction, or you agree with Sigfried Giedion, who in effect said that when it comes to architecture, construction has occupied the place of the unconscious since the nineteenth century.[3] This is not to forget what might be outmoded about such statements, like similar ones made by Viollet-le-Duc, sucked as they are into the orbit of functionalism—even if only on a preventive basis, as was the case with Schelling.

La Tourette: A Conceptual Work?

Le Corbusier apparently only went to L'Arbresle three times: the first time, in 1953, to find his bearings on the land; the second time, to visit the building site prior to the consecration of the monastery that took place before the completion of the works; and the last time, on his return from Agadir in 1960, when he could see the whole thing finished and had time to chat with the members of the community.

On May 4, 1953, less than a year after Father Couturier, in the most imperative way ("Corbu, it's just the thing for you!"), had gotten him to agree to build a monastery and a short while after receiving the official commission, Le Corbusier spent a whole day at the site. In the afternoon, as the clock struck four (confirmed by the position of the sun), he dashed off a quick

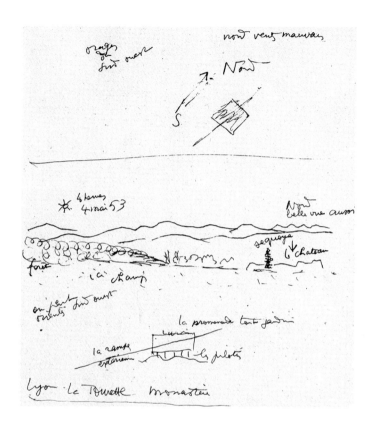

10.2
Le Corbusier, Panorama sketch of La Tourette site, May 4, 1953. © F.L.C./ADAGP, Paris/Artists Rights Society (ARS), New York, 2015.

panorama opening to the north onto the chain of the Lyonnais Mountains ("also a beautiful view" is noted), with "forest" written to the left, followed, in the "here" where the building would find its place, by "fields" (coupled with this important detail: "sloping, in a southwest direction"); mention is made on the right side of a "sequoya" [sic] and the nearby "castle." At the top of the page are "southwest storms" and "bad north winds," as well as an unfinished outline of a square volume, with an arrow running through it noted "S —> North." At the bottom, below the panorama, a drawing of a rectangular box sits on what are described as "pilotis" planted in the undulating ground; the horizontal ridge line of the box begins with a delicate doodle labeled "roof garden promenade." The whole thing is crossed, as though crossed out, in peremptory fashion, by a diagonal line, paired with this caption: "external ramp."

This last motif grew in importance and assumed different forms through a series of variations that culminated in the first state of the project in April 1954, only to be abandoned bit by bit as the project evolved. Le Corbusier went so far as to imagine a complicated network of ramps ("the system of aerial pathways"[4]) clinging to the wall of the church and leading to the cloister set up on the roof terrace. He let himself be talked out of this without ever resolving the problem posed by transferring the cloister to the top of the buildings. At issue here was not just the program or the set of monastic rules, but the concept that directed the entire work, and the overall scheme was soon established: in terms of cubic volume (analogous to what Father Couturier suggested to Le Corbusier), a U-shaped unit, which contains the private living quarters and public areas of communal life, the library, and study rooms, is connected like an open drawer to the volume of the parallelepipedic church, but separated from it by a rather dizzying gap on the right side, opposite the entrance, which is crossed at the top by a bridge in the form of an air traffic lane connecting the roof terrace of the church to that of the monastery buildings, thus producing a distortion or apparent warping of the block. Within the quadrangle defined by the high blank wall of the church and the inner walls of the monastery, themselves punctuated by wide picture windows on the level above the communal areas and by narrow strip windows running the length of the corridors on the two levels occupied by individual cells, is a network of galleries or "conduits" in the form of a cross, through which the wings of the monastery communicate with each other as well as with the church on what would be the "ground floor," and which Le Corbusier himself spoke of as a cloister when not simply referring to them as conduits or canals. The empty parts of the quadrangle are cluttered chaotically with various small structures, staircases, and mock casemates. One of these edifices sits at the bottom of the high wall of the church and corresponds to the sacristy; it is bristling with the famous "light-machine-guns" (*les mitraillettes*) designed by Iannis Xenakis.

Referring to the part assigned to Xenakis in the design process leads us to wonder about the respective roles played by Le Corbusier and his studio in the development of the project and its realization. The part Le Corbusier himself played would have been limited essentially to the design, in which he involved Xenakis early on in his capacity as a studio engineer, a role that was beginning to require him to assume greater responsibilities. Le Corbusier said to him, "I have a project that will suit you perfectly; it is pure geometry."[5] Even if what we understand by "geometry" here cannot be reduced to the use of a ruler and precision sizing—any more than to the introduction a posteriori of geometric volumes like the cube of the oratory, set on a cruciform base and capped with a pyramid—it is certain that Le Corbusier determined the initial course of action in a fairly elliptical fashion, with a few sketches, then asked Xenakis to work out the proportional relationships between the different parts with a

10.3
Le Corbusier, La Tourette, Éveux-sur-l'Arbresle, France,
1953–1960. Looking west through the gap between
La Tourette's church and monastery, with the bridge
connecting the roof terraces of the two buildings in the
distance and the sacristy and its "light-machine-guns"
in the foreground. Photo: Hubert Damisch.

Modulor and to draft the first plans for the project proper. Xenakis worked continuously on the project, whereas Le Corbusier followed the progress at some remove, though he did show up after the community's budget was revised downward and it became necessary to cut one level from the convent block and do away with the rooftop vaults, among other things. His interventions were further limited, after 1955, to going along with the decisions made by his collaborators after arbitration, though he managed later to modify them.[6] In the actual building phase of the project, André Wogenscky, the head of the studio, took charge until 1958, though he put the on-site management in the hands of the aptly named Fernand Gardien. For strictly economic reasons, those in charge of the main building work were given free rein to impose most of the technical solutions, from the prestressing of the structural concrete and the reduction of the height of the pilotis, which meant a lowering of the monastery as a whole, to pouring concrete in forms for the church.

Whatever the consequences may have been, the handling of the project as Le Corbusier understood it implied a sharp division between the tasks of design and those of execution; at the same time, the project was characterized by a drastic opposition between the coherence of the formal approach and the anarchy of the management of the building site, an opposition intensified by the scattering of the team and the mobility of the individuals in charge of the project. On this point, one can only agree with Sérgio Ferro and his colleagues: if Le Corbusier had wanted to, he had the authority and the necessary skills to resolve this paradox; the fact that he did not do so means we are forced to consider that what might look like avoidance was actually an integral part of his approach.[7]

The emphasis placed on the formal aspects of the project and his indifference to the concrete conditions of its realization do not, however, mean Le Corbusier was a "conceptual" artist

10.4
Le Corbusier, La Tourette, Éveux-sur-l'Arbresle, France,
1953–1960. Altars in the side chapel. Photo: Hubert
Damisch.

before his time, in the sense that someone like Sol LeWitt understood the term some years later.[8] Le Corbusier was certainly in a constant search for concepts, whether graphic or discursive, but not to the point of claiming to achieve control of the various aspects of the building process by conceptual means. Whether we are justified in saying that the firm imposed its texture (raw concrete) on the body of the building, Le Corbusier was no novice in that regard. And if bandying about the term *brutalism* in relation to La Tourette smacks of delusion in the constructive order, the surface effects associated with the job of striking the formwork were no less in vogue at the time.[9] This fact is nowhere more clearly demonstrated than in the church and the sacristy, where the reality of lumpy cement washed with vivid colors undeniably evokes the monochromes of Yves Klein. Paradoxically, the space allotted for material accidents in La Tourette meant that, at the implementation stage, the constructive aspect was translated by a kind of overflowing of the substance the building is made of: the cement pourings vie with the many traces of a transubstantiation that in places takes on a quasi-pictorial quality. It is as though the architecture, in its very conception, had taken up the genealogy that makes it a metaphor of construction in order to reverse its terms, leaving it up to the building to develop its effects.

The Slope

The downward slope of the site is assumed to be one of the major components of the project, as Le Corbusier said: "I came here. I brought my sketchbook along as usual. I drew the road. I drew the skyline, I put in the direction of the sun, I 'sniffed out' the topography. I decided on the place where it would go since the place was not at all determined. By choosing the place I committed the criminal or decent act; the first move to make is to choose the nature of the location and then the nature of the composition you

10.5
Le Corbusier, La Tourette, Éveux-sur-l'Arbresle, France,
1953–1960. The oratory with its cruciform base and
pyramidal roof. Photo: Hubert Damisch.

will produce in such conditions."[10] This extract from Le Corbusier's widely published interview with members of the La Tourette community in 1960 poses a number of questions. It does indeed look like the choice of what Le Corbusier calls the "place" or "location"—in other words, the site—had the force of a prior logic, essential within the framework of the architectural project and just like the operation Alberti describes in *Della Pittura*, which for the painter consisted of first delimiting the space of a painting before undertaking to paint within these limits. (Remember that at the time when he conceived his plans for La Tourette, Le Corbusier devoted part of each day to his work as a painter, which he saw as more than a source of inspiration—indeed, as the path that had led him to architecture.[11]) That there was a "move" or gesture there, in the architect's own terms, comes down to saying that there was nothing "natural" about such an act and that as far as "nature" goes, the location, as much as the composition that was called upon to take place there, was a function of a linked decision; far from corresponding to some kind of framing, the choice of place (or location) made no sense in the final analysis except in light of the project, provided that this one could, at its best, transform the terrain into a "site" and succeed in establishing (or constituting) it as such.

It is therefore appropriate to take Le Corbusier's other declaration with a grain of salt:

> *The place dictated the architecture. The terrain was on a sharp incline: a small valley sloped downward, opening on to the plain, and it was surrounded by forest. The building was designed from the top down: the composition begins with the roof line, a great broad horizon, and it ends in the downward slope of the ground on which the building comes and sits by means of pilotis—load-bearing columns. From the horizontal summit, the building*

10.6
Le Corbusier, La Tourette, Éveux-sur-l'Arbresle, France,
1953–1960. La Tourette as seen from the southwest.
Photo: Hubert Damisch.

*defines its organism as a descent: the loggias form a
"brise-soleil," then come the classrooms, studies and library and, below this, the refectory and the cloister in the
form of a cross that leads to the church.* [12]

In fact, the way in which Le Corbusier dealt with the steep slope
on which the monastery is set makes it hard to accept that the
place "dictated" the architecture. It would be more correct, more
in keeping with the "truth" in which the said architecture feeds
the fantasy, and even more in keeping with the Corbusian aesthetic, to say that it was entirely up to the architect to confer on
the place its status and value as a site—the same way he did for the
Chapel of Ronchamp. Le Corbusier did this while taking no notice of the slope, the better to play around with it later by trans-
posing it to another register, another key. [13] Father Couturier was
thrilled that Le Corbusier followed his advice and paid a visit to
the abbey at Thoronet: "You notice how they used all the inclines
of the ground there, without trying to hide them, even where the
church is. I'm sure that delighted you." [14] It scarcely makes sense
to want Le Corbusier to use the slope at L'Arbresle. Certainly, he
did not try to hide it. But everything proceeds as though, having chosen to set up the monastery starting from the top of the
slope where the access road stops, he resolved the problem that
placing it in such a spot posed in two different, that is, opposing,
ways, depending on whether he was handling the church or the
monastery buildings.

As far as the church goes, excavating and filling up the terrain
gave it a nearly horizontal base; in the monastery buildings, Le
Corbusier initially pretended not to notice the difficulty by re-
versing the terms of the problem. This he was later compelled
to candidly—though not without an apparent paradox—explain:
"Here, in this terrain that was so mobile, so receding, descending, flowing away, I said: I'm not going to make the base on the

ground since the ground gives way or else it will cost as much as a Roman or Assyrian fortress. We don't have the money and this is not the time. Let's make the base high up, at the horizontal of the building at the top, which will then square with the horizon. And we'll measure everything else from this horizontal at the top and we'll get to the ground when we touch it." Le Corbusier went on, increasing the shock value such a statement might have: "It is like La Palice, but that's just how it is. That's how you get a building that's very precise at the top and that defines its organism, bit by bit, as it descends, touching the ground as best it can."[15]

A terrain "so mobile, so receding, descending, flowing away": all these terms count, even the order in which they follow each other, with mobility coming first, only to be parsed under the three forms of flight, from descent to liquidity, the building having to accommodate itself "as best it can" when it comes to touching ground that flows away. We know that on this score the construction firm would have been given free rein to deal with a resulting network of supports that look, for the most part, like pylons rather than pilotis and which don't all make the grade in terms of constructive rationality (to say nothing of the strange "combs" designed by Xenakis to support the atrium). But if the ground runs away at the very moment the building manages to touch it (to touch it but not leaning on it from the outset—not, at least, at the level of the concept), the question of the area left empty at the center of the quadrangle remains unsolved. As Father Couturier also wrote to Le Corbusier: "On the ground floor, people normally move through the quadrilateral of the cloister and the latter, given the Lyonnais climate, should probably be glazed, unless it is combined with an internal circulation system." But what sense can the notion of a ground floor have in the context of a project that played with the incline in such a way that any notion of a ground level was literally stripped of any foundation, the ground simply lacking its place (in the Lacanian sense

10.7
Le Corbusier, La Tourette, Éveux-sur-l'Arbresle, France,
1953–1960. A conduit raised above the sloping
ground. Photo: Hubert Damisch.

10.8
Le Corbusier, La Tourette, Éveux-sur-l'Arbresle,
France, 1953–1960. Xenakis's "combs." Photo:
Hubert Damisch.

of *manque à sa place*)? Nor was a cloister, classically defined as occupying the perimeter of a central space, reduced in this particular case to a hole delineated on three sides by the facades of the communal buildings and on the fourth by the wall of the church.

Le Corbusier's solution turned the whole project upside down, giving the conduits, or galleries, of the circulation system—glazed, as Father Couturier had advised—the form of a cross that marked a perpendicular within the quadrilateral. If there is circulation, it involves a whole play of inclines aimed at bringing together the parts of the block located at different levels. This organization, which has all the appearances of a cloister in negative, manages to substitute its own system of inclines for the natural slope of the ground. Therefore, if it is true that the place played a crucial role in the genesis of the project and its structuring, the organization paradoxically denies the natural slope of the terrain and internalizes the very notion of slope, while the building seemingly works against the natural slope, pretending to take no notice of it. The building does this by increasing the number of inclined planes and occasionally matching them up, as in the case of the gallery that runs along the bottom toward the church entrance, with "undulating" plate-glass walls in trompe l'oeil perspective. Even the Richard Serra–like heavy bronze door, pivoting on its axis in this passage (in the musical sense of the term, knowing the importance Xenakis attached to this aspect of things), borrows a little of the resolutely contemporary resonance that we have every right to ascribe to La Tourette.

The Last Post

One reason for the—at times suspect—critical interest in La Tourette, if not the attraction critics acknowledge that the monument exerts, may well be connected to the fact that, not content with putting himself at the service of a faith he did not share,

10.9
Le Corbusier, La Tourette, Éveux-sur-l'Arbresle, France,
1953–1960. The glazed conduits seen from above.
Photo: Hubert Damisch.

10.10
Le Corbusier, La Tourette, Éveux-sur-l'Arbresle, France,
1953–1960. Glazing detail of the conduits. Photo:
Hubert Damisch.

Le Corbusier seems to have made a clean slate of a number of his principles there, beginning with the system of the famous "five points of a new architecture." Certainly, there are the pilotis, the long strip windows, and the roof gardens. The monastery buildings are indeed up in the air, well off the ground, and even if we cannot really say that the garden goes underneath the house, the terraces on which wild grasses grow, though failing to correspond to the usual notion of a cloister, nonetheless take up what was in the on-the-spot sketch dashed off during the architect's initial visit to the place. But the windows stretching like one continuous slit along the entire length of the corridors of the living quarters have no impact on the monks' accommodation, with their cells opening on to the exterior through so many loggias, which give the upper two floors of the facade the look of a beehive. Even the communal areas, the chapter hall, the classrooms, the study rooms, and the refectory revive, by way of a so-called free plan and in the broadest definition of the term, the great tradition of the hypostyle hall—right down to the treatment of the cylindrical section supports striated with vertical grooves. Is what we are dealing with here—to take up the title of Ford Madox Ford's novel—the last post? The last avatar of the column? The fate of the hypostyle hall? A column that would happily truncate, on a symbolic plane, the never-ending rhetoric of the post (postmodern, postimpressionist, postindustrial, poststructuralist, postmortem . . .)? The column subsisting merely as a fetish, with beams inserted in its stem instead of resting on top of it, is enough to give a Japanese feel to the columns of the chapter hall or the refectory, a feel reinforced by the grid of windows musically composed by Xenakis. (I note in passing that one of these columns, at the southwest corner of the monastery, goes through the floor to touch the ground and enrich, like a footnote, the eclectic repertoire of the pilotis, among which it takes on the figure of intruder.)

The reference to hypostyle architecture, taken in its broadest sense without forgetting the possibilities of transposition between construction in wood and construction in stone or concrete, is worth insisting on as a reference, especially since no trace of it is to be found in the church. We are dealing here with two radically distinct places, architecturally as much as functionally, but which are in a dialectical tension emphasized by the opacity of this somewhat negative volume, thrown up as though to bar entry to the monastery. Open to the public through a little low doorway, the place of worship is treated like an almost blind, minimalist volume, an immense box, dark and empty, with no openings other than a few slits that in no way resemble windows: one vertical, running the full height of the building in the corner to the right of the altar, and two others above the stalls, whose slanting recesses allow indirect light to well up as though pregnant with the vivid colors of their paint. But to claim it has the exterior of a bunker, not to mention a megalith,[16] is sheer nonsense, delusion. The walls of formed concrete, cast and applied in successive layers, may well look rough and somewhat archaic: they nonetheless retain the thinness of the metal skeleton that was part of the original plan, as well as a surprising lightness, given their height, which is revealed by the small number of openings punched into them. It looks like a hull with rectilinear and perpendicular edges, or an envelope that is definitely rigid but whose actual minimal density is enough to minimize any appearance of brutalism. The more compelling allusion would be toward an analysis not conducted in strictly tectonic terms—as are, moreover, the references to hypostyle architecture.

It is clear enough that the contemporaneity that we are attributing to La Tourette both as milestone and model has to do with the fact that part of its activity as a theoretical object comes down to determining in what sense there is or can be architecture in the present day. To do so, we must accept in return that the

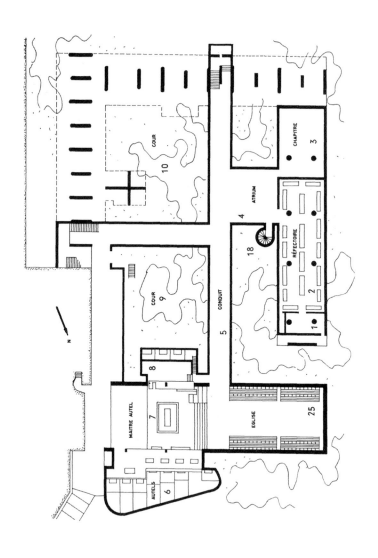

10.11
Le Corbusier, La Tourette, Éveux-sur-l'Arbresle, France,
1953–1960. Level two plan. © F.L.C./ADAGP, Paris/
Artists Rights Society (ARS), New York, 2015.

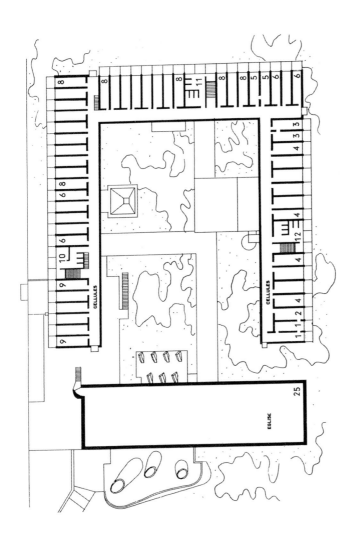

10.12
Le Corbusier, La Tourette, Éveux-sur-l'Arbresle, France,
1953–1960. Level five plan. © F.L.C./ADAGP, Paris/
Artists Rights Society (ARS), New York, 2015.

valence of the word *construction* will vary depending on whether we place ourselves in the realm of the project, of its realization, or somewhere in between the two. Schelling's formula defining architecture as a metaphor of construction and Giedion's pronouncement giving construction the position of architecture's unconscious may well prove to be important today to the extent that they both play on two notions that go together and whose reality is indisputable. In the first instance, the notion of resistance—if we accept that the same goes for the resistance of materials as for all other forms of resistance, made as it is to be overcome or diverted—is mobilized to other ends. Second is the notion of conversion, in the Freudian sense of *Umkehrung*, of the translation into an image, a metaphor, or a symptom, of a thought content that can only be expressed via such a detour: from the project stage, the concept has to translate into graphic terms; even if it were to let itself be thought through at the outset in constructive terms, the transition of the building to architecture would still itself correspond to an operation of a conceptual order, which for Le Corbusier came down to the descent of geometry into the field in which builders operate. Poincaré used to say that one doesn't do geometry with chalk, signifying that geometry is an abstract thing. Yet, as etymology would have it, geometry did in fact begin with the tracing on the ground of some figure, just as Socrates had the Slave of Meno do. It was left to Le Corbusier, breaking with the ground, to do geometry with concrete.

The Horizontal

If the authors of one of the best works on La Tourette are to be believed, Le Corbusier only needed a one-day visit to the spot and to read a few letters from Father Couturier to trigger the "stronger than ever" geometric inspiration we know about. (But what exactly do we know about it? What do we know about geometry as a source of inspiration? What does it—geometry—have to do in all this?) There is something else that concerns the evolution of the project: "The geometric part of the four-sided plan (and of the elevation drawn starting from the 'horizontal at the top') will not be gone back over. Starting with this geometric decree, the second phase of the project is elaborated in counterpoint through the convolutions of ramps, cloister, staircase, atrium that complicate the initial grid."[17] It really is as a "decree," the decision of some higher power, that we should read the idea of a building "conceived from above," one that would touch the ground "as best it can. . . . It is not something that would occur to everyone. It is one of the original aspects of the monastery—highly original."[18] A decree from on high, one that would be geometric to the extent that it would revive the founding gesture, consisting of geometry's cutting all ties with the very earth where it originally found a place to inscribe itself? Viollet-le-Duc argued that the Gothic cathedral was conceived and should be thought of from the top, starting with the layout of the vaults and their groins, whose linear repercussions would then have determined the form and the section of the supports and their distribution on the ground. At La Tourette (and this is what makes it so contemporary, at its most advanced), Le Corbusier went even further down the road of a reversal that seems to attack the very idea of construction, inasmuch as the latter presupposes something like a ground that would act as its base. Such is the virtue of the model that he imposes the idea—even more than the form—of a structure, one to be thought of in strictly internal terms. This is the case with a number of so-called virtual objects that architects work with today, the idea of a base or foundation being "suspended," so to speak, or—phenomenology *oblige*—placed in brackets. Geometry begins here, when it comes to La Tourette: the setting of the base at the top at the building's horizontal, along its ridge line, with the intent "to square with the horizon."[19]

The decision (the decree) to reverse the normal order of things and take them from the top needs to be linked to the desire, clearly asserted from the first drawing from life in May 1953, to stress and reinforce the contemplative purpose of the cloister by perching it on top of the monastery terraces. Sérgio Ferro rightly emphasizes that in the first version of the project, acroteria 1.83 meters high visually isolated the contemplative circuit of the surrounding landscape, which Le Corbusier felt was a "disastrous distraction," whereas a sort of belvedere formed by a suite of small vaults sheltered the circuit. Today, those terraces open directly to the sky, and the added load of dirt intended to combat seepage has raised the wild-grass-covered ground to such an extent that you have to make an effort not to let yourself be caught out by the opening up of the landscape and to remain within the experience Le Corbusier had in mind. Although Le Corbusier was not a man of faith, the idea of a retreat was not foreign to him, on the condition that it was appropriately translated into architectural terms: on the condition that architecture organize it, impose its geometry on it, and offer it something more than just a shelter.

Everything in Le Corbusier's commentaries confirms that something like thought was indeed at work in all this. La Tourette is not only that *machine à émouvoir* whose spirit Colin Rowe claimed to bring to light. Le Corbusier said he accepted the commission because it was not just a matter of a place of worship but also involved a set of residential buildings. We must still consider not only what is implied and meant by a *machine à habiter*'s being able to be inhabited, if not haunted, by an idea (or its phantom) but also what might be implied, or meant, for an idea to have a *habitat*. There is something else that goes even further and truly marks the gap between architecture and construction. That is the impact that architecture can have on thought, not only providing it with models and metaphors—which construction already does—but also putting thought to work, as La Tourette manages to do. It is clear that Le Corbusier abandoned himself to an experience—one that each and every person passing through can have—in choosing to place the base at the top, when the experience of the world is to let the ground take the weight and gradually extend toward the horizontal: something that, in phenomenological terms, Husserl called "the openness as horizontality that is not completely conceived, represented, but that is already implicitly formed."[20] Husserl also wrote that each of us derives our "historicity" from the respective ego that is *domiciled* in it: "If I am born a sailor's child, then a part of my development has taken place on the ship. But the ship would not be characterized as a ship for me in relation to the earth—as long as no unity would be produced between the ship and the earth—the ship would itself be my 'earth,' my homeland."[21]

No doubt, having your residence or habitat on land is not the same as having it at sea, but as Joseph Conrad wrote, it is not only on the seas that land can come to be missing. At La Tourette, everyone is in the same boat, starting with the apprentice monks who were supposed to perfect their personal development there; the ground is definitely missing from its place, right up to the ridgeline of the terraces, which was originally designed in such a way as to seal what Husserl called "the opening of the landscape." If there is an actual base, it is not to be sought anywhere other than in the edifice itself, such as it opens onto the sky; the spiritual experience urged upon the brothers obeyed the same program, the same discipline, the same geometric decree as the veritable challenge constituted by the present state of things for the visitor admitted to the roof terraces.

If the ridgeline of the terraces today squares with the horizon in the opening of the landscape, the effect is due, as has been said, to it (the ridgeline) being lowered, which followed the laying down of what today no longer has anything of the roof

10.13
Le Corbusier, La Tourette, Éveux-sur-l'Arbresle, France,
1953–1960. Roof terrace. Photo: Hubert Damisch.

garden about it. But another, less immediately apparent feature demands to be taken into account: the slight incline of the roof of the church in the opposite direction to that of the terrain, which is another manifestation of the process of internalizing the slope. This incline is all the more pronounced because it begins crudely, with all the appearances of a second-rate remedy, in one of the forms close to the ridgeline, before gradually shifting upward toward the top. The effect is that the ridgeline of the church vies with that of the monastery, with "the church, naturally, dominating the whole," as Father Couturier wrote to Le Corbusier, imposing itself so effectively as a horizon that it results in a kind of conflict translated into an apparent distortion or warping in the articulation of volumes, which is further accentuated by the jutting bridge thrown over the dizzying caesura opening onto the landscape below. If there is geometry, in the circumstances it accommodates itself to—if it doesn't actually result from—an apparent wavering, though carefully calculated, in what comprises the primary foundation of the experience of the world, whether imagined, represented, or implicitly *deformed*: "horizontality." The church dominates the whole, squaring with the horizon, imposing its own horizontality at the expense of that of the convent buildings.

Walking

The experience in question here is not only of an optical order. The whole body is implicated, if not what Husserl called the flesh ("the flesh is unique by way of its being experienced as my total organ and as articulated into distinct organs in which I [*Ich*] am the functioning 'ego' [*Ich*]"[22]). Le Corbusier made no mystery of this: "The monastery of La Tourette was realized on the basis of this essentially human program: the tough life of the preaching friars. As at Ronchamp, it was a matter of a program for hearts and bodies on a human scale. . . . This monastery of rough

10.14
Le Corbusier, La Tourette, Éveux-sur-l'Arbresle, France,
1953–1960. View of La Tourette from the south.
Photo: Hubert Damisch.

concrete is a labor of love. It doesn't talk to itself. It lives on the inside. It is inside that the essential happens."[23] As we have already seen, this could be interpreted in two ways: in a spiritual sense and in an architectural sense. For it is indeed in terms of architecture, and only in terms of architecture, that Le Corbusier would have understood and been able to respond to the commission that had been passed to him by men of faith (not having a valid answer, in that specific sense of the term, does not imply leaving the question open). This brings us back to the idea of a *promenade architecturale* and, even more crucially, to the notion of *circulation* that Le Corbusier never stopped making—if you will forgive the expression—one of the articles of faith of his architectural creed.[24]

There is no doubt that the *promenade architecturale* corresponds to one of the key articulations of the project as Le Corbusier understood it. Based on La Tourette, Colin Rowe masterfully reconstructed the almost dialectical stages of a circuit designed to offer at every moment and at every turn fresh views and insights, which, in Husserl's terms again, participate in the same "style of emergence" in which spatial, qualitative, and temporal perspectives come together. With the notion of a promenade—even in its virtual, if not phantomlike, aspects—the architecture opens itself to a form of experience, which the arts of memory have put to good use. This leaves the orator to worry about arranging his discursive material, in his mind, in the rooms of an imaginary building that he only had to walk through, always in his mind, in the desired order, when the time came, so as not to lose the thread of his argument.[25] But there is nothing of the theater of memory about La Tourette, even though the model for the architectural promenade was copied from the Acropolis of Athens. Nor is the experience it offers merely a matter of perspective. Wherever the lumpy raw concrete walls make the strongest demands on our attention, it is their tactile aspect, rather than their optical one, that does so.

From the stairs of the residential floors to the inclined ramps of the conduits, another kind of experience imposes itself that we might describe as kinesthetic. Certain of the fathers were concerned at having the impression of "going up Mount Sinai."[26] The idea was not in itself inappropriate, but you only have to see the young brothers racing downstairs to the church or climbing upstairs to pace around the rooftops in any film of La Tourette to understand that the experience urged on any subject (or, to use Husserl's words again, any "functioning 'ego'"). Traveling through the place is not reduced to a promenade across an essentially visual space but occurs through the experience of walking. Husserl analyzes it in terms similar to those Le Corbusier used to describe the way in which La Tourette, thought out from above, comes to meet the ground as best it can. "In the purely tactile realm, I thus experience in walking—insofar as I periodically displace my legs above the ground, one after the other, egoistically—the unity of the endless surface of the earth. . . . But something else intervenes here, too: when I walk I don't touch the ground, I meet it. And in doing so, I put all my 'weight' on it."[27]

This also returns to what Le Corbusier said of the way in which the project of La Tourette was entirely thought out not only from the top down but also from the inside out: "Walking is from the first a part of those phenomena constituted in perspectives through the play of all the kinestheses together. And this occurs already in closed spaces, in which everything becomes accessible in the normal way and everything is thus constituted in the same way as real things spatiotemporally exterior to one another. Closed space, however, is closed the way a thing can be closed and it has its exits out into open space."[28] You could not put it better or give a more explicit form to the thinking that inhabits

La Tourette and that inscribes it, phenomenologically as much as architecturally speaking, in time—a time that is well and truly our time.

11.1
Barcelona Pavilion, a 1986 reconstruction of
Ludwig Mies van der Rohe's German Pavilion for the
International Exposition, Barcelona, 1929. © 2015
Artists Rights Society (ARS), New York/VG Bild-Kunst,
Bonn. Photo: Erich Lessing/Art Resource, NY.

11 THE SLIGHTEST DIFFERENCE: MIES VAN DER ROHE AND THE RECONSTRUCTION OF THE BARCELONA PAVILION

I don't like to say columns, the word has been spoiled.
—Le Corbusier, *Toward an Architecture*[1]

On the initiative of the architect Oriol Bohigas, who presided for many years over Barcelona's municipal building programs, the pavilion Mies van de Rohe designed to represent Germany at the 1929 International Exhibition (which had immediately been destroyed when the show closed) has been reconstructed. For decades, the monument existed only on paper, in the form of a folder of period photographs and a few sketches and preparatory plans (now kept at the Museum of Modern Art in New York), together with a welter of miscellaneous commentaries, but in 1986 the Barcelona Pavilion was returned to us in concrete and marble, glass and steel (we would say "in flesh and blood," if it were a person) on its original site at the foot of Montjuïc, with all of the attendant consequences in terms of both its reception and Mies's work as a whole.

Today, engaged as we are in a general revisiting of the values of modernity—the same values found in the Barcelona of Cerda, Gaudí, Sert, and Bohigas, but also of Picasso (the return of the pavilion does not sit well with the caricatural critique of the "postmodernists," who have too quickly condemned the limits and even the alleged bankruptcy of "modern" architecture)—what might be the meaning of such an operation? And what might be the impact of the reconstruction of the most emblematic work of this particular master of the modern movement (who perhaps represents the hardest, most imperious, and most intransigent core of that movement) and, for those who confuse architectural criticism with the criticism of ideologies, also the most intolerable work? Beyond the coup for local commerce and tourism, should we see it as a profession of faith, reiterating anew the message of Mies's 1929 architectural "manifesto"? Or would it be rather a call to order (Let's not let ourselves be taken in: modernity is not, or is not only, or exactly, what they would have us believe), or even a way of fending off a certain critical discourse that sees in Mies's oeuvre a mere series of "empty prisms," characterized by the reduction of the image, pure form without content, set into invariable types? These same supposed "empty prisms" have tended to work as symbols, if not symptoms, through a characteristic rhetorical reversal, to the point at which they have embodied what Manfredo Tafuri describes as "the fantasies of European intellectualism."[2] For a French intellectual like myself, who made the trip to Chicago at the beginning of the 1960s burdened with the images of the architectural press and influenced by Tafuri (who worked hard to give architecture the place it holds in contemporary culture), that "fantasy" could not fail to be striking. As may well be, in the current context, the reconstruction of a mythical monument par excellence that looks to have, once again in the order of reception, a semiexperimental scope.

I spoke of a "monument," but a *monument* in what sense? Its construction long planned with the consent of Mies himself and carefully prepared, reflected upon, even orchestrated, the reintroduction of one of the lost prototypes of the so-called International Style into the built environment does not appear to be precisely a return of the repressed. In fact, the "identical" nature of its reconstruction might have posed a greater problem, meeting with resistance on a number of fronts (to say nothing of the cost of the endeavor, a factor that also weighed heavily on the fate of the original building). The influence of the pavilion was felt from the very outset, the latest round of debates on modernity having little impact. There is no history of architecture, no matter how "critical," that does not give the Barcelona Pavilion a special place, value, and significance as an example to be followed. If we can apply the word *monument* to it, merely on the strength of having seen a few graphic documents that recreate its appearances (with the ambiguous authority typical of architecture photography) and allow a reasoned analysis of it based on the floor plan, it is because the trace it has left in the archive or memory of the modern movement corresponds, historically as well as formally, to a kind of successful "clean-up operation."

As unusual as the pavilion was and remains, in principle and in practice, the vicissitudes of history having conferred on it an almost ideal, even mythical, value (even if photography attests to the reality of its provisional existence), this object has never stopped functioning simultaneously as a paradigm and a memory device. As a paradigm, it worked to propose, at the reduced scale of a relatively light single-story structure, a schema for declining and conjugating the parameters of the architecture that we correctly hold to be characteristic of a certain *moment* of modernity. As a memory device, if a paradoxical one, it conjured up a memory of this moment (all the better to cover its tracks) so that such a schema seemed to overlap with proposals put forward in fields outside architecture—notably, painting and sculpture. This seemed to imply the serious revision of the boundaries between practices, the specificity of which was obstinately stressed by the modernist ideology, while at the same time admitting that such practices might share a common denominator, as in the mandatory first-year course still taught at the Bauhaus for all students (whether they wanted to go into painting, sculpture, architecture, or *design*) at the time Mies was about to become head of the school, a year before the opening of the Barcelona exposition. One of the issues the Barcelona Pavilion raises, the subtlest perhaps, ultimately bears on the limits (which I would call disciplinary) of a history of architecture and especially of modern architecture on its conditions of possibility and on the meaning, in this instance, of the word *history*. It is not certain that now having at our disposal an "identical" reconstruction of the Barcelona Pavilion will help us get a clearer picture of this.

The reconstruction (or should we say reproduction?) should at least lead us to reflect on the diverse species or modalities presented by the architectural object. In this regard, Mies's oeuvre does not escape the common rule: any overview that one might offer presupposes that we compare terms that are not necessarily of the same nature, or even the same level. Whether we are dealing with the spectacular projects for transparent office blocks designed for Friedrichstrasse, from 1920 to 1922, the residential tower blocks built on the shores of Lake Michigan in Chicago from 1948 on, or, within a narrower time frame, the 1923 Brick Country House project that Mies built a few years later at Guben and Krefeld, the connections risk being misleading, as much on an aesthetic as on an ideological level, as we will later see. In another register and to a lesser degree, the comparison between the prevailing image of the Barcelona Pavilion in the architectural press and the reconstruction offered to us today might also be misleading—even if the only reason for the uneasiness the operation is likely to cause is the *gap*, which some will see as insurmountable, between the mark left by the prototype on the imagination and its rediscovered reality.

What was it about the prototype, then, that the fact of reconstructing it, of reproducing it (almost) identically, is enough to change its meaning—or at least to alter its impact, in the same way that a new edition of a bronze sculpture can lead to a shift in the way we look at what was held to be the original? How can the very thing that makes for its originality (which no one is contesting) be affected by its *replication*? It has often been noted that the Barcelona Pavilion registers a break with the archetype of the primitive hut, of the house conceived as a cube, a closed box. If "shelter" there is, it is in a quite different sense, one illustrated today by the windbreak shelters erected at bus stops, or at a particular service station in Montreal, which was once presented to me as being by Mies (or his atelier), but which monographs and catalogs routinely fail to mention. In the absence of the glass doors the architect had taken down for the occasion, most of the 1929 photographs bring out the separation of functions between the flat roof—supported by two rows of fine vertical steel posts, cruciform in profile and set back—and the glass or marble partitions that seem to slide perpendicularly between the two parallel slabs of the base and the roof, creating cantilever effects that are partly illusory, while the *cella* (to the rear of which once stood the statue by Georg Kolbe) appears out of line, ajar, the way a drawer or a box of matches might be (an option that Mies systematically played with in his patio house projects of the 1930s). Meant to represent Germany itself, sitting alongside the exhibits of the country's main industrial firms, the pavilion did not answer any well-defined purpose. As far as function goes, or its value as an exhibition or representation, it did not show anything and did not exhibit or present anything but itself, made as it was to be entered and traversed both physically and by sight. It was a place that promoted a kind of circulation that was even more visual than pedestrian, without anything to block one's movement, save for the two famous Barcelona chairs, placed there in expectation of the inaugural visit of the royal couple and then left in place like an empty figure of absence or of a presence always deferred.

The reconstruction today milks that figure for all it is worth, as Mies himself tried to do in the lobbies of the apartment buildings along Chicago's Lake Shore Drive.

Beyond Kolbe's sculpture, the two Barcelona chairs, and a few stools of the same design, the Barcelona Pavilion housed no other object or work of art. No display cabinets, no pedestals, no supports, no surfaces for hanging anything on, either; the marble, onyx, and glass of the walls, as well as the vertical panels that demarcated, divided, and articulated the site or, better still, *marked* it, ruled out the very idea of such things. Instead, the panels themselves, in their potentially sumptuous materiality, became the equivalent of paintings, stretching out *recto-verso* to the dimensions, if not to the very density, of the wall or partition. Was that due to the ascendancy of the model constituted by the Barcelona Pavilion on paper, an ascendancy confirmed by the 1942 museum project for a small town in which the image of *Guernica* played the role of a wall? I have never been able to look at the large-scale paintings of Jackson Pollock or Barnett Newman, or even certain canvases in Monet's *Nymphéas* series, without seeing in them the desire that haunts a certain kind of modern painting to replace the wall to the point of superseding any notion of hanging—I would even go so far as to say making the wall obsolete. Architecture, of course, is familiar with the opposite temptation, which sometimes dreams of opting out of the very determinations that define architecture in order to practice freely on the blank page.

Mies made at least one graphic study for the interior of the Barcelona Pavilion that directly illustrates what I am saying. In that study, there is a thin vertical bar consisting of two parallel lines neatly drawn with a ruler and corresponding to one of the metal supports I mentioned. (Nothing here allows us to use the term *column*, either in the look of the drawing or in the function of the support, which is deliberately blurred and even erased, as

11.2
Ludwig Mies van der Rohe, German Pavilion,
International Exposition, Barcelona, 1929. Interior
perspective. Museum of Modern Art, New York. ©
2015 Artists Rights Society (ARS), New York/VG
Bild-Kunst, Bonn. Image © The Museum of Modern
Art. Licensed by SCALA/Art Resource, NY.

it is in reality in the building. If my thinking thus far makes any sense, it is in inciting the reader to measure precisely how much the discourse on Mies's oeuvre would be altered, even transformed, if we made it a rule—at least provisionally and as an experiment—not to use the word *column* in its regard. A number of tirades about his alleged "classicism" would then certainly lose their raison d'être.) On either side of the bar and drawn along the axis of the page, without being able to be precisely located in depth but letting itself be glimpsed on the left, parallel to the outline of the inscription, there is the beginning of a speckled marble panel, behind which a fragment of a glass partition emerges, given rhythm by vertical mullions, while the right side is filled with a more complex device. Seen in perspective, that presents two marble panels set at a right angle, in front of which sits a tiny glass panel, identifiable as such by effects of transparency and reflection that are quite obviously calculated, even if something like a cloud seems to pass through, driven by some mysterious wind. It is as if architecture, concerned as it is with its own limits, intended here to compete with painting at a moment when painting attempts to escape its own identity—something it could only succeed in doing by borrowing painting's tools, including those of collage (as in the concert hall project of 1943), but not without the constraint of the plan still asserting itself more strictly than ever.

The constraint of the plan: criticism has always fallen into the trap denounced by Le Corbusier, a trap set every time the plan (in the architectural sense of the term) is supposed to be taken as the generator of the surface and the volume, so that all that can be seen is a network of signs that act like a mosaic, a decorative panel, in the two dimensions of the plane (in the geometric sense of the word).[3] The same illusion led Alfred Barr to make a connection between Mies's Brick Country House project and Theo van Doesburg's 1918 painting, *Rhythm of a Russian Dance*, based on analogies that could hardly be described as formal, in the strict sense of the term, being in the final analysis merely picturesque. As Peter Eisenman[4] clearly saw, if van Doesburg's work might have taught Mies anything, it would have been the extent to which Mies could have used it as an argument for radically subverting the figure-ground relationship that seems to be the basis of all perception and first and foremost any apprehension of a painting. But this trait only appears if we consider the plan of the country house or the plan of the Barcelona Pavilion as the projection on the ground of a device that can only be fully developed in the three dimensions of architecture. In Barcelona, every partition but also every opening—the solids and the voids—functions in turn as a background in relation to another partition, another opening—another solid, another void—in an endless exchange that mobilizes only "figures."

In this context, the vertical supports correspond to so many marks, and even incisions, made on or in the void, in the immediate proximity of surfaces that do not themselves enclose any volume, caught as all of them are between the floor—that "horizontal wall," as Le Corbusier defined it in terms introduced by Alberti—and that other kind of *wall* that is the flat roof, laid on two rows of set-back posts. The same roof is drawn directly in the floor plan, in a twist that is revealing here, motivated as it is by the constructive system. If the architecture is no longer bound by the rule that governs walls, it is because it has shifted its impact onto the horizontal walls, where it lodges in the intervals, because the vertical elements do not seem to have the function of supporting so much as of manifesting openings and measuring gaps. The glass box of the Farnsworth House (the plan of which dates to 1946, though Mies built it in 1950) is built between two apparently identical slabs, one clearly detached from the ground and the other overlaying the first and doubling it at a distance marked by two rows of metal posts of the I-beam type. In the

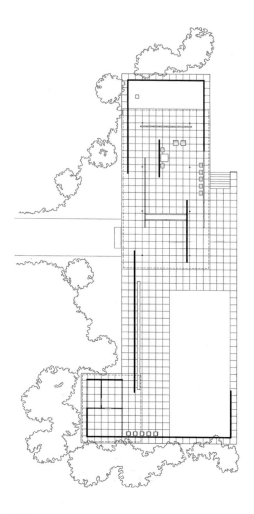

11.3
Ludwig Mies van der Rohe, German Pavilion,
International Exposition, Barcelona, 1929. Floor
plan. Drawn by the Mies van der Rohe Chicago office.
Museum of Modern Art, New York. © 2015 Artists
Rights Society (ARS), New York/VG Bild-Kunst, Bonn.
Image © The Museum of Modern Art. Licensed by
SCALA/Art Resource, NY.

square-plan Fifty-Fifty House project, the four posts that hold up the roof (itself consisting of a square network of metal sections soldered onto a steel plate) are not laid at the corners but in the middle of each of the four sides of the square. Both projects bear witness to a similar separation between the structure, in the classical sense of the term, and the volume, which is marked by the essentially transparent surfaces.

Architecture is thus reduced to a paradoxical volumetric game in which the diaphanous space occupied by a transparent body, defined simply by its bones and by the effects of reflection produced at its surface, or by a body with falsely labyrinthine consonances, articulated by a set of vertical planes unevenly distributed between two horizontal slabs of variable area, interferes with an essentially linear constructive structure without ever merging with it. That game, based as it is on a repertoire of simple elements and an economy of means taken to the extreme, inevitably parallels the practice of the twentieth-century avant-gardes, whether the neoplasticist or constructivist avant-gardes of the 1920s or the minimalist or conceptual avant-gardes of the 1960s. The comparisons are, of course, misleading, but they should not be ignored, since it is on these kinds of similarities and anachronisms, and even blatant misinterpretations, that what we call the history of art, which includes architecture, is in reality only partly built. The retrospective glance we cast, through the lens of our own day, over the artworks of the past, however recent they may be, is no less relevant, in this regard, than the effort to understand their genesis in the terms of the times that saw them come into the world.

Just after World War I, Mies van der Rohe was directly involved in the experiment of the avant-gardes of Europe, first as a director of the architecture section of the Novembergrüppe, created in the middle of the revolutionary period, and a bit later, between 1922 and 1923, when he provided active support for the review *G*. Edited in Berlin by Hans Richter, Werner Gräff, and El Lissitsky, *G* published some of Mies's reflections in the form of aphorisms on architecture, as well as several of his projects, starting with the Friedrichstrasse office blocks. *G* was short for *Gestaltung*, as indicated by the publication's subheading, *Material zur elementaren Gestaltung*: *Gestaltung* in the sense of an active, dynamic development, a shaping; *Gestalt* in the sense of an ordering, a configuration, potentially unstable, random, an organizing process that always has to be started over again and therefore is distinct from its static sense, which is inseparable from the idea of completion. The word could not help but resonate with the emphasis Mies persistently brought to bear on the act of constructing and the idea of construction. If it is anachronistic to try to deal with his work from the position of our contemporary discourse, the confusion might be less the fault of the critic or the historian than that of the period we live in, with its antitechnological bias and the lack of interest felt by a number of architects in problems that are strictly constructive; construction has ceased to be both the matrix and the regulator of architecture (but how long can this last?).

The adjective *elementaren* in the subheading counts as much as the word *Gestaltung* here, suggesting a kind of shaping that comes down to its elements, its principles, and is reduced to the essential or, better still, taken to the limit, to the threshold beyond which the concept of construction ceases, purely and simply, to develop. We are a long way, here, from any idea of skill, from any extravagance, from any technological *dramatization*. If the Barcelona Pavilion established itself as a model of technical perfection, worthy as such to represent Germany in the circumstances, this is first because of the clarity and precision of the assembly of the different elements involved in its construction, the cleanness of their bones as much as the beauty of the materials, the combination of precious marbles, carefully machined steel, and faultless glass panels. Things had developed by then from the *misérabilisme* cultivated by an entire section of the avant-garde, by Dada and constructivism, partly out of necessity, partly out of virtue, for some time after the end of the privations following World War I. In this respect, the prototype pavilion was actually more in tune with the "minimalism" of the 1960s, which more easily accommodated "high-tech" effects than the deliberately parodic and derisive elementarism of the 1920s. As for the technical improvements that were brought to the reconstruction, I cannot see how they would change the building's impact today.

If the pavilion is (or was) a prototype, then the question, as I have hinted, is how its reconstruction may alter its meaning or impact, though this will no doubt have less to do with the historical than the theoretical order. The idea that a visually repetitive architecture, with which the name of Mies van der Rohe is associated, by definition lends itself to *reproduction* is commonplace—but experience has refuted the accompanying ideas of invariable types, the end of the unique object, the *unicum* in the series. For me, as a lover of architecture, my discovery in the early 1960s of the Seagram Building, the Lake Shore Drive apartments, and the buildings of the Illinois Institute of Technology was a revelation that nothing since has been able to shake. In spite of appearances, and with a few exceptions that I only discovered later, there was scarcely any relationship between what was revealed to me then and what had been presented to us in France and elsewhere as "modern" architecture, or even a mode of construction inspired by Mies's example (I was then in the Paris of the building of the Maine-Montparnasse skyscraper, the reconstruction of the Seine waterfront, and, shortly after, the development of La Défense). If the difference was striking, the reason was unclear. I could, of course, see that it was not only a matter of planes, surfaces, and volumes, or of materials, lines, proportions, or technical perfection—even though all of these considerations had their importance. It took me a while to realize that, to the contrary, one had to privilege the objects over the series, or types, while taking very seriously the celebrated, but incredibly enigmatic, motto that Mies gave himself: *less is more*.

That, one might say, is a matter of economy, even when it comes to difference—in relation to which the so-called identical reconstruction of the Barcelona Pavilion easily looks like a parable. Now reproduced, the model has lost its value as a monument and become nothing more than a double or doublet, one of a pair, a life-size maquette, something like the Esprit Nouveau Pavilion perhaps, reconstructed a long way from Paris on the outskirts of Boulogne, or, if the project goes ahead, Melnikov's pavilion among the "follies" of La Villette: curios at worst; museum pieces at best (and are things any different—and in what context!—with the restored Villa Savoye?). The parable (which means comparison, *parabola*) shows us that despite its repetitive appearances, Mies's work does not lend itself to reproduction, in the strict sense of the term, and that if there is a series there, then its generative principle is to be found not in repetition or some recurring typology but in the patient, obstinate, methodical search for the minimal deviation, the minimum perceptible difference between two individuals that all the signs suggest merge, and in which precisely lies the difference eliminated by reproduction. But that would still count for little if the difference were reduced to a simple variation. Difference, in Mies, was the object of real labor, prompted by an intention, if not a concerted calculation. It fabricated a *story*, a story that was exclusively architectural, so that we are entitled to speak of the labor of the work—the very labor of which the reconstructed Barcelona Pavilion is today like the recovered emblem, the recaptured trophy.

The labor of the work is thus easily confused with that of the difference; the architecture is no longer thought of as being of the order of the supplement (the decor) or of value added to the building (did New York City not try to tax the Seagram Building for its architectural quality, that which indeed made all the difference?) but as a kind of passage to the limit, in the serial process, to the experience that is, so to speak, liminal, bearing as it does on the differential thresholds between "less" and "more."

I will mention here just two examples that are in fact complementary. The first was supposed to lead gradually, via the suite of buildings on the IIT campus, to the elimination of the element that I hereby refuse to describe as a "column." Crown Hall, the home of the College of Architecture, may well follow its predecessors, as inserted in the volumetrics of the overall project, but it derives from a kind of architecture that, if not suspended, is at least *en suspension*, or hanging, a goal Mies never stopped pursuing his whole career, beginning as early as the late 1920s in the Mannheim theater project with its reticulated slabs, supported by set-back supports made redundant by the external porticos. In both cases, the technical apparatus, which I would describe as the "grid," is transferred from the vertical surfaces to the horizontal surfaces, as in the spectacular demonstration of this procedure at the National Gallery in Berlin.

That transfer leads to the second example of work on the "slightest difference" that I want to invoke here, which concerns the relationship between solids and voids. Le Corbusier was distressed at seeing holes that pierced a wall, "holes that are passages for man or for light: doors and windows," that destroy the form instead of accentuating it: hence the idea of resorting to grids or checkerboards on surfaces.[5] Here, too, Mies's work on the grids of his facades, from one project to the next ordered by the interplay of calculated differences, paradoxically makes perfect sense in relation to the model proposed by the Barcelona Pavilion—an architectural device in which no wall is pierced by holes, where the passage of bodies and light is reduced to a play of intervals and transparencies.

In the days of *L'Esprit Nouveau*, Le Corbusier saw the factories of America as the "reassuring first fruits of the new age,"[6] an era that Mies, as a close reader of Max Weber, would have been more tempted to identify with the triumph of bureaucracy. However, it would be making a groundless accusation against him to characterize his architecture as "bureaucratic." The Seagram Building, which differs markedly from the early proposals for Friedrichstrasse in 1921–1922 and again in 1933 for the Berlin headquarters of the Reichsbank, takes its place in a different series, inaugurated by the low-rise tower blocks on Lake Shore Drive and continued in Toronto, and is entirely "other" from that of the commercial office buildings of the Chicago that received Mies in 1938.

The same "monuments" that are the products of the forces and technological instruments used by Mies and developed to his advantage tend, with distance, to lose their burden of reality and to operate in the hallucinatory mode of paper architecture. The reconstruction of the Barcelona Pavilion will be justified when the Catalan capital becomes one of the obligatory stops on a pilgrimage that starts in Berlin and leads, via New York, to Chicago, justified for all those who do not confuse history with the cult of relics or ruins, who are not easily taken in and can claim to have seen with their own eyes, touched, and explored the monuments of a modernity captured at the very real moment of its difference.

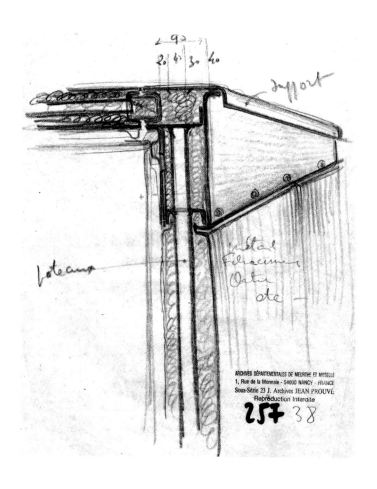

12.1
Ateliers Jean Prouvé, sketches for l'Unité d'habitation,
Marseille, Le Corbusier, architect, 1946. Fonds des
Ateliers Jean Prouvé. Archives départementale de
Meurthe-et-Moselle. © 2015 Artists Rights Society
(ARS), New York/ADAGP, Paris.

12 ARCHITECTURE AND INDUSTRY: JEAN PROUVÉ, OR THE PARTI OF THE DETAIL

If we built a plane the way we build a house, it wouldn't fly.
—Jean Prouvé[1]

Just after World War II, French architecture suffered incredible impoverishment, which was partly cultural but made worse by the abdication of a profession transformed, by its own admission, into a syndicate of vested interests. In that impoverished state and precisely for the inept policies adopted not only by a group or a class but also by the ruling class as a whole, Jean Prouvé's beautiful and melancholy venture looks exemplary: Beautiful because his architecture was neither nostalgic nor utopian, but resolutely contemporary; in the absence of any major buildings, let alone signed works, and long without recognition as an architect, he was nevertheless an architect, engineer, and builder, and the sole French professional with an international following. But also melancholy, for were it not for the energy and modesty of one who was able to start again from nothing three times, only to set out once more on a new career at the age of seventy (a career that until then had been ruled out by an "order" issued under the Vichy regime), the enterprise to which he devoted his life could have appeared to be a failure. If failure there was, it most certainly was not the fault of Prouvé or his idea, but of society itself.

At a time when society was called "industrial," Jean Prouvé, in feigned naïveté, took the word literally. After all, architects were alone in denying the need to industrialize the building process, even though every government in the world had finally put industrialization on their programs, fifty years after Walter Gropius and Le Corbusier had made it a cornerstone of the modernist project. How is it that housing was, and still is, the only thing not to benefit from the industrial "miracle," and that of all industries, as Prouvé observed, "Building is the only industry that does not advance?"[2] Even more important, how is it that "all production relations being equal, some periods of the past offer us a far more highly industrialized architecture than our own, based on extremely sound and well-defined techniques"?[3] Surely, these perceptions result from the fact that people confuse technology and industry, and if industry, in its present form, is unable to respond to demand, or if its responses are inadequate, the reason is that it does not just obey the imperative of rationality. However, we know very well that the "housing question" is not just a technical issue but also a political one. Unable to formulate this question correctly, both the revolutionary movement and the reformist movement deprived themselves of an instrument that was quickly appropriated by fascist ideology. The industrialization of building no doubt answers to economic necessity, but economics is always political. The experience of Prouvé, after that of Gropius, demonstrates this all the more obviously, since unlike the Bauhaus experience, it was supposed to hinge directly on an industrial practice.[4]

Not that Prouvé ever had a head for politics, and still less for revolution. His declared, or "ingenuous,"[5] position was more that of a skilled craftsman, a "master," though in a very different sense from the masters of the École des Beaux-Arts: "A new type of architect must therefore be called into being who would quite simply be an industrialist—and why not? Personally, I can see no other hope. Such an architect, head of an industry, will be listened to, followed and not merely consulted. And in the long run he will find this very pleasant."[6] The reference to the content-ment of an architect who would double as a captain of industry should not be taken lightly. It directed the destiny of a man who discovered the métier of construction by paths that were any-thing but academic—a man who, contrary to received opinion, was not even an engineer and who only had training as an artisan. The son of Victor Prouvé, a painter and decorator of the École de Nancy, he opened his first wrought-iron workshop in Nancy in 1923. It grew rapidly and in 1925 acquired equipment that en-abled the production of work "adapted to architecture." Incorpo-rated in 1931 as a *société anonyme*, the Ateliers Jean Prouvé were associated with a number of avant-garde projects in the prewar years (including the Buc flying club [1935] and the Maison du Peuple, Clichy [1938], with the architects Beaudoin and Lods). At the same time, he worked to establish the principles of a metal architecture based on the most advanced techniques of shaping very fine sheet steel, such as those used in automotive, railway, and aeronautical construction, but it was only in 1944, at a time when the demand for reconstruction seemed to require mass production, that the Ateliers moved to Maxéville on the outskirts of Nancy and attained a properly industrial scale. However, the firm's very success also led to its rapid destruction, as its capital development led to Prouvé's elimination by Aluminum Fran-çais's offer, in 1953, to establish him in Paris to design "his style of forms." Prouvé found the proposal unacceptable, and on Le Corbusier's advice, he opted to shut himself away for a "long and joyless period," in fact keeping himself busy exclusively *design-ing*[7]—as he understood it.

Nothing could have been more opposed to the working method Prouvé had pursued for more than thirty years. It would be hard to overemphasize the sense of rejection and the absolute break involved in his choice of an occupation without promised financial advantages, a designer cut off from the workshop and the construction site. How can we accept that the same man who never stopped fighting for the idea of industrialized architecture preferred to withdraw from the game the moment the firm that bore his name succeeded in drawing attention to its international importance and could at last expect to achieve an industrial scale? Is it that, like so many of his predecessors (remote or immediate), Prouvé was not able to shake off the mentality and habits of the artisan, that he was incapable of making the leap he had nonetheless anticipated? Such a suspicion is quickly formulated, but in fact it only ignores the real questions. These may be considered thus: (a) Were the proposed solutions genuinely *economic*, in the accounting sense of the term, for a production ruled by profit and an industry that failed to embody, in all its sectors, the progressive, rational character desired by Prouvé? (b) Did Prouvé's very method, his conception of work in the shop and on site, contradict in principle the relations of production and the modalities of the division of labor that then prevailed in the industry? (c) Did the concept of prefabrication he hoped to develop coincide with the ideological as well as the economic and political functions assigned by the system to architecture and, more generally, to building and the construction industry ("When building goes, everything goes")?

The answer, in terms of economy (and so-called rationality), amounts to a few words, or rather, a few figures: in the prevailing conditions of the time, metal construction used forty to fifty kilos of material per square meter. The shift from the use of roughly tooled beams to highly machined elements made of fine, folded sheet steel brought the ratio down to 20 kg per square meter. In the automotive industry, shaped sheet steel was sold at double the price of the raw material, and in the building industry the price of a beam rose as high as three times the price of untreated material. That being the case, we can easily see that in relation to standards of production and of cost-effectiveness based essentially on the quantity of raw material used—the statistics by which the relative levels of development of national economies were then assessed—Prouvé's proposals were not necessarily made to win over the directors of Aluminum Français, who wasted no time taking control of the pilot factory in Nancy.[8] In a completely different context, in an industry that had developed in a different direction from French industry, Buckminster Fuller (whose firm presented a number of points in common with Prouvé's) met with the same resistance. If the building industry had scarcely progressed since the halcyon days of reconstruction in Chicago at the end of the nineteenth century, this is because it had nothing to do with "doing more with less," which was the first article in both Fuller's and Prouvé's credos.[9]

Such accounting data, I dare say, bear little weight in relation to the fundamentally transgressive effects of a method that did nothing less than undermine the distinction and division between the tasks of conception and those of execution that characterize industrial production. The assertion that the architect should be, or once more become, a man of the construction site not only runs counter to the evolution that made the architect at worst a businessman or at best a lawyer,[10] but also introduces an added distinction between conceptual architects and building architects, often with disastrous results. Prouvé's concept responds to a fundamental principle: when it comes to *constructing*, it is not enough to draw and then consign the project to a design office to make the necessary adjustments for the building's stability and proper functioning. *You do not calculate folded sheet metal, you experience it* (the assertion being true, in certain respects, as far as the most advanced concrete techniques go); objective data was to be gained from the everyday experience of the workshops. Hence, the precept that became the most enduring feature of the course Prouvé taught at the National Conservatory of Arts-et-Métiers: *draw nothing you cannot build*. This precept forbade not only futuristic schemes and uncontrollable utopias, but also any form of work or study that was marginal or outside the atelier ("The designer must also be able to discover his mistakes quickly and recognize them in advance; there must therefore be a constant dialogue between the designer and the constructor who must work as a team. . . . One should design merely what can be executed, but always in the most advanced manner and without recourse to imitation."[11]).

The idea of teamwork, whereby the architect would take on the functions of a "master craftsman" (which justifies the reference to past eras of architecture), was not new. It was evoked, among other ideas, in the initial organization of studies at the Bauhaus, as Walter Gropius had conceived it, imposing his approach despite the resistance of many he had wanted to associate with his endeavor but who remained committed to an individualist ideology of artistic creation. However, whereas the Bauhaus ateliers still functioned on an artisanal and hierarchical basis and depended directly, through the Preliminary Course, on what we might call "formalist" teaching (without that being in any way pejorative in itself), the work in the Nancy ateliers and the on-the-job training they allowed took from the outset a very different turn toward a resolutely industrial direction, based on a set of determinations and technical choices that called for new relations of production. Prouvé was still only an artisan blacksmith when he set to work producing tall gates and doors made of simple steel strips, cut and rigorously standardized, which soon caught the attention of Robert Mallet-Stevens. It was just a step from there to the use of sheet metal, steel as much as aluminum, which was delivered in rolls and stiffened by shaping on a roller as well as by folding and pressing, to make movable partitions and facade panels with translucent elements: the step from artisanal production to industrial production. As early as 1930, the lessons learned from shaping sheet metal and the possibilities it opened up led to the development of a project for a small metal house on stilts. Here again, Prouvé's research happened to overlap with certain experiments conducted in Germany.[12] In fact, Prouvé could only have subscribed to the criticism Gropius leveled at prefabrication systems that aimed not to mass produce the constituent parts but to propagate the house as a whole (a procedure favored in France by various ministries for obvious ideological reasons as much as for profit motives). Those prefabrication systems rivaled, in their mediocrity, ugliness, or absurdity, the products of repetitive housing, a result of a falsely artisanal practice.[13] But the technological advance the Nancy ateliers had was such that it soon enabled development of a prefabrication system that was much more rigorous and structured than the simple assembly of vertical and horizontal slabs designed by Gropius in Dessau.[14]

A built object, whatever it may be, presupposes a constructive idea. "The builder spontaneously envisages it completely finished in space. He is inspired by familiar materials, the *parti* is decided on. After that, it gets built."[15] But what does *parti* mean? Certainly not what Beaux-Arts schools teach under that label, which has led, as we are all too well aware, to monuments of incredible academic pretension or to technical aberrations. Prouvé's goal was very different in nature and was defined by a radical departure from the "organic" ideology that then passed for theory when it came to architecture. Nothing could be more opposed to that goal than the idea that a building ought to be designed as a totality in which the relationship of the parts to the whole is conceived in terms of expressiveness, with each element having to show in its form and appearance that it belongs to a preestablished order, just as for Viollet-le-Duc the profile and section of the base of a Gothic pier expressed the set of determinations that the system assigned to load-bearing members. However, that was because such a support was far from constituting one of the generative elements of a system that was rigorously deduced, if Viollet-le-Duc is to be believed, and conceived as a whole from the top, starting with the vaults. In fact, the break marked by the practice of someone like Prouvé in relation to the ideology of the expressive totality had already been put forward as a theory in Viollet-le-Duc's *Dictionnaire raisonné*, based as it was on "details," the alphabetically listed elements of French architecture from the Middle Ages. If we had to sum up Prouvé's contribution to a form of contemporary architecture (and to a theory about architecture), we would have to adopt the rule that he made his own, to think of a building starting from the elements that reveal its generative principle. The "alphabet of structures" systematically introduces constructive propositions that are not at all deductive in nature but quite the opposite, deriving directly from their fabrication in a factory. Close to the techniques favored by the automotive industry (a constant reference in Prouvé's practice, as in Fuller's), the techniques used for folded or pressed sheet metal and later extruded aluminum gave birth to a series of elements—porticos, shells, stands, and so on—whose sections and profiles required more careful study so as to combine resistance and lightness. Gradually, and starting with a portico (Meudon houses, 1949), a shell (Mame printing works, Tours, 1951, Zehrfuss), a stand (Source Cachat refreshment stall, Évian Spa, 1956, Novarina), and a reticulated roofing block (Petroff system, Total service stations, 1969), a set of rigorously complementary elements came to be defined, dry-assembled by bolting or clamping. Sometimes the system was designed starting from the support, sometimes starting from the roof, with the Palais des Expositions in Grenoble (1967) combining the flourish of clustered tubular supports with the rigidity of a reticulated roof. In every case, the principle of assembly was deducible from the generative element, designed from the very beginning in constructive terms.

The same rule applied to furniture (for Prouvé, there was no difference between the construction of a piece of furniture and the construction of a house). Here, it is interesting to note that Prouvé systematically rejected the technique of bent steel tubes used at the Bauhaus by Marcel Breuer to make prototypes for a few chairs that are now widespread, whereas the furniture developed in Nancy from 1924 to 1950 did not enjoy the same broad commercial distribution. This is because bending a tube with a constant section, as in Breuer's famous Wassily lounge chair, does not conform to any manufacturing principle nor open up any constructive possibilities. Here again, to quote Prouvé, "I found curved steel tubing unsatisfactory, while sheet steel inspired me to fold, joint, score and then weld it. This produced areas of uniform strength and strict outlines which were set off by the attention paid to detail and by the quality of the finish."[16] A desk or a chair rests on the same type of supports as a house. Construction, for Prouvé, equals assembly: assembly of complementary elements, defined step by step, beginning with the generative element, such as the independent metal frames that were called on to rest on struts (as in monolitic concrete infrastructure), a platform and stabilizing central core, including wet rooms (kitchen, bathroom) and pipes, designed to take the industrialized elements of the superstructure, including the lining and covering panels (the Alba house, 1950, of which the house known as abbé Pierre's house, 1953, is just a variation, incorporating a central metal block). The "alphabet of structures" was an integral part of the course Prouvé taught at Arts-et-Métiers—a course in comparative anatomy, as he called it, and which we would like to have seen published or, better still, filmed.[17] Doubtless, drawing (but drawing informed by half a century of practice and workshop training) has never more clearly *revealed* (another word dear to Prouvé's heart) the mechanical engineering involved in a tower with a central core or in a cement dam or a railway carriage in steel section. It was always with renewed amazement that audiences—or, more precisely, spectators—witnessed, week after week, the production and updating of a veritable structural iconography in which analytical rigor vied with demonstrative evidence.

If we accept Lévi-Strauss's opposition between the *bricoleur* who makes his constructions with bits and pieces picked up here and there, which he may then divert from their original purpose, and the engineer who develops the elements of the machinery he designs as a function of a well-defined project, then Prouvé deserves to be called an engineer, even if some of his projects have a deliberately "mécano" look and even if he was not officially qualified. The distinction took on its fullest theoretical (and no doubt political) significance when Prouvé advocated "closed planning," as opposed to "open planning" that directly entrusted the study and realization of building elements to certain industries only to impose them on architects to achieve serial production. For Prouvé, "a committed building industry must be able to put before the authorities practical models of dwellings to accept or reject, but not subject to argument."[18] That was the engineer speaking or, more precisely, the constructor—the sole credential Prouvé claimed for himself (and one that Elie Faure had applied to Cézanne). Of course, these kinds of constructors are also great "deconstructionists," those who attack a system's most fundamental structures, whether material, technical, or ideological and institutional. For Prouvé, a house was not just a "machine for living," as Le Corbusier scandalously put it, but an "object to be built."[19] It was an object, a machine; its proper working did not accommodate any bricolage, but implied the opposite: strict subordination of the different components to the constructive idea translated into structural elements.

Take just one example: Prouvé had the right, on a number of well-established grounds, to claim himself as the inventor of

12.2
Jean Prouvé, Jean de Mailly, Henri Depussé, Nobel
Tower, Paris, 1967. Curtain wall with CIMT panels.
Photo: Jean Masson. © Archives départementale de
Meurthe-et-Moselle.

the curtain wall, the lightweight and continuous facade with no load-bearing function and made up of panels simply attached to the peripheral structure, which seems to have been used for the first time in its complete and systematic form in the Maison du Peuple in Clichy. That "festival of steel," of "folded sheet steel,"[20] is not a well-known building; nonetheless, it was a real technical and architectural event. Prouvé's invention went on to enjoy its now familiar success, for a time asserting itself as the most conspicuous and immediately distinctive feature of so-called modern architecture. If Prouvé showed himself so reticent in relation to the very notion of a curtain wall and the use of facade elements mass-produced by industry (including even those marketed by CIMT, one of the big French railway material companies that managed to hold on to this "ideas-provider" for nearly ten years), then it was because for him this particular element could not be reduced to a simple outer cover adaptable to the most diverse structures in order to provide—at the cost of a few theoretical and economic misinterpretations!—the look (if not a mask) of modernity. For him, the curtain wall was an integral part of a structure whose elements could not be separated.

The curtain wall does not, strictly speaking, have a load-bearing function, but this is not to say that it has no structural value. The potential distortions of large plates of glass and metal panels[21] attest to the fact that, even when "hung," a glass-and-steel or aluminum facade is not an inert element, but may play a role in a well-conceived constructive economy. The mistake—common to all structural thinking aided and abetted by the play of metaphors—is to confuse structure with skeleton[22]: hence the unnatural association of the curtain wall with massive structures of a size and, above all, a weight out of proportion with the demands of construction or the imperatives of safety. "Unnatural" in the sense of going against the economic—in every sense of the word—imperative of lightness, which is satisfied by the curtain wall when used in a resolutely constructive or structural way, as a skin stretched over a skeleton from which it cannot be separated and to whose stability or, more precisely, rigidity it contributes by its very elasticity and its resistance to the elements (consider the facades, today largely disfigured, of the Centre National des Industries et des Techniques at La Défense in Paris, or the facades of the Palais des Expositions in Grenoble, which are equipped with large, composite stiffeners). The curtain wall also solves a number of problems shared by any architectural structure, including thermal insulation, lighting, ventilation, sun protection, and so on. By the same token, we can see how the inclined glass facades on single-story buildings designed by Prouvé and his team (the Évian Spa bar, the Villejuif school buildings) are not only a "style" feature, but also take part in the play of forces and tensions that corresponds, for example, to the Y-shaped stanchion, set up in unstable equilibrium and only taking on its full structural functions once integrated into a constructive system in which every element contributes to the cohesion and rigidity of the whole.

Against any kind of bricolage and "design" ideology, Prouvé, refusing to accommodate the demands of workshops that would have ensured the fabrication of "forms of his style," preferred working with a few selected architects, those who were more respectful of his ideas than the financiers. Yet such was the quality of the components developed by his design office that when they were adopted by architects worthy of the name "constructors," they marked indelibly the apartment blocks in which they were used (Jaoul-Minguerin House, 1969, by Jean-Claude and Carine Drouin; the National Institute of Fishing, Nantes, 1970, by Olivier Vaudou; the extremely beautiful Rotterdam Medical Faculty, 1968–1969, by Van Emblen and Co., in association with CIMT). Indeed, such was the generative capacity of the "alphabet of structures" that the system tended to produce ever more complex combinations of different structures. This could be said of the project (developed at the same time as that for a small house with a central support core) of high-rise apartment blocks with a central concrete core of various sections, to which peripheral structures (floors, etc.) in metal or cement were to be connected, complemented by its curtain wall. Similarly, the project for the Tour Nobel at La Défense (1967–1969, De Mailly and Depuissé) combines all of the innovations that had been developed at Maxéville between 1945 and 1952. The truly avant-garde project for the Ministry for National Education, the first project that would have been officially credited to Prouvé jointly with Belmont and Swetchine, was rejected because of the resistance of the users and the abdication of the authorities, doomed to remain in boxes, leaving us only to catch its echo in Norman Foster's Hong Kong and Shanghai Bank, or in Rem Koolhaas's project for the Bibliothèque de France, also too innovative for its inventiveness to be perceived.

One of the merits of the "structural iconography" developed by Prouvé is that, in its principle, it constitutes the best antidote to the partly promotional fascination with the image, which is one of the scourges of contemporary architecture. The most recent example of this is furnished by Dominique Perrault's winning entry for the competition for the Bibliothèque de France, which won for its image, a true *architecture parlante*, of four open books represented by the corner towers. On a more theoretical level, there are at least two implications in Prouvé's work that demonstrate its scope, both practical and conceptual. One of the paradoxes of his endeavor is that, in its methodical development, it overcame some of the oppositions (if not contradictions) among materials commonly ascribed to architecture: concrete versus metal, plastic, and so on. For Prouvé, such distinctions were meaningless; if there was any opposition, then it was played out not at a level of the material but of the use that could be made of it

("What worries me is what people do with the new materials, or more precisely, what they do not do."). Here, the design history of the great parabolic horseshoe canopy of the Centre National des Industries et des Techniques is revealing. In 1955, with the constructive solution not yet determined and metal and concrete still in competition, Prouvé was called in as a consultant, suggesting a very light version, composed of a network of factory-made stainless steel domes, which required original mechanical assembly lines.[23] Although his proposal met all the criteria listed by its engineer, Pier Luigi Nervi, prestressed concrete ultimately prevailed. Yet Prouvé's position was elegantly nuanced:

> *I admire the tremendous achievements of reinforced concrete construction, particularly bridges and dams, but I have always been much more doubtful about the use of this material in large apartment-blocks. I found the arrangement of pillars and beams, as in timber or steel structures, a disappointment. Because it can flow, it seemed to me that concrete should give rise to a very different articulation, more closely related to the requirements of living areas. I could conceive cylinders, large funnels with equally varied and adaptable sections, curtains and cellular structures. I also visualized these skeletons enveloped in lights skins made of metal, glass or wood.*[24]

Prouvé's last projects—for the university dormitory in Nancy, where the individual student cells would have rested on steel cantilevers and tie beams connected to a concrete structure, and the study for the housing unit in Marseilles, designed to house entirely prefabricated duplex apartments in a concrete cellular structure, the way bottles are housed in their racks—were destined not to be realized. In retrospect, they seem utopian, but they were not unrelated to the proposals put forward by the British group Archigram. Actively engaged in promoting the idea of an architecture composed of mobile, replaceable, interchangeable elements connected to alterable structures, Archigram drew on the imagery of science fiction, as opposed to what we might call the *experimental* utopia of Prouvé. Running counter to a "brutalist" interpretation of the art of Le Corbusier and the massive, monumental architecture of his apartment block at Marseille, the idea of an evolving, adaptable, mobile, and even ephemeral architecture would seem better adapted to the needs of the era,[25] even as today it would seem to respond to the demands of ecology. Prouvé never stopped insisting on the speed of mounting and demounting, the ease of transportation and assembly of the prefabricated elements, some so light they could be put together in the air (an image that in truth speaks volumes, but is already stamped for us with the seal of nostalgia). All of these qualities took on a precise meaning in the context of the postwar period and reconstruction program.

In the aftermath of the war, and in the face of the piles of rubble where the totalitarian project would finally be realized, Prouvé's enterprise stood out for its modesty: the modesty of an architecture that seems to have been vaccinated against the fantasy of the "beautiful ruin" and the ideology of "reconstruction." His was an architecture concerned above all with lightness and delicacy, one ready to remain in the background—to erase itself, when the time came, without leaving any traces other than in the memory of men and the imagination of builders.

13 ARCHITECTURE IS . . .

The Undecidable

Looking at the range of issues debated in the architectural press today, one would be tempted to claim that everything seems to be relevant for the architect. Since Alberti, the curriculum traditionally assigned to the architectural apprentice has amounted to the same range and diversity as the training required today for becoming a psychoanalyst: The architect has had to be versed in all matters, in mathematics as well as in the humanities, in history and mythology as well as in economics and technology, and be able to design, to speculate, and even occasionally to philosophize. Time has passed without making things any easier for the architect. My reference to psychoanalysis is just a way of pointing to what Rem Koolhaas calls the "hazardous mixture of omnipotence and impotence" that architects are currently experiencing when they deal with problems that preclude, on their part, any form of conscious mastery. As Rem used to say, the architect is entitled to the unconscious.

Let us start by playing, in a philosophical mode, with the word *anything*, which was chosen to conclude the Any series of conferences. If architecture is "anything," or if anything deserves or, more neutrally (for *deserving* introduces an idea of value, or evaluation), if anything is to be labeled as "architecture," then what is it? Architecture as (a) thing; the "architectural" thing; the thing "architecture": as has been the case in other Any conferences, we seem to be confronted with multidisciplinary approaches that tend to pull apart the object under scrutiny. In *Anybody*, Cynthia Davidson refers to the body as being dismembered in the process and being if not destroyed, then at least dissected. "Anything" sounds different, for the invocation of the "thing" points toward some sort of unity, regardless of the prefix *any*. As Heidegger put it, in everyday life we do not encounter the "thing" as such, only the individual things that surround us. In terms of architecture, things are buildings and/or images, projects, plans, models of buildings, anything that is commonly held to belong to the realm of architecture, whatever that means. This leaves us free to extract—or to "abstract"—from such a multiplicity a general idea of this art and its whereabouts.

Of course, this involves operating from a totally different perspective than Heidegger, whose questioning in *Die Frage nach dem Ding* moves toward what he calls "thingness": toward what turns *one* thing into *a* thing, the condition of its being a thing ("Was das Ding zum Ding be-dingt"). Nevertheless, we may benefit from some of his remarks. First, *das Ding*, the thing—in French, *la chose*, from the Latin *causa*—commonly refers to an affair, a process in the judiciary sense; a matter of debate, an issue that calls for the judicial faculty, a "case" to be studied and solved. Second, beyond the world of everyday experience, things belong to different varieties of truth—or, to use Wittgenstein's term, things present themselves under various aspects. To paraphrase Heidegger, the sun is not one and the same thing for the peasant and for the astrophysicist; the body is not one and the same thing for the dancer or the biologist. In the same way, a house is not one and the same thing for the contractor who builds it and for the client who inhabits it, not to mention the diverse components, the various aspects of the "case," that the architect who designed it may have been playing with. Being a thing means precisely this: that one and the same thing allows for diverse (and eventually mutually exclusive) varieties of truth.

At first glance, it seems that one way of addressing the issue of what architecture is, or is supposed to be, would be to explore what it is not, or is not supposed to be. Such a move would lead us back to the issue of specificity, which Rosalind Krauss raises in *Anymore*. Strangely, dealing with architecture as a "thing," the "architectural" thing, the thing "architecture," not only means differentiating between what it is and what it is not (architecture being defined as "anything but . . ."); it also, at a deeper level, implies reconsidering the very relationship between what architecture is, or is supposed to be, and what it is not, or is not supposed to be. If, as far as architecture is concerned, there seems to be no room for "anything but . . . ," then this is due not only to the range of issues that are of relevance for the architect, in terms of both practice and theory. Historically speaking, the "specificity" of architecture has always been challenged by the need for the art to confront demands that were by no means "artistic." More fundamentally, one has to recognize in architecture's present willingness to cope with what seems to be most foreign to it—time, movement, instability, shapelessness, and so on—a characteristic of its condition at the end of the millennium. Hence "undecidability," a keyword of the Any series and a concept that may seem contrary to the idea of specificity.

I would briefly like to test this keyword of *undecidability* in terms of dimensions, both temporal and spatial. From Koolhaas, we learn to stop thinking of architecture as being part of some quasi-utopian "things to come," the way the modernists did. Rather, his exploring the Pearl River Delta or flying over Lagos is revealed as a way of measuring what is actually going on and how far things may have gotten out of control, in the traditional and most problematic sense of the word. It would be too easy, and overtly repressive, to decide that such developments are anything but architectural. Nonetheless, they certainly challenge the commonplace view of architecture as planning or building for the future. The new modes of producing architecture force us to reconsider to what extent, and no matter what purpose or lack of purpose, the notion—the stage of the "project"—is inherent to architecture, whether built or not. (Similarly, new architectural mediums, new tools, and new machineries of conception force us to reconsider the related concept of "projection.")

"Paper architecture" has been an integral aspect of architecture since the period of *perspectiva artificialis* provided a valid model and tool for both the art of building and that of painting. Geometric projection was used in both arts not only to represent objects or buildings as they appeared or were to be seen but also to conceive or, according to the terminology of the period, to invent or to compose them. This technique was used first to construct the scene (the grid, the checkerboard) on which the invention, the composition, and eventually the *istoria* that for Alberti represented the supreme goal of painting was to take place, including its architectural setting. It took several centuries before the painter was no longer satisfied, metaphorically speaking, with throwing ideas against the wall, as an architect might do on paper, and began, nonmetaphorically, to project paint directly on to the canvas, the only intermediary being the gap between the hand and the surface. But to what extent does the word *projection* apply to Jackson Pollock's drip paintings? The question is relevant to architecture insofar as it suggests a radical transformation of the idea of projection, rather than the concomitant notion of the project as such. It implies that the interval between the project and its realization strictly corresponds to the distance induced by the mode of projection itself—allowing or not for the possibility of a critical distance, or distanciation, specific to architecture (at least to paper architecture), if not to painting.

The problem is that the corporate museum architecture of the 1950s—the "white cube," as Brian O'Doherty has labeled it—provided the perfect setting for Pollock's drip paintings, as well as for Barnett Newman's antithetic attempts toward the sublime, Jean Dubuffet's explorations into the *informe*, or formless, and, later, for Frank Stella's and Ellsworth Kelly's alternate geometries. It was as if its own form of strictly repetitive, quasi-mechanical abstraction would itself accommodate different types or modes of painterly abstraction, be they based on automatism, meditation, calculus, or a combination of all three. This may seem to be a simple play on words, but what is at stake is the very idea of abstraction, the matter being one of comparison: In what terms, at what level, from what point of view, and playing in how many dimensions are we going to tackle the issue of abstraction in architecture or in painting? In stylistic terms, what would allow for an approach both formal and historical, in which abstraction would be considered a period style characteristic of the twentieth century (given that the century is now over)? Or are we to deal with abstraction in generative terms—with abstraction as a process that is independent of any particular stylistic manifestation, a process that is intrinsic and, in different ways, foundational to any form of art, be it labeled representational or nonmimetical, figurative or constructive?

Fifteen years ago, Gillian Naylor tackled this issue in a particularly instructive article, the title of which is itself problematic, because it refers to a specific moment in the history of modernism—the foundation of the De Stijl movement after World War I—and to Theo van Doesburg's attempts to demonstrate architectonic ideas that were in accordance with the twentieth-century artists' "grand vision of placing man *within* the painting instead of in front of it."[1] In asking "abstraction *or* architecture?" Naylor questions whether the harmonies and values of painting could be translated without compromise into three-dimensional form. The question may sound odd, for we spontaneously (and in many ways mistakenly) think of architecture as an abstract art in its very essence, just as we do of music. Nonetheless, the matter was of real consequence at a decisive moment in the rise of what was to be called "abstract art." The debate among the founding members of De Stijl resulted in a schism between the artists (painters and sculptors) on the one hand and the architects on the other. Meanwhile, van Doesburg aimed desperately at realizing in material form what he believed the other arts had already achieved in an imaginary manner. Material form was understood as three-dimensional space, whereas modern painting was supposed to have reduced corporeality to flatness—that is, to the two dimensions of the plane or the surface. What matters here is the assumption that painting, at that time considered "the most advanced form of art," had by then paved the way for modern architecture. Conversely, a useful approach to the relevance or nonrelevance, the working (or nonworking) value of the idea of abstraction today, would be to consider how and in what ways abstraction operates in the field of architecture at a time when painting has ceased to be the trailblazing medium it was in the first decades of the twentieth century.

According to Naylor, it was easy for van Doesburg to demonstrate architectonic ideas that incorporated all of the qualities De Stijl artists attributed to painting, because most of his projects remained in model form—that is, on paper. However, the twentieth century did not usher in the ability to conceive the relationship between architecture and painting in transformative terms. Five centuries earlier, Alberti's approach to the problem of ornament was already entirely dependent upon the passage, or shift, from the two-dimensional space in which the painter operated, in terms of *composition*, to the three-dimensional space the architect dealt with and in which *construction* was to take place. We know of Alberti's definition of the column as "the first ornament of architecture"[2]—a definition in line with Bertold Brecht's famous proclamation that the proletarians were entitled to the column and had the right to enjoy it in their dwellings. However, how are we to understand Alberti's statement that he borrowed this ornament from the painter, together with architraves, bases,

capitals, pediments, and other such things, as found in his treatise on painting, written some twenty years before his text on
architecture?[3] How could painting serve as a reservoir of forms
for architecture unless we think of these forms in terms of "ornament"—that is, in bidimensional terms?

The word *composition* does not appear in Alberti's *De re aedificatoria*, but in *De pictura* it corresponds to the second part of
painting, immediately following *circonscriptio*: once the painter
has delineated the surfaces, a figure is "composed," in projective
terms, then it is time for him to assemble or "compose" these elements on the picture plane as in a puzzle or a work of marquetry.
In the same way, according to Alberti, the process of writing sup-
poses first the tracing of letters and second their combination
into words on a sheet of paper. *Compositio* thus relates to projection—that is, to the two dimensions of the projective plane. Significantly, in *De re aedificatoria*, when Alberti begins to deal with
the different orders of columns, he directly refers to the same
paradigm of writing. Starting with the capital, which identifies it
as part of the "order" to which it belongs, the column is described
as a succession of profiles that assume the shape, when projected
on the plane, of different letters: an *L,* followed by an *S,* an *I,* and
so on. The column as ornament is thus reduced, projectively
speaking, to a succession of elements that are assembled on the
plane in the same way as letters on a page. To put it in Derridean
terms, ornament, considered in its linearity and bidimensional-
ity, is supposed to be supplemental to architecture in the same
way that writing is supposed to be supplemental to speech. It was
as *ornament* that the architect borrowed architraves, capitals,
bases, columns, and pediments from the painter, thereby adding
value to his art.

As far as composition is concerned, architecture therefore
had to operate in the two dimensions of the plane. One may
find it astonishing that Alberti, of all people, made no room for

perspective in *De re aedificatoria*, even though he offered the first systematic exposition, in *Della pittura*, of the method by which it became possible to represent building as it appears in three-dimensional space. According to Alberti, architecture first had to settle within the two dimensions of the plane and to "compose" with painting in order to develop its own distinctive mode of representation—one that excluded any illusion of depth or distortion of volume that could alter the sense of proportion. It is remarkable that in the twentieth century, under pressure from painting (then considered the dominant medium), modern architecture still faced the same challenge, yet with a radical reversal of the problematics of ornament. The same Adolf Loos who held that "ornament is crime" found no better way to eliminate or repress it than to systematically apply an abstract and planar facing or coating over the built structure; whereas the members of De Stijl were still dependent, in "composing," upon the interplay between vertical and horizontal planes, conceived, according to Bart van der Leck's definition, as "the delimitation of light and space."

Given that I have been considering the thing "architecture" retrospectively, one might ask: How does this relate to the present? If architecture is something more than a productive agency (for example, a way of thought), then how are we to deal with the models it is actually working on? Pierre Rosenstiehl, a French mathematician and friend of mine who specializes in *taxiplanie*—that is, the study of the nature and properties of different varieties of planes—makes a very simple demonstration of the kinds of problems we are confronting today at the juncture of diverse disciplines, diverse ways of thought, and one that incidentally also points toward a new alliance between mathematics and the arts: Imagine a piece of paper. It presents itself as a two-dimensional sheet. If I crumple it, I get a kind of sphere or ball that is three-dimensional in volume. If I then uncrumple it, I have something neither bidimensional nor tridimensional, but what we might call "planar." (I could simply fold it; the result would be the same.) Planes should not be seen or considered as mere surfaces, reducible to two dimensions. Unlike surfaces, planes have a kind of *thickness*, in that they allow for different modes of wrinkling, crumpling, folding and unfolding, overlapping, interweaving, and interknitting. These are all operations that architects are currently involved in, so we have to rely on their practice—even if it is strictly "virtual"—in order to learn how to think in topological terms. This calls for taking into account new and other mediums and technologies, new and other abstract procedures and machinery, which, to paraphrase Greg Lynn, present architecture with yet another possibility to both rethink and retool itself, just as it did with the advent of perspective and with projective and stereometric geometry.[4]

Space, time, architecture: the theoreticians of the modern movement were at pains to add a fourth dimension to the game of architecture. Suggesting that art be considered as a way of thought no longer operates exclusively in either the two dimensions of paper architecture or the three dimensions of the built environment, but in the in-between. At the same time, it dismisses the opposition between vertical and horizontal, which directly relates to the idea of undecidability that was fundamental to Any's approach to architecture. It also induces a new approach to the notion of construction and to the ideas of form and formlessness, an issue that was debated at length in the *Anybody* volume. Can we still pretend that architecture is anything but formless, a mere matter of form, when it deliberately operates between form and formlessness and confronts the *informe* at the risk of shapelessness itself being turned into a *constructum*? A move is required that would correspond to the shift from architecture as setting the stage for history to architecture being practiced as a game that can be looked at under different conditions.

(Consider, for example, Peter Eisenman's use of the grid, no longer seen as a checkerboard or a support for any kind of board game but as an integral part of the game itself, whose variations, deformations, and transformations allow for its constant restructuring and redefining.)

I want to end with a question around not the idea of "anything but . . . ," but the idea of "anything like . . ." Even if we were to follow Fredric Jameson in getting rid of the concept of the aesthetic and in accepting the idea of beauty as definitively outdated (something which I doubt; it may rather be a matter of displacement or relocation), then there would still be the incentive to see the distinction between, or simply the existence of, "good" and "bad" architecture. To put it more radically, there will still be the urge to decide whether anything exists that could be labeled "architecture" tout court. Where does architecture begin? And where does it end? Where, to what extent, and within what limits is architecture at play? The thing "architecture," or the "case" of architecture, calls not only for study but also for critical evaluation and judgment, leaving room for debate (a debate concerning aesthetics, according to Wittgenstein) and for choices that correspond to specific moves. *Undecidability* was, indisputably, the right keyword for the project. What will come next is another story—maybe another thing.

Construction

Not unlike the previous Any conferences—occurring each year at the same time but always in a different location—this Anymore conference, located (as the prefix *any* demands) under the sign of a generalized epistemological wandering, is subjected in 1999 (the last year of the millennium) to a temporal horizon. Although taking place in Paris, it is also subject to an ideological and institutional horizon. An effort of accommodation imposes itself, accompanied by the invitation to deal with the absence or lack—a

13.1
Jean Dubuffet, *Group of Four Trees*, 1969–1972.
Photo: Anna Robinson-Sweet. © 2015 Artists Rights
Society (ARS), New York/ADAGP, Paris.

particularly sensitive matter in this building (Cinémathèque française), situated as it is under the invocation of the author of *Eupalinos*—not so much of an "architectural culture" as of a clear notion of what the conjunction of those two words, *culture* and *architecture*, connotes and what the implications of that conjunction are. What place does architecture occupy in what one might call the culture of our time? Under what species might one consider architecture as symptomatic of the state of that culture and its aims? If indeed there are aims, which would be architecture's own? What relationship does culture, or whatever it is that now takes culture's place, entertain in general vis-à-vis architecture? More profoundly, more secretly, what link, considered fundamental, can one discover between the very concept of culture and that of architecture?

I will address my remarks to this last question. Allow me to introduce it via the detour of an anecdote that for me possesses the quality of a moral fable. In June 1982, during its annual convention that year in Honolulu, the American Institute of Architects awarded the painter Jean Dubuffet a medal accompanied by a certificate with the following inscription:

> *THE AMERICAN INSTITUTE OF ARCHITECTS*
> *Is honored to confer this*
> *AIA MEDAL*
> *On JEAN DUBUFFET*
> *Artist, sculptor, and iconoclast.*
> *His works provide not only scale, focus, color and*
> *texture but clear insights into the nature of the*
> *architecture they complement—its space, volume,*
> *structure and surface—blending architecture*
> *and sculpture into a single entity.*
> *Robert M. Lawrence, President[5]*

Dubuffet did not make the trip to Honolulu to receive his medal. However, six months earlier, in a letter dated December 22, 1981, he thanked Robert Lawrence for the honor the AIA had conferred on him: "I am especially moved to receive from the Institute the award mentioned in your letter, and I am truly happy that American architects have chosen in this way to demonstrate the interest they have in my work. I do believe, it is true, that my work points in a direction that can inspire architecture to explore rich possibilities, possibilities where we would begin to see new structures from which symmetry, rectilinear elements, and right angles would be excluded."[6]

The contradiction between the two discourses is patently obvious—that is, the contradiction between the words of the certificate conferred by the AIA (words that show every sign of having been carefully weighed) and those of the recipient, who takes exception to them in anticipation. The certificate makes implicit reference solely to the works—monumental sculptures of more or less huge dimensions—that well-known architects such as Gordon Bunshaft, I. M. Pei, and, more recently, Helmut Jahn commissioned from the artist. These were works that those architects expected (the text leaves no mystery about it) would reinforce the effects of the structures with which they were associated. Whereas in his letter of thanks, written before he could have been aware of the wording of the certificate, Dubuffet stands rather distant from seeing his contribution to architecture as something like a complement—or should one say supplement?—something that, far from affecting it in its form, on the contrary merely emphasizes its worth, reaffirms its message, and (the AIA would express gratitude to him for this) helps in understanding the nature of the work. Instead, it is precisely on the terrain of architecture—in the very domain of architecture itself—that Dubuffet comes to intervene, and in quite another direction and toward quite a different goal—as he had already done when he published his first "edifice" projects in 1968.

The entire affair is all the more edifying—the exact word—in that Dubuffet never made a secret of his feelings (likewise, never in the least mitigated) about the architecture said to be "modern." Nor did he hide the disquiet he felt seeing an out-and-out modernist such as Bunshaft interested in his works to the point of collecting them—indeed, to the point of commissioning his *Group of Four Trees*, though you would have to say the work looks rather good at the foot of the vertical, rectilinear, glass tower that is the Chase Manhattan Bank of New York (as does *The Tree Stand*, adjacent to the cement snows courtesy of Marcel Breuer, at the ski resort of Flaines). In Paris, one might well think that Dubuffet's *Tower of Figures* is implanted on the Ile Saint-Germain at Issy-les-Moulineaux less in defiance than as a knowing wink of the eye on the edge of the contemporary metropolis—located in the immediate surroundings of what young architects regard as "the city on the periphery," that strange urban ensemble that (in introducing itself into the interspace) has come to despoil the binary play of oppositions between the city and its suburbs. Analogously, the *Tower* models the opposition between sculpture and architecture and imposes itself as a kind of interrogation of what can become of architecture when it has neither the rights to the city nor, for that matter, the right to be cited.

I have chosen Dubuffet to introduce my remarks less for his contribution, by itself resolutely peripheral, to the architecture of its time than for the attack he never ceased to press against the general culture and the control it exercises on the arts. When the time came for him actually to *construct*, necessity compelled him to borrow knowledge from the domain that partook of what can only be called a technical culture, hereinafter pushed to the point of academicism. In this sense, there is no art more "cultural" than architecture. In fact, Dubuffet was the first to recognize that human beings were irremediably situated in a culture and in particular could extricate themselves only partially—through art—from the cutoff from reality that language imposes. Let us begin, then, with regard to this concern, with the division that language imposes (at least in the West) between architecture and construction—a division that Dubuffet implicitly endorsed in his writings without really examining the matter more closely and without excluding, as one will see, all culture seen as "technical."

What in fact does one read in *Prospectus* under the title "Edifices"? That the sculptor of the *Tower of Figures* was assisted in the interior design of the work by an architect, to whom we owe the general plans and the two models, the closest of which to the final configuration is named *Le Gastrovolve*, in reference to the involuted character of an apparatus whose exterior aspect of perfect compactness leaves no doubt that it defers to the constructive norms of the most advanced modernism:

> The construction of the edifice shall be based on the principle of hanging the entire exterior envelope on the arborescent interior apparatus of the Gastrovolve, which, made as it is entirely out of concrete, will support the work. The floorboards will be cosmetic. The exterior envelope will be lightweight and thin, and simply attached in the manner of a curtain wall. It can also itself be made of concrete, but of small thickness, though preferably of stratified epoxy resin. In the latter case, a network of stiff materials, joining the meandering black tracings of the exterior decoration, can be used if needed—notably to strengthen the entire dome covering the highest room, which forms the cupola roof, of the building, etc.[7]

The moral fable, one might say, begins to take shape. The same Dubuffet who denied that the creation of art was the business of specialists did not hesitate to consult a professional when it came to erecting his *Tower*. This man, who could not find words strong enough to denounce architecture that he judged lacking,[8] used techniques that were the very techniques of architecture itself. The moral that emerges from this story could take the form of a question: What does it signify for architecture that it is constructed and, perhaps even more significantly, that it is *constructed* in such a particular manner? What do all these facts and practices signify, not only for architecture as a concept but also for architecture as a phenomenon of culture, through the prisms of which we can see something of culture's own architecture?

On the concept of architecture, Jacques Derrida has opportuncly reminded us that it is itself a *constructum*, and whatever presents itself as an "architecture of architecture" has a history and is itself historical from one part to the next. This remains very much the case even if we accept that it is a *constructum* that we inhabit, even as it inhabits us, and of a heritage that comprehends us even before we have made the effort to consider it.[9] One might object to the notion that every concept, beginning with the concept of culture, is more or less constructed—if the remark did not have the effect of obliterating the relationship (apparently a sensible but highly problematic one when you think of its history) that the concept of architecture clearly maintains to that of construction: a relationship of difference as much as of similarity. In this sense, Derrida is right to say that "from its ancient beginnings, the most basic concept of architecture has been constructed."[10] However, why would one not add (and why did Derrida not add) that this concept had been *architectured*, as is suggested by the lovely formula that insists that there is an "architecture of architecture?" It is not only because the verb *architecturer*—which entered the French language soon after the distinction was made between architects and engineers—has to be handled with caution, signifying (if I am to believe the *Petit*

Robert dictionary) "construire avec rigueur." Rather, the reason should be sought on a deeper level, somewhat approaching the heading "architectural culture": architecture as a fact of culture, culture as inhabited by architecture as much as it inhabits architecture, culture informed by architecture as much as it informs architecture.

This philosophy attributes to architecture the idea of construction—together with all its additional resonances, including even Kant's definition of *architectonics* as "the art of systems"—but does not necessarily signify that all there is to architecture is construction. Nor does it allow one to suppose that the two are equivalent in the sense that the concept suggests—whether it is the concept of architecture or that of construction. Conversely, the image of God as the architect of the universe appeals beyond the idea of construction; the universe is not thought of purely in technical terms (in Kepler's time, the mathematics applicable to architecture were at a very rudimentary stage and were almost entirely empirical), but also in aesthetic terms: regularity, symmetry, harmony, and even composition (harmony of the spheres, composition of forces, etc.), if not beauty itself. The dictionary distinction between *construire* and *architecturer* was justified by the rivalry that emerged in that constructive century par excellence, the nineteenth, between the professional groups heretofore constituted and which proclaimed for themselves disparate cultures: technology for the one, art for the other. However, it all went contrary to reason in that the diverse functionalisms insisted there was no "truth" in the matter of architecture other than a constructive one, at a time when the use of new materials, particularly iron and concrete, went hand in hand with the development of methods of calculation, in the literal sense of the word. Beyond its obvious tautology, the formulation that architecture is architectured also abandoned the idea that architecture is constructed. The question that concerns us here—that of "architectural culture" in its ideological as well as institutional aspects—is essentially tied to the difference, indeed to the conceptual split, that exists between the verb *architecturer* and the verb *construire*, between *art* and *technique*.

In his writings on cinema, Roland Barthes was not afraid to assert that the dream of every critic was to be able to define an art by its technique.[11] This hope was paralleled by those linguists who laid claim to abstracting the condition of meaning so as to study language by its strictly technical, not to say constructive, aspects—in anticipation of recognizing an order that, in being presented as functional and therefore susceptible to entering into resonance with other morphological forms (mathematical, musical, etc.), can then take its place in the semantic order. One could say, a fortiori of architecture. Responding to this issue, I will allow myself to reproduce something I wrote more than twenty years ago as part of a research project, collectively undertaken, on the function of the sign in modern architecture; it was a period in France that was dominated by our readings of Manfredo Tafuri and the journal *Oppositions*. I refer to a text that for obscure reasons was never circulated but that, despite being somewhat dated, still has relevance today:

> *To formulate in semiological terms the question of the relationship between architecture and construction, the notion (if not the illusion) of a functional order as a prerequisite to any semantization, from which every constitution or institution of sign would necessarily borrow, soon imposes itself. If architecture has the right to present itself as a language (though it does not see itself as "talking"), it is in the measure by which the form of expression that corresponds to the first instance of the operation of the semantization of functions models itself, directly or indirectly, on a supposedly coherent*

functional order. Each architectonic member is under-
stood to maintain with the ensemble in which it insets
itself, as well as with each of the other elements the lat-
ter is comprised of, a "reasoned" relationship (to revive
Viollet-le-Duc's expressionism). If architecture can seem
to function as a language, it is because, to begin with,
it presents the model of an arrangement, of a construc-
tion, of a structuration anterior, logically speaking, to
the very operation of meaning. It is the model, one might
say, of a double articulation, the masonry itself having
to satisfy—in order simply to hold—a certain number of
structural constraints, without which there would be no
question of architecture, no more than one of language
or, in parting, of culture. [12]

Architecture, then, is not simply a matter of *supplement*: a
supplement of rigor (according to the dictionary), a supplement
of meaning (with all the risks of failure we know these days), a
supplement of beauty (architects are among the last people in
the world not to be afraid of the word)—beauty that it could flat-
ter itself to have discovered in construction, as the functionalist
aesthetic would have it. Schelling's definition of architecture as
the "metaphor of construction" does not necessarily imply that
the proper meaning of architecture, let alone its truth, is to be
found in construction; note that Gothic architecture and its linear model of a constructive system possess in their details none
of the rigor of the working drawing. However, a whole aspect
of architecture also derives from the category of the *mask*—and
indeed the exterior envelope of Dubuffet's *Tower* acts as a mask,
one whose figures deny in dissimulation the constructive apparatus of modernity. It is a design, let us say in passing, that itself
represents a challenge to the traditional norms of construction,
be it the suppression of supporting walls replaced by suspended

panels, the out-of-line floor planks, or the truly revolutionary constructive role subsequently assigned to pressed glass and the like—in effect, all those things that are now part of the legacy, of the vulgate of architectural modernity. This, however, should not lead one to underestimate the work of deconstruction from which the vulgate derived. As Derrida insists, contrary to appearances, deconstruction is not an architectural metaphor:

> *The word should, the word will, name a kind of thinking about architecture, a kind of thinking about the work. To begin with, it is not a metaphor. One can no longer rely on the concept of metaphor. [This relates to Schelling's formulation of architecture as a "metaphor" of construction.] Deconstruction, then, should deconstruct—to begin with and as its name indicates—the construction itself, the structural or constructivist motif, its patterns, its institutions, its concepts, its rhetoric. And deconstruct as well strictly architectural construction, the philosophical construction of the concept of architecture, the concept the model of which governs the idea of the system in philosophy as well as the theory, practice, and instruction of architecture.*[13]

It is a matter, then, of culture and of thought—if such things exist. The architecture we call *modern* did more than just instigate this project. It also precipitated a break with the principle of discontinuity, which construction had until then supported, by imposing new structural models in continuous veils—unthinkable until the invention of prestressed concrete—with the parallel demise of the distinction between the vertical and horizontal, upon which what Derrida called the *ject* of the project (*le "jet" du projet*) had been grounded.[14] This is to say nothing of the montage of elements—girders and crossbeams, which Viollet-le-Duc's dictionary says nothing about, because they correspond to a level of structural articulation inferior to the formal and semantic units identified in the *Raisonné* (column, base, capital, arch, vault, etc.): the equivalents in language of what would be the level of articulation of phonemes in relation, semantically, to that of words.

Walter Benjamin did not fail to see in the precocious expression of architectural modernity that iron construction represented the first instance of the principle of montage—in a way that was neither metaphorical nor rhetorical, but strictly mechanical. "Never before," one reads in the notes of *Passagen-Werk*, "was the criterion of the 'minimal' so important. And that includes the minimal element of quantity: the 'little' and the 'few.' These are dimensions that were well established in technological and architectural construction long before literature made bold to adapt them."[15] Montage as a modality of construction took quite another turn with iron. Thus Marx, whom Benjamin quotes, writes: "It is only after considerable development of the science of mechanics, and accumulated practical experience, that the form of a machine becomes settled entirely in accordance with mechanical principles and emancipated from the traditional form of the tool that gave rise to it." To which Benjamin adds, "In this sense, for example, the supports and the load, in architecture, are also 'forms'"[16]

But the principle of montage does not correspond simply to a new modality of construction as much as it does to one of form, emancipated in theory from every kind of anthropomorphism and every kind of organicism. As its corollary, it appeals to the possibility of de-montage—not to be confused with deconstruction. Not that de-montage lacks theoretical, to say nothing of "deconstructive," instances, which suggests that a building is an object obeying a transitory principle, but in fact it demonstrates that it was built to last. For example, a clause was inserted into the land concession act related to the construction of the Crystal Palace that stipulated the building's demolition after the closing of the 1851 London Exposition (to the great consternation of the London public).[17] More extreme examples were those buildings that lacked foundations, quickly erected in their locations, as in the manner of the houses of Jean Prouvé or even of a structure dropped onto the ground by helicopter, as with the geodesic domes of Buckminster Fuller. The fact that architecture has come to the point of even repudiating the idea of a foundation is something that we should not accept without consequence, especially in what passes for "architectural culture." An architecture that will leave no trace of itself, not even ruins, spells a utopia that risks announcing itself to be as disastrous as its totalitarian antithesis. However, in an architecture that, without ignoring the preeminence of residential quarters, would instead of looking for some foundation rather expose them to every manner of variation and displacement, to every manner of transformation—an architecture of wandering, then, in its concept as in its realization—a thought, if not a culture, could find there a point of departure.[18]

Time

As far as space and time are concerned, Hegel has a way of classifying the arts that is paradoxical inasmuch as it is simultaneously generative and subtractive—generativity depending in this case on subtraction, and even proceeding from it. Architecture and sculpture come first in this classification because they take place and operate in the three dimensions of the objective world. Next comes painting, the concept of which implies the elimination of one dimension—that is, three minus one; painting develops itself up to the point of being converted into a pure magic of color that is nevertheless still of a spatial character, bound as it is to the two dimensions of the wall or the picture plane on which the

13.2
Robert Mallet-Stevens, Villa Noailles at Hyères,
France, 1923–1925. Photo © Jacqueline Salmon,
1996.

interior self, the "subject" as we call it, projects itself in the guise of permanent configurations of forms and color. Last comes music, in its seemingly linear, one-dimensional, and ephemeral mode of manifestation—that is, three minus two; music, as Hegel writes in his *Lessons on Aesthetics*, does not proceed so much from the disappearance or subtraction of one more dimension of space than it does from the suppression of spatiality in general. The main task of music is to make manifest the most intimate self, the deepest subjectivity, the ideal soul, resounding, finding an echo, in the pure and permanently flowing element of time.

Architecture and music thus correspond to two opposite poles, traditionally referred to as the arts of space (architecture, sculpture, painting) and the arts of time (music and poetry). Far from assigning it the first rank in the hierarchy of the arts, Hegel considers architecture the most incomplete of all, claiming that it is unable to adequately express the spiritual through the use of materials concerned mostly with obeying the laws of gravity and therefore reduced to providing an external environment with only symbolic significance. Music, on the other hand, is thought to be the "romantic" art par excellence, because it deals with a material as insubstantial as sound—a material which, in turn, implies a double negation of exteriority; space is nullified by the way in which the body reacts to a mere vibration, which is thereby converted into a mode of expression of pure interiority.

The strictly conceptual opposition of space, as the element of exteriority and objectivity, and time or duration, as the element of interiority and subjectivity, is contradicted by the reality of movement. Movement is defined in terms of space and time, or perhaps it is space and time that are defined in terms of movement. Form in music is related to movement, just as movement is related to form. This calls for further investigations into the fabric of time, a fabric that, in spite of its alleged "linearity," allows music to reflect itself in the mirror of form and structure

13.3
Robert Mallet-Stevens, Villa Noailles at Hyères,
France, 1923–1925. Photo © Jacqueline Salmon,
1996.

13.4
Robert Mallet-Stevens, Villa Noailles at Hyères,
France, 1923–1925. Photo © Jacqueline Salmon,
1996.

and thereby recognize the spatial image of its development, its construction, and its architecture. But if, according to Friedrich Schelling's famous metaphor, architecture is nothing but "frozen music" (*eine erstarrte Musik*), how are we to define music? As "defrosted architecture?"

In the story of *Amphion* as told by Paul Valéry (who used it as an argument for a "melodrama," set to music by Arthur Honegger), a temple is built through the agency of music. Having received the lyre from Apollo, the mortal Amphion gives birth both to music and architecture when he begins to play it. The stones move and assemble themselves into a temple. Hence the challenge for the composer, who refrains from making use of all the resources of his art until they are developed in Valéry's story of Amphion's touch. The same is true for architecture, which at first was to be presented more as a simple exercise of movements and combinations than of structure or composition. In the same way that music retrospectively reflects itself in its own architecture, architecture projects itself in its own generative, not to say musical, process. But its relation to time and to its fabric goes deeper than a succession of choices and displacements, a mere succession of moves, as in a game or a play; it involves—or relies on—a kind of movement or dynamic inherent to its own fabric and which requires, in order to become visible, an approach other than metaphor, an approach that involves the medium of images according to their own movement, their own circulation, and their own dynamics.

Painting was for a long time associated with architecture. With the Renaissance, linear perspective became a common basis for both arts and provided architects and painters with an instrument that allowed them to commute freely between the actual three-dimensional space of architecture and the two-dimensional plane on which it was represented. This seemed to exclude any consideration of time or duration, except for the

13.5
Robert Mallet-Stevens, Villa Noailles at Hyères,
France, 1923–1925. Photo © Jacqueline Salmon,
1996.

representation of ruins and decay or of the building process it-self. The transformations that could take place within the frame of perspective all implied, in one way or another, a displacement that could be treated according to the same geometrical lines on which the comparison between architecture and music relied; any attempt to make room for the representation or expression of movement and its dynamics had to conform either to the rules of proportion or to the principles of harmony.

This state of affairs was radically altered by the discovery of photography and the invention of the cinematograph. Accord-ing to Walter Benjamin, not only did photography change the very notion of art by replacing the question of photography as art with the notion of art as photography (that is to say, mechanically reproducible), it also called for a transformation of the whole Hegelian system of the arts. Benjamin, among others, noted that photography provided a better hold on an image, a work of art, and especially a building than could be obtained from dealing with the object itself. But this not only derives, as he thought, from the reductive aspect of photography and its greater mastery over a three-dimensional object (especially architecture) by the elimination of one dimension. What photography and, more-over, film reveal is that architecture cannot be considered only as an art of space; room has to be made, in its practice as well as in its concepts, for time and movement.

Hegel's lessons left no room for photography and film. He was still free to consider architecture and music as the two op-posite poles of art: one static, related to the laws of gravity as they operate in space, and the other dynamic, corresponding to the movement of sounds as they take place in time. Painting, as it eventually developed into a magic of color, emancipated itself from the reign of matter only to enter the field of appearances. As far as movement was concerned (and, according to Aby Warburg, it was of great concern to Renaissance art), painting succeeded

13.6
Robert Mallet-Stevens, Villa Noailles at Hyères,
France, 1923–1925. Photo © Jacqueline Salmon,
1996.

in evoking, representing, or "expressing" it in a more or less illusionistic way but did not succeed in actually producing, or even "imitating," it. For movement, as Gilles Deleuze later put it, not only takes place in space, as something that occurs between objects; it also expresses duration, in the Bergsonian sense, as something that, in opposition to time, cannot be divided into parts. The same applies to music, the movements of which actually take place in measurable, divisible time in such a way that one can deal with it in terms of composition, of structure, of architecture. However, the movement of sounds—their *tempo*, even their color, and most of all, their rhythm, as they echo, according to Hegel, the rhythms of the heart and the soul—are more a *matter* of duration than of time: a matter of duration as Henri Bergson describes in *Matter and Memory*.

The discovery of photography dramatically altered the classification system of the arts. For photography, from the very beginning, has been related to both space and time. It relates to space as the element in which the project is actually taking place, and that allows for the reduction of the "view," the object, or the model to the two dimensions of the photographic image. It is related to time as well, as the inescapable condition for imprinting the image on the sensitized plate or paper. It is related to time but not to duration, because the time of exposure implies the elimination of movement ("Stand still!" "Ne bougez plus!"). The subsequent development that led to the "snapshot," or the *instantané*, allowed photography to deal with movement, but only by fixing it, having it "frozen." For a long time, photography was thus torn between two poles of attraction: on the one hand, the analysis of movement as it could be caught and represented through a succession of snapshots, and on the other, the image of stability. Here, of course, the paragon was architecture, which resists the ravages of time and surpasses the living model or still life in its ability to stand still in front of the camera.

The arrival of film disposed of the alleged opposition between the arts of space and the arts of time on which the traditional classification of the arts had relied. A new turn was given to the notion of "projection," which, since the Renaissance, had been a component of the arts of *disegno*—architecture, sculpture, and painting. Projection was no longer considered merely a geometric process related to the two dimensions of the plane but a dynamic one involving a third dimension—the dimension of time—inseparable from the mechanism of the camera and the running of the film. With regard to architecture, the move was of great consequence, for the cinematographic approach meant dealing with architecture in terms not only of time but also of movement and, through it, of duration.

In his 1932 lecture, "The Story of Amphion," Valéry referred to duration as the equivalent of memory and the equivalent of form: "*duration*, that is to say memory, that is to say form."[19] If when listening to music we supposedly have to memorize its developments in order to "understand" it, in the same way that we supposedly have to memorize the first words of a sentence in order for it to make sense in our mind when completed, it doesn't mean that musical form is to be thought of in terms of space, as something we can only access in retrospect. Projection plays its role in the process, in a dynamic and prospective way; form is present, form is perceived, form is at work, on the move, for the listener, from the very beginning of the execution of a sonata as well as for the uttering of a sentence.

But what about architecture? What are we to learn about it from or through photography? What are we to learn about it from or through film? And no less important, does film outdate photography, make it irrelevant, with regard to architecture? I recently raised this issue in a short book that I worked on with the French photographer Jacqueline Salmon, about Robert Mallet-Stevens's Villa Noailles in Hyères, one of the incunabula of

13.7
Robert Mallet-Stevens, Villa Noailles at Hyères,
France, 1923–1925. Photo © Jacqueline Salmon,
1996.

modern architecture. The issue was all the more relevant in that Mallet-Stevens himself first worked as a set designer for the film industry (he designed, along with Fernand Leger, the sets for Marcel L'Herbier's *L'inhumaine*, a film that was conceived and received as a manifesto in support of modern architecture). The tension between film and architecture was also at stake in a film on the villa that was commissioned from Man Ray by the Noailles in 1928, *Les Mysteres du chateau du dé* (The mysteries of the castle of dice).

In looking at Salmon's photographs and at Man Ray's film, one must be attentive not only to day passing into night, as reflected in the photographs, but also to the analogies and the differences between the two approaches to the building, analogies and differences that culminate in Man Ray's rhetorical figures of movement (Man Ray being, first of all, the great photographer we all know). His film starts with a wide-angle, 360-degree pan of the terrace, with its openings on the outside, and then ignores the Mediterranean landscape (just as Salmon will, seventy years later) to shuffle into the house, through its corridors, staircases, and tunnels, and raise the eye toward the stained-glass grid that corresponds to the sky of the great salon. Here, the handheld camera slowly slides over the metallic grids on which the collection of paintings was stored and, turning upside down, finally ends up back on the terrace. It is a dramatic circular move that echoes the pan of the terrace and also turns the building upside down. I find it to be a good introduction to the notion of "defrosted architecture" inspired by Schelling and to the relations between architecture and what I called the fabric of time, its texture, and, by the same token, its relation to space. It is a good introduction to the way in which architecture addresses the eye and the body through the movement of the camera, just as music addresses the ear and the body through the movement of sound.

13.8
Robert Mallet-Stevens, Villa Noailles at Hyères,
France, 1923–1925. Photo © Jacqueline Salmon,
1996.

History

Ours is a time that seems to have no way of dealing with history other than as strictly retrospective, in the past tense. A time that doesn't want to know of any form of ideology other than the laissez-faire, the mere and mechanical submission to the rules of the "market." A time that leaves no room for utopias other than the degenerate, as in Disneyland. A time that precludes any projection into the future, unless evolutionary, in terms of profit, fiction (so-called science fiction), or fantasy, in the guise of identity or of virtuality, which in some way is the same (there is no identity but virtual, no virtuality but "identitarian" [*identitaire*], both in trompe l'oeil). My thesis is that no matter the conditions, architecture indicates the new paths (or nonpaths), the new ways (or nonways) that are or could be—I dare not say "or should be"—the ones of history (or nonhistory) today. Architecture also indicates the margin of "play" (in the sense of play in a machine or gear) that is left, beyond irony, for any form of creative, critical, or subversive activity.

1

Is there any way for a building, public or private, large or modest, to be declared "historic" or a "landmark" without reference to the past or to "style?" Is there any way for architecture to deal with "history" in its very process or activity, as well as in its appearance, in terms of structure or form? One of the most common criticisms of modernist architecture is that it had no concern for history. Indeed, the ideology of modernity implied a rupture with the past, under the labels of newness or rationality or both. As Walter Gropius once said: "Modern architecture is not a new branch added to an old tree, but a new growth, that sprouts directly from the roots."[20] The architecture of the "moderns" involved a projection into the future, the very notion of "project" being related to the forthcoming dimension of time, to the opening of things to come, things to conceive and construct, things to "plan" and to "project," eventually to the detriment of the remnants of the past: project and utopia hand in hand, as Manfredo Tafuri recognized.[21] For the constructivists, history had to do with expectations rather than with memories; with looking forward rather than with looking back; with construction rather than with conservation.

Architecture is not only a product of history, a product to be studied, analyzed, and criticized in relation to its context, conditions of appearance, or possibility. Architecture is an essential thread in the fabric of history, most especially in the fabric of "context." It is an agent, or tool, in the making of history, in the development of new forms not only of dwelling but of production and sociability, of power and exploitation: new modes of historicity. This may sound like mere commonplace, but it needs constantly to be reassessed. The very activity of building, of projecting, is by definition future oriented. Even the great monuments that celebrate the past are a way of getting rid of it. Adolf Loos claimed that the tomb is the epitome of architecture: It is, first, a way for the living to come to terms with the dead, a way for people to come to terms with death itself. This is part of history and part of architecture, but only one part of it.

No one has better formulated this issue in contemporary architecture than Fredric Jameson—the same Fredric Jameson who, in a daring move, shifted gears from "postmodern" to "postcontemporary," as if even contemporaneity, such as we have to live it, think it, be part of it, is already and irremediably lost as such; as if we could live it, think it, be part of it only in retrospect; as if history, be it contemporary history, history in the present tense, had from the start to be narrated in the past tense while failing to attain any form of coherence. Peter Eisenman's project for the University Art Museum in Long Beach, California, is perfectly in tune with such a scheme, taking its form from—to quote Eisenman—"the overlapping registration of several maps" corresponding to various time zones, the coordinates of which are incompatible: "Beginning with the settlement of California in 1849, the creation of the campus in 1949, and the projected 'rediscovery' of the museum in the year 2049. The idea was to imagine the site in the year 2049, 100 years after the founding of the university and 200 years after the period of the gold rush."[22] Projecting into the future equates with reducing the future to its own archeology, with making up for the lack of deeper layers of time, the lack of "history" in the past tense that is supposed to be characteristic of America.

I quote, somewhat freely, from Jameson's *The Seeds of Time*:

> *Now the new individual building does not even have a fabric in which to "fit," like some well-chosen word . . . rather (consistent with the freedom of the market itself) it must replicate the chaos and the turbulences all around it. . . . Replication means the depoliticization of the former modern, the consent to corporate power and its grants and contracts, the reduction of social conscience to manageable, practical, pragmatic limits; the Utopian becomes unmentionable, along with socialism and un-balanced budgets. Clearly also, on any materialist view, the way the building form falls out is of enormous signifi-cance; in particular the proportion of individual houses to office buildings, the possibility or not of urban ensem-bles, the rate of commissions for public buildings such as opera houses or museums (often recontained within those reservation spaces of private or public universities, which are among the most signal sources of high class contemporary patronage), and not least the chance to design apartment buildings or public housing.*[23]

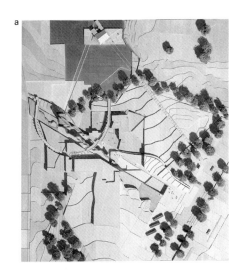

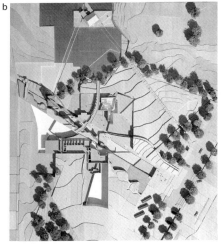

13.9a, b
Eisenman/Robertson Architects, University Art
Museum, California State University at Long Beach.
Presentation model for phase 4, with (a) and without
(b) roof, 1986. Courtesy Eisenman Architects.

From the small private house rebuilt by Frank Gehry to what Jameson calls "the grandiose new totalities" of Rem Koolhaas, the contemporary (or shall we say the postcontemporary?) praxis of architecture demonstrates the narrow range of possible interventions left to architects in a world in which any form of planning has been subverted by building regulations and zoning laws that are applied in a strictly defensive and negative way; at the public level, the process of decision is reduced, at its best, to a choice between different moves that mechanically follow the weakest lines of resistance. The paths of "history" are such that today there seems to be only one creative way of dealing with this: to accept the constraints and to try to take advantage of them in order to develop new ideas. (As Koolhaas likes to say, in a Goethean way, with respect to New York City zoning laws: "The more you stick to the rules, the more freedoms you have." The *more freedoms*, in the plural.)

2

Among the types of public buildings that are publicly or privately commissioned today, Jameson mentions opera houses and museums—that is, buildings explicitly related to the issue of history or "heritage." Strangely enough, he omits airport terminals, yet these are among the most important public commissions today, and they may eventually be turned in the future into museums, as train stations already have been (think of the Musée d'Orsay in Paris; in Washington, DC, a former department store is being turned into an opera house). For the moment, the museum is desperately attempting to resemble a terminal, with its halls, counters, escalators, zones of gathering, security booths, shops, parking lots, and herds of tourists that make us believe that museums are enjoying a vogue that equals one of the great pilgrimages of the past, even though the number of visitors they attract is in fact constantly declining.

The museum as a terminal, inside or outside the city: Not very far from here, set in the park of Upper Veluwe, is the Kröller-Müller Museum, a good example of the museum as part (in Jameson's terms) of a reservation space. Here in Rotterdam, when the city council agreed, in 1928, that a new museum was needed, it seemed logical that the plan for the building retain the parklike character of the same site on which the museum of architecture, the Netherlands Architecture Institute, stands today: "A tranquil stretch of land in the midst of the city's hustle and bustle."[24] Similarly, the Museum of Modern Art in New York has for a long time been conceived as a public oasis, an island of culture in the center of the metropolis. In fact, the architects who recently participated in the competition to remodel the museum were asked to treat it as a "campus"—that is, as a reservation space under high-class patronage.

The great collections that historically have been developed into museums were by no means restricted to a retrospective view of artistic production and to the celebration of antiquity or the great schools and periods of the past. When Vélazquez was commissioned in 1629 to go to Italy to buy works of art for King Philip IV of Spain, he mostly acquired paintings by his contemporaries or immediate predecessors. The first museums were not conceived as monuments of the past and still less as tombs or funerary sites, but rather as repositories of models for living artists. Things changed when, in the eighteenth century, the erudite sense of history and archeology overrode the concern for the present and when, partly due to the success of the salons, the art of the past and the art of the present were sharply divided, while at the same time the institution as such pleaded for continuity, often to the detriment of living art.

A symptom of the way in which we now deal with history is evident in the same split between the art of the past and the art of the present that gave way to the creation of museums of modern art, a split now reverberating inside those relatively new institutions as a split between modern and contemporary (and postcontemporary) art. The best way to avoid the apparent contradiction between the diverse approaches to history seems to be to dodge it by carefully isolating each layer of time in its own container, thereby avoiding or preventing any form of communication, exchange, or contamination among them. The museum has become some sort of air terminal, but in opposition to the imaginary one, or to what I would call the "paper museum"—in the sense in which we speak of "paper architecture"—it doesn't offer flights to all destinations.

In 1979, referring to Cesar Pelli's model for the new Museum Tower, Bill Rubin (then director of the Museum of Modern Art) declared: "This new building solves the problems of the past but not the future—you can't predict what art's going to do." We are aware of the problem that curators at the Centre Georges Pompidou face with each new installation because programmers in the 1970s thought they could predict where art was heading and what it would need: a museum without walls. But we also know what an extraordinary challenge the spiral of the Guggenheim Museum still offers to artists forty years after its completion. This is exactly what makes it "historic" in the sense I am trying to suggest.

Not only do we not know what art is going to do, it also looks as if one of the main concerns of art was to deceive any prediction, to evade any enlistment. This doesn't mean that plans for new museums, or for the remodeling of existing ones, should only solve problems of the past, as Rubin put it. The "historic" quality of a project depends on its capacity to generate a margin of play as well as a set of situations to which both the visitors and the artists must react. As far as the museum is concerned, this means breaking with the strictly linear development of a master narrative. Frank Lloyd Wright's scheme for the Guggenheim Museum represented a drastic move beyond Le Corbusier's Mundaneum, a museum that developed concentrically as a snail shell, providing no room for any confrontation or short circuits, not to mention the impossibility of introducing a new piece into the game without having to reorganize the entire itinerary. In the Guggenheim Museum, the visitor is allowed, at any moment along the spiral, to take a transversal view, either upward or downward, backward or forward. In a recent show there, Ellsworth Kelly played systematically, and dramatically, both on the constraints that the spiral form imposes and on the possibilities it opens.

A museum is at once a narrative and a system that assumes an architectural form: a narrative that "precipitates"—in the chemical sense—according to constant accretions and redistributions; a system that corresponds to the mapping of diachrony into synchrony, of succession into simultaneity, and through which one has to open a path in some transversal way. When the new Boijmans Museum opened in 1935, it was much criticized for its traditionalism by the adepts of the modern movement. However, due more to its intricate plan than to its technically advanced system of lighting, the building retains an extraordinary quality. Distributed on several levels, with a circular hallway at the crossroads of various possible itineraries, it functions according to an unprecedented principle, mirroring in its very structure the evolution of art—itself ramified, arboreal, bushlike—and the multiple pathways of its history.

We still need to learn from Marx that history is not only a matter of narration. We still need to learn from Lucien Febvre and Marc Bloch, creators of the French school of Les Annales, that history has to be constantly rewritten according to the needs and anticipations of new generations. In the museum, such rewriting takes the form of new additions and the remodeling of former parts. For the curators at the Boijmans, it meant dealing simultaneously with ancient, modern, and contemporary art. My own move in the exhibition that I curated there is consistent with this. *Playing Chess and Cards with the Museum* amounts to an experiment in having art from the past working, with no intermediaries, with art from the present and vice versa. It is an experiment in the ways in which history can be dealt with not only according to sequential lines but through simultaneity and the constant confrontations, overlappings, and short circuits of which the history of art is constituted.

3

A more delicate, even painful question concerns the uses and abuses of history and the uses and abuses of architecture in a "museum" like the United States Holocaust Memorial Museum in Washington, DC, a structure, according to its supporters, that is specifically about the nature of memory.[25] This issue seems to defy any attempts to deal with it in a seemingly detached and objective way; hence, I will only pinpoint in the most discrete way two problems of special relevance to my argument here.

First, the problem of linearity: Notwithstanding the architects' efforts to provide visitors with a succession of choices between different itineraries and to induce (here again, I borrow freely from different sources) "a sense of imbalance, distortion and rupture," the story of the Holocaust unfolds linearly on three levels surrounding "a large hollow interior that resembles another hall of arrival" (itself described as both "a non-place and a central space")—that is, strictly speaking, another kind of terminal. How are we to deal in a narrative way with an event so beyond measure that it not only evades the grasp but blasts the very notion of it? I do not want to sound polemical, but the way in which the story starts in 1918 and implacably continues to 1945, with General Dwight D. Eisenhower discovering the atrocities of the death camps; the way in which the tale is told to play on the sense of guilt that Western democracies should develop for having refused to welcome the great numbers of refugees who would have otherwise supposedly been allowed to leave Germany; the claim that one would have had to wait until 1942 and the Wannsee Conference for the Nazis to engage in the "final solution"; and, last but not least, the tale abruptly ending on the two interrelated historical destinies left to the Jews after the Holocaust, the State of Israel and the American Jewish community; all the supposed subtleties of the setting lead to the same conclusion: there is no way to deal in critical terms with such an endeavor other than strictly architecturally. At stake is no less than the capacity of architecture to ensure a visible grasp on an unspeakable past—for the enormity of the event, the way in which, as Jean-François Lyotard once put it, it destroys all instruments of measurement, is measured by the way in which it implies the negation of any form of bigness other than the merely quantitative, as well as the total, or totalitarian, elimination of any architectural trace or any archeological remnant of the boundless atrocities that took place on the premises.

There is no other way to discuss such a "monument" in the etymological sense of the word than the strictly architectural. A more general question concerns the different ways in which architecture can relate to history today, the different ways in which architecture can deal with the challenge of history.

This leads to the second problem, that of style: The way in which the architects of the Holocaust Museum played on style reveals the degenerate Nietzschean way in which we now indulge in dealing with history in stylistic terms—starting with the "architectural language" of the Hall of Witness, conceived as "an ironic criticism of early modernism's lofty ideals of reason and order that were perverted to build the factories of death,"[26] and ending, regrettably, with an unbearable touch of so-called concentrationary atmosphere. One is forced to watch a sequence of events in strict chronology down to a horse-stable barrack treated as the canonical representation of German camps. In a way, the Holocaust Museum, in its limitations and given the issues it raises, amounts to an urgent call for the museum to come to terms with history in ways other than the merely retrospective and narrative, in the past tense. An urgent call for architecture to be "historic" in ways other than the stylistic, mimetic, or allegorical. An urgent call for architecture in the future tense, the future of metaphor.

14.1
Edward Weston, *The Great Cloud, Mazatlán*, Mexico,
1923. Oakland Museum of California, The Bell Fund.
© 1981 Center for Creative Photography, Arizona
Board of Regents.

14 BLOTTING OUT ARCHITECTURE?
A FABLE IN SEVEN PARTS

FOR PHYLLIS LAMBERT

You can't build clouds. And that's why the future you dream of never comes true.
—Ludwig Wittgenstein, *Culture and Value*

1 Weston's Cloud

In the summer of 1923, when the old tub that was slowly taking Tina Modoti and himself to Mexico made a stopover while trailing down the coast of Baja California, the photographer Edward Weston took a shot of a great cloud whose shape had caught his eye: "A sunlit cloud," he writes in his *Daybook*, "which rose from [Mazatlán] bay to become a towering white column." A few days later, he noticed the roll of film was damaged, but he went about repairing it as soon as he was settled in Mexico and went on to produce several enlargements of an image that, far from being reduced, in his words, to a matter-of-fact shot, somehow fulfilled an intention he seems to have deliberately kept vague.[1] How could it be otherwise? From the moment the cloud becomes a phenomenon—*phenomenon*, not object—it eludes all intentional purposes along with any essentialist position, having only an accidental and transitory presence and being a function of strictly external causes and conditions, leaving us, moreover, completely free to project our fantasies on to it. (Where Weston saw a column, we might be more tempted today to see a hint of the atomic mushroom, minus the cap.)

2 Brunelleschi's Mirror

With the passing of the weeks, and as intense and dramatic as life in Mexico seemed to him to be, Weston never ceased to be as fascinated by the walls bathed in sunlight as by the clouds—"the marvelous clouds," to echo Baudelaire. "They alone," Weston writes, "are sufficient to work with for many months and never tire."[2] But the fact that the photographer could be interested at the same time in textural effects resulting from the play of light on walls of stone, brick, or clay and effects of a very different kind to which cloud formations lent themselves leaves us to imagine that we are witnessing a play of oppositions between the architectural (or constructive) sphere and the atmospheric sphere. Mark Wigley notes that "atmosphere seems to start precisely where the construction stops,"[3] in order to contrast this assertion with the idea of an "architecture of atmosphere" that would be based on a notion of atmosphere different from a strictly meteorological one: a "built" atmosphere that emanates from a building or from its image or representation, to say nothing of its ruin. In terms of graphic design, Le Corbusier could well condemn those seeking effects not restricted to a more or less stenographic line, but he did not get as far as the cult of the abstract line that generates its own specific atmosphere.[4] From this perspective, what sense would it make to stop at the element of air, an element as apparently foreign as the cloud is to any notion of construction, graphic or otherwise, and to architecture itself, defined in Le Corbusier's formula as "the masterly, correct, and magnificent play of volumes brought together in light"[5]?

Weston compared the great cloud of Mazatlán to a column. Contrary to any architectural construct, it remains that a cloud cannot be enclosed or delineated, still less circumscribed according to a well-defined outline that, as we read in Alberti's *Della Pittura*, provides the names of the surfaces and volumes that can be generated from it: "It is by their 'edge' (*l'orlo*) as much as by their 'back' (*il dorso*)," their "skin," their external envelope, that circles, squares, and triangles are defined, along with spheres, cubes, and pyramids.[6] In this sense, and it is certainly what Leonardo meant in texts that are rightly celebrated, the cloud is like a stain or mark—a *blur*—that escapes the essentially graphic clutches of Euclidean geometry and, by the same token, accentuates by default the bond between art and geometry that was formed in Ancient Greece more than two thousand years ago and is fundamental to and characteristic of Western culture. In his famous opuscule *The Origin of Geometry*, the philosopher Edmund Husserl explained accurately how, born at the foot of the pyramids with the sage Thales, the invention of geometry presupposed as its precondition the constitution of a base, a ground, of sensory experience which itself would have gone through the elaboration and production of regular architectural volumes, among other things, before moving on to clearly defined edges, such as were obviously involved in said pyramids.[7] Paul Valéry had the same idea in *Eupalinos*, in which Phaedro reminds Socrates of the buildings they saw put up in Piraeus and the engines, the efforts, the flutes that tempered them with their music, "all those incredibly precise operations, that progress at once so mysterious and so clear," linked obviously to the progress of geometry: "More than anything else, what confusion seemed to go hand in glove with order! What solidity, what rigor sprang up among all those threads that yielded all those perpendiculars, along all those fragile strings stretched out only to be leveled by the growth of beds of brick."[8]

In *The Origin of Perspective*, the title of which deliberately parodies that of Husserl's opuscule, I tried to show how, from Brunelleschi to Desargues, the work of the perspectivists has repeated this same scenario and in turn prepared the ground, though by other means, for the developments of modern geometry in its descriptive and projective aspects.[9] In this context, we must return yet again to the founding myth that the first of Brunelleschi's "experiments" constitutes on the subject. I will limit myself here to recalling how, if we are to believe what may well be a mere fable or tall tale (albeit one of utmost consequence), Brunelleschi painted on a small square panel a perspective view of the Baptistery of San Giovanni in Florence as it appears from inside the central doorway of the Cathedral of Santa Maria del Fiore. He is then is said to have punched a conical hole in the *tavoletta* corresponding to the building's vanishing point so that, by turning the thing over and putting his eye to the reverse side, he could see the image in a mirror. We will say nothing here of the theoretical implications of what effectively presented itself not so much as an experiment than as a demonstration in due form: essentially, the projective coincidence of the point of view and the vanishing point that is the image of it in the blueprint of the painting—a proposition that we take for granted today, but which was at the time a major discovery, one that would prove decisive for mathematics as well as for philosophy. What matters here, forming an integral part of this other fiction we are dealing with, is that once the baptistery and its surrounds were represented in perspective and in the greatest possible detail, it remained for Brunelleschi not to depict the sky but—as his biographer strongly puts it—to show it or, literally, to demonstrate it (*a dimostrarlo*) as it stretched above the line of the rooftops. He manages to do this by resorting to the subterfuge that consists of inserting a burnished silver mirror in its place, in which air and sky are reflected as much as the clouds that could be seen in it "driven by the wind when it was blowing."[10] (It is impossible not to think here, as far as "cloud traps" go, of the shimmering bluish facades of modern architecture and, in a radically inverted perspective, of the mirrors Robert Smithson laid out in remote spots in the Yucatan in order to capture, mixed with the ash and mud that sullied them, something of the skies and clouds of the Mexico of which Weston was so fond.)[11]

The time would soon come when clouds would find a way to record themselves directly within the frame as a pictorial species or, in a more properly graphic form, as though appliquéd or left blank within the tight weft of lines (or dots) of which the sky is made, following a convention that Roy Lichtenstein so spectacularly mined. Doubtless, a cloud is not entirely formless, because we are sometimes tempted to see zoomorphic or anthropomorphic figures in clouds, not to say landscapes or fictional architectural shapes sculpted by the wind, as in a Mantegna painting, in which cloud formations rival his piles of antique ruins in intensity. However, if there were forms or figures in this particular case, they were explicitly marked as transitory, just like the clouds passing in Brunelleschi's mirror "driven by the wind when it was blowing." It is their nature as unpredictable shapes, devoid of any permanence, in constant movement and perpetual transformation, to which clouds owe the fact of having caught the attention of a number of photographers and filmmakers, hot on the heels of the painters, in the first half of the twentieth century. But the fact that architects have more recently come to use an element so apparently foreign to the reign of the built environment for their own ends—this smacks, yet again, of a fable or some kind of fiction that may well be worth a closer look.

3   Diller + Scofidio's Cloud Machine

In the summer of 2002, at Yverdon-les-Bains, on the banks of Lake Neuchâtel in Switzerland, I photographed a strange, thick,

14.2
Roy Lichtenstein, *Cloud and Sea*, 1964. Enamel on
steel. © Estate of Roy Lichtenstein.

14.3
Diller + Scofidio, Blur Building, Exposition Pavilion,
Swiss Expo, Yverdon-Les-Bains, 2002. Blur hovers
over Lake Neuchâtel; clouds hover over the Swiss
mountains. Photo: Hubert Damisch.

oblong-shaped cloud that seemed to float some distance from the shore above the surface of the water. It seemed to float, or—to put it more accurately, since the choice of words is fairly crucial here—it seemed to be in a state of levitation above the lake. As I examined it more closely, I could make out fragmentary glimpses of a metallic structure momentarily showing through the cloud at certain points and emerging from it as if following it in its end-lessly changing shape, seemingly enveloped by it in the manner of a celestial body endowed with a more or less opaque, nebulous atmosphere.

I sought out the two people I call the authors of the thing ("thing"—not object or phenomenon), Elizabeth Diller and Ricardo Scofidio, at whose invitation I arrived at the scene to visit what they first called a "cloud machine" before limiting them-selves to the more succinct and programmatic title of Blur. Ini-tially, Blur was conceived as one of several attractions organized around sites retained for what styled itself as "Swiss Expo 2002." The directive obeyed by the exhibition—which was in the best possible humor—is not relevant here: while playing on an exten-sive media gamut, it made much of architectural objects that were at the least incongruous and whose iconic range rivaled their critical function, much as occurred elsewhere with projects de-signed by Jean Nouvel and Coop Himmelb(l)au. There is no need, either, to go into the financial ups and downs that progressively blurred and watered down the outlines of the original project, only to wind up giving the cloud machine complete autonomy as the centerpiece pavilion, though it had originally been designed as part of a collaborative attempt at a "media landscape"—what-ever we care to make of such a term. Two features, however, de-mand to be retained. The first seems to imply an oblique way of eluding the network of structural determinations that can limit architecture on a conceptual as much as on a constructive level. The second corresponds to a calculated shift from the medium in which architecture works to the formal media operations and interactions to which architecture may lend itself.

4 The Work of the Concept

The Diller + Scofidio project presents a number of features or aspects typical of a conceptual work, beginning with the fact that it gave rise to the publication of a book, *Blur: The Making of Nothing*, which is like the work's archive, providing an otherwise ephemeral embodiment with a kind of lasting quality at once textual and iconic and comparable to that to which a number of contemporary productions can lay claim, whether arising from performance or not: the lasting quality of a fable or, better still, of a work of fiction.[12]

I will return to the problem posed by the term *blur*, a term that may mean a number of things and may assume different forms as noun or verb with a flexibility that goes to the heart of the matter. First, I need to remove any doubt. One can, of course, not take Diller + Scofidio's discourse seriously and can see their cloud machine as a mere gadget, one no doubt clever as well as spectacular, but definitely of a flippant order, without any real speculative or architectural implications. I have chosen to take the opposite view, one which leads to concern for the thinking that might subtend what presents itself less as an object than as a machination of "nothing" or of absence (the making of nothing). This sends us back to our original paradox: in what way might architecture form a pact with clouds without exposing itself to becoming the victim of determinations strictly foreign to its own order?

Wittgenstein writes that "you can't *build* [bauen] clouds. And that's why the future you *dream* of never comes true," thereby implying that dreams have no more consistency than clouds and that we are incapable of building anything essentially oneiric or fantastical—which leaves hanging the whole question of utopia,

14.4
Diller + Scofidio, Blur Building, Exposition Pavilion,
Swiss Expo, Yverdon-Les-Bains, 2002. Blur from
across the lake. Courtesy Diller Scofidio + Renfro.

14.5
Diller + Scofidio, Blur Building, Exposition Pavilion,
Swiss Expo, Yverdon-Les-Bains, 2002. Blur's Angel
Deck "in the clouds." Courtesy Diller Scofidio +
Renfro.

along with that of narrative.[13] Yet, in a quite different context, Wittgenstein also wondered about the modalities according to which a concept might be brought down to what one can see, leave its imprint there, and, literally, *inform* it, in the manner in which Jacques Lacan compared the setting up of the Signifier to the descent of the Holy Spirit:[14] to begin with the concept of outline, from the moment that nothing like lines or strokes exists in nature. But the issue is not limited to how the concept fits into the field of the perceptible. The issue bears on the way in which the concept can be put to work and, more to the point, can be put *into* work. Blur is the manifestation of this, if not the manifesto; the performance, if not (as I hope to show) the performative.

For an example of how a concept may be evolved along lines peculiar to architecture, we might look at how the idea of structure was handled in this particular case, along with the design and construction, properly speaking, of the machine, as well as the effects the latter was supposed to produce, which were neither exclusively visual nor constructive. A brief description will show how an ovoid metallic structure suspended from four incredibly skinny tubular piles sunk deep into the water and lake bed at a point where it is particularly loose, and working essentially in tension as a tensegrity system, was coupled with a network of pipes punctured at regular intervals by apertures, out of which mist was sprayed at very high pressure. The accumulation of the mist in jets at the periphery of the structure produced, on contact with the ambient air, the fog or thick cloud through which visitors were invited to roam after donning blue raincoats handed out at the entrance to the ramped bridge slung from shore to machine. The whole thing involved considerable technology. The flow of the water through the nozzles and its output as atomized mist were designed to be regulated by a computer from a built-in weather station, which adjusted the strength of the spray according to atmospheric conditions and wind direction.

14.6
Diller + Scofidio, Blur Building, Exposition Pavilion,
Swiss Expo, Yverdon-Les-Bains, 2002. Construction of
the Blur structure at night. Courtesy Diller Scofidio +
Renfro.

I would like to come back here to the use of the concept of structure and whether we understand this in a strictly constructive, tectonic sense or whether we take it in its epistemological sense as having to do with structuralism. What implications can the idea of a cloud structure have and, further, what effect can what we are forced to call the fantasy (or fiction) of a building whose primary components are steel and fog have on the very concept of structure? As Diller + Scofidio put it to the technical team with whom they discussed the terms for testing what claimed to be a cloud of dots: "We do not intend to make a volume of space covered with fog. We intend to make a building of fog with integrated media."[15]

Is not "building" saying too much or a mistranslation? If we take this text on its own terms, what is involved here is merely a matter of "making" (to make a building of fog), the idea of the building being directly associated with consideration of the paradoxical material that is fog—a material whose production has now become, as we learn in *Blur*, a veritable industry, particularly big in Switzerland, with its engineers, technicians, and machinery. This is in obliviousness to, or should we say the fogging up or blotting out of (both possible equivalents for the word *blur*) that other material associated in a privileged way with the notion of built structure, steel. Paradoxically, as far as so-called primary materials go, priority was given, phenomenologically speaking, to the "cloud" element, with architecture succeeding where perspective failed, at least as far as Brunelleschi conceived it: I mean, contrary to Wittgenstein's assertion, by building a cloud, if not by building *in cloud*, as we speak of building in wood, in brick, in stone, in steel—or, to put it another way (without resorting to metaphor), by using cloud as a material with a structural application. This is something that seems to go without saying for steel, but once cloud is brought into play we are forced to rethink the concept of structure and, without actually rejecting it, to try to inject a bit of elasticity into it, its share of fuzziness—something that is, again, far from obvious. Blur has nothing of the poststructuralist about it and still less of the poststructural. However, insofar as an honorable role must be given to architecture in the genealogy of the very notion of structure, we have a right to expect that the sometimes unpredictable evolutionary mutations in building would be of consequence for the future of structural thought and affect its economy.

Now, do not misunderstand me: if in the circumstances one is justified in speaking of a "cloud building," then this is less in terms of construction or function than in relation to the play of opposition the /cloud/ element is caught up in, play with a patently symbolic dimension (by putting the word between slashes, I aim to set it up in the position of signifier). We saw this with Weston and his interest in both the walls and clouds that Mexico laid on so abundantly. In a similar vein, I would cite the wonderful book in which the biologist Henri Atlan attempted to explore the notion of system and the organization of the living being in reference to the two extreme poles constituted by crystal and smoke.[16] By way of anecdote or symptom, I might add my own amusing discovery, as I was strolling through the online library catalog of the Canadian Centre for Architecture, of a paper titled "Steel for Bridges," delivered at a meeting of the American Institute of Mining Engineers in Philadelphia in 1881 by a certain John W. Cloud.[17] That a name like John Cloud could have been worn by a man with a marked interest in steel construction I see as the index of a symbolic determination based on the same kind of structural opposition between steel and cloud that Diller + Scofidio wanted to play around with.

For myself, I can clearly see what fixed determinations the interest I felt from the outset in the Diller + Scofidio project complied with—to the point at which I accepted writing about it even before I saw it, walked through it, and "breathed" it—I mean,

14.7
Diller + Scofidio, Blur Building, Exposition Pavilion,
Swiss Expo, Yverdon-Les-Bains, 2002. Misty details
of Blur. Photo: Hubert Damisch.

14.8
Diller + Scofidio, Blur Building, Exposition Pavilion,
Swiss Expo, Yverdon-Les-Bains, 2002. Misty details of
Blur. Photo: Hubert Damisch.

beyond the beauty of the thing, which I would qualify as "pneumatic." This thing ("thing," I repeat, rather than object) is in fact located at the intersection of two of the principle axes of what I see as my work: on the one hand, the comparative approach of the fate, which I see as paradigmatic, of the sign or /cloud/ element in Western art and the art of the Far East, and on the other, the reflection on the specifically architectural determinations and resonances of structuralist thought as it was first systematically expressed by Viollet-le-Duc. If the architectural fiction conceived by Diller + Scofidio speaks to me, it is because it plays precisely on the articulation between these two apparently opposed, if not incompatible, axes of reflection.

5 Pavilions

As surprising as it was, the Diller + Scofidio project was not without echoes or precedents—from Mies van der Rohe, who wanted to *punch through the clouds* and whose facades actually have nothing of the shimmering about them, to Coop Himmelb(l)au, founded in 1968 with the desire to make "an architecture as floating and changing as the clouds,"[18] and, above all, to the Pepsi Pavilion for the International Fair at Osaka in 1970. This was a geodesic dome covered in an artificial fog created by Fujiko Nakaya, who treated it as a sculpture, as we would expect. If we look at Diller + Scofidio's gambit more closely, the deal remains no less drastic: not only, as the authors of *Blur* insist, are we not dealing here with a *built* fog, strictly speaking, the way the Coop Himmelb(l)au structures, hung out like "skies," could be said to be built, but also, more importantly, as sparkling as it was, the Pepsi Pavilion still adhered to the norm of a shelter firmly anchored to the ground and with the aim to serve as a theater for a whole series of performances and representations.[19]

Even though it has its place in the tradition of exhibition pavilions, the Blur does not fit into the tradition of provisional

14.9
Fujiko Nakaya, fog installation at E.A.T.'s Pepsi
Pavilion, Expo '70, Osaka. Photo: Skunk-Kender
© J. Paul Getty Trust. Getty Research Institute,
Los Angeles.

structures intended to serve as showcases for mercantile production, from the Crystal Palace to Melnikov's pavilion for the Paris Exhibition of Decorative Arts of 1925. Nor does it fit into the tradition of pavilions designed as so many advertising panels for one type or another of housing. Blur was certainly not inhabitable in the sense in which the villa-apartment block cell presented by Le Corbusier at the Esprit Nouveau Pavilion in 1925 was. Yet there most certainly was a proposition here that had something to do with the idea of an inhabitable place, a place where it would be good to breathe, and to breathe differently, by inhaling a different air, one charged with the purest of waters—in vaporized form. And if there was nothing really to exhibit or show here, then a person could still go to the bar upstairs to take the waters once more, this time as mineral water, still or sparkling, everything playing on the juncture of the two elements of water and air with nothing earthy muddying them.

The only other precedent for the project that I can come up with is the German Pavilion designed by Mies van de Rohe for the International Exhibition in Barcelona in 1929. Without being in any way nebulous, this pavilion broke its ties with the archetype of the house conceived as a cube and instead imposed the idea of an enclosure devoid of any linearity, as shown in the series of photographs of the reconstructed pavilion, now called the Barcelona Pavilion, presented in 2001 by Thomas Florschuetz under the title "Enclosures." Just as important, apart from a statue (*Evening*, by Georg Kolbe), the German Pavilion exhibited nothing other than itself, with the two Barcelona chairs that served for the reception of the royal couple during the opening ceremony just sitting there, empty, like an emblem of absence or of some endlessly deferred expectation.

A new and rare example of an exhibition pavilion with a strictly self-referential, not to say reflexive, purpose, Blur went one step further to the extent that self-exhibition was coupled with

14.10
Thomas Florschuetz, *Enclosure III*, 2001 (Barcelona).
© 2015 Artists Rights Society (ARS), New York/VG
Bild-Kunst, Bonn.

self-regulation in meteorological terms. Aside from the fact that strict economic considerations meant abandoning electronic media attractions such as underwater projections, the machine ultimately met the initial criteria of integrating the interactive concept of "media-architecture" under the title "cloud." The operation that aptly calls itself Blur is in effect the equivalent of a fable or fiction that one might describe as media based.

6   Architecture in Absentia

I have said how the idea of the cloud (cloud machine) was gradually replaced in Diller + Scofidio's discourse with the word *blur*, which can be read equally as either a noun or a verb. The noun denotes the effect produced by the strict conjunction of the steel structure and the fog that emanates from it, blotting out its contours, each linear element being coupled, so to speak, with its negation in actuality. (That it was necessary to double up the apparatus instead of getting the structure itself to produce the cloud could be seen as a flaw on the conceptual level, without this having much resonance on the phenomenal level.) The verb takes on the prestige of a performative: what Blur accomplished was merely the same as what it said or described.

In the manner in which the storm clouds that invaded vaults and cupolas in the baroque era fogged up the architectonic, the blurring of lines and of any overly precise volumetry results first if not in the dissolution then, at the very least, in the loosening of the ties that architecture might maintain with geometry—and perhaps in their transformation within the perspective of new geometries able to give the fuzzy its due alongside various effects of surface and texture, as already happens with shimmering.[20] Does this mean going as far as claiming it as a manifestation of a utopia—not of the absence of architecture, but a different kind of radical utopia, involving architecture in absentia, an "absent" architecture or one on the verge of absenting itself: an architecture in suspense, literally and figuratively, and all the more sophisticated in its operation and effect because all other forms of architecture were vying with each other to wipe it out? Curiously, the same Walter Gropius who made himself, at least in his writings, the apostle of a fluid and transparent architecture, yielded (in what we might describe as a critical moment in history) to the fantasy of an architecture that would work toward disguising itself, camouflaging itself, by drowning not in clouds but in the greenery. Holed up in London after having fled Nazi Germany, Gropius argued: "With the development of air transport, the architect will have to pay as much attention to the bird's-eye perspective of his houses as to their elevations. The utilization of flat roofs as 'grounds' offers us a means of re-acclimating nature amidst the stony deserts of our great towns; for the plots from which she has been evicted to make room for buildings can be given back to her up aloft. Seen from the skies, the leafy housetops of the cities of the future will look like endless chains of hanging gardens."[21]

These words have a peculiar resonance today, appealing to an experience of architecture seeking to escape the earthbound limits of the *promenade architecturale*, as well as those of gravity, and opening itself up to the sky. Certainly, there was no need to wait for the conquest of the air and the development of aerial navigation for the idea of a bird's-eye view of architectural forms to make itself felt; from three-dimensional models to axonometrical plotting, a certain distance had already been taken regarding frontal perception, the horizontal. What remained to be seen was to what extent such a view could be affected—not to say radically altered, if not foreclosed—in what was its very object by the attack on the World Trade Center. From now on, architecture would have to be considered as a potential target, exposed in its structure—if not its very being, in what it might contain of the provocative—to the most devastating assaults. That, at least, is what some critics would like to persuade us of, not missing an opportunity to shamelessly flaunt their hatred of density, the skyscraper, and building tall, which they hold partly responsible for the event at a symbolic level. It amounts to a singularly perverse form of rhetorical terror, one condemning thought, and one that should be categorically denounced.

7 A Chinese Fable?

No more than Gropius could imagine, while he was writing *The New Architecture and the Bauhaus*, that bombs would soon rain down and flatten the stony deserts of the great cities of Europe, could Diller + Scofidio have conceived Blur and the thick cloud that emanates from it in terms of target and camouflage. Putting aside the effect of context, we need to look elsewhere entirely, within a comparative perspective—one that is accordingly radically nonterrorist, which is enough to confer upon it, here and now, a strategic impact. The way in which architecture seems in this particular case to wipe itself out and cut its ties with the ground to enter into levitation is not in fact unrelated to the way Chinese painters of the Ming dynasty initially liked to represent palatial architecture as viewed in aerial perspective on a background of dense clouds, above which mountains seemed to float. The Jesuit father Matteo Ripa, from whom the emperor commanded a suite of engravings featuring one of his summer palaces—the art of engraving being then unknown in China—soon saw how he could turn this to his advantage:[22] the empty area, left blank, to which the white cloud cover is reduced as it stretches from one side of the paper to the other over a view of a few pleasure pavilions, corresponds (in its function as sheer spacing) to one of the most constant features of Chinese landscape painting—in anticipation of the new genre of the architectural view, invaded by a stream of thick clouds that drown out or partly dissolve contours and from which emerge the high, curved roofs

Sei chi guon in. Gran pietra che guarda i pesci = Gajineta recreazione fabricate sora un bel pezzo di monte—

14.11
Matteo Ripa, engraver, after Shên Yü, *Gran pietra che guarda i pesci (Watching the fish from a rocky outcrop)*, 1713. Copper-plate engraving on paper. From an album of views of the Chinese imperial palaces and gardens at Jehol in Manchuria. DR1981:0072:015, Collection Centre Canadien d'Architecture/Canadian Centre for Architecture, Montréal.

characteristic of Chinese architecture as though floating at the surface of the clouds or flying above them, as mountains used to do in the Song dynasty. These same roofs have been seen by some as the image of the totemic bird of the Shang dynasty (c. 1600–1046 BCE),[23] itself partly mythical; as Oswald Siren, one of the first great Western connoisseurs of Chinese painting, as well as Chinese architecture, put it, they seem "to soar over the colonnades."[24]

If we take a closer look at one such view of the Forbidden City in Peking during the Ming era, we note that, apart from the golden clouds in which architecture is absent or dissolves, the gap between the rim of the roofs and the beams that serve as architraves is itself filled by what looks like packing or cotton of a different color, here bluish, resembling curling clouds and justifying the comparison between the two types of structures and between the effects they each lend themselves to. If building in wood as it has been practiced in China for over 3,000 years was based on the combination of columns and beams, then it did not proceed by stacking along the lines of the Greek temple, but by the use of stress—the same as the steel structure that formed the foundation for Blur. As Siren further notes, the beams did not rest on the columns but went straight through them, or were fixed to them by notches and pegs, without the use of any nails— these being reserved for other uses considered permanent, such as sealing caskets—while offering the external appearance of an architrave connecting the whole colonnade, itself reduced (conceptually speaking) to the subordinate function of simple support.[25] In big buildings, the architrave sometimes seemed to rest on brackets (*lianzhu dou*) attached to the columns, but what comprised the actual system of brackets—one of the main articulations of Chinese architecture—sat above the architrave to support the lower purlins of the roofing while introducing extra distance between the architrave and the main beams. Later,

14.12
Detail from *Palace City in Beijing*, Ming Dynasty,
Museum of Chinese History.

these brackets were multiplied with gay abandon, not only directly above the posts but all along the architrave. They were sometimes packed so closely together that they themselves came to look like cornices. Siren concludes, "They [the brackets] lose their function and become pure ornament, a sort of beard beneath the roof."

What is important, within a comparative perspective, is that not only the brackets (reduced for the most part to a supposedly decorative function) but also the blocks (*tuofeng*) themselves, placed at the end of one beam to support the next beam, came to look like clouds or lotus flowers in the Ming and Qin dynasties. Siren feels compelled to remark, "Parts are used that no longer have any material reason for being and that disguise the true building processes. The forms are the same as before but no longer make much sense." This is so much the case for Siren that he finds that whereas the wood architecture of Ancient China had the principal merit of being eminently logical and appropriate to its ends, as it was guided by the laws of the material used, it then lost what amounted to its immemorial soul when the original building principles began to be eclipsed by what he calls "decorative tendencies." The only problem is that if there were decorative tendencies, then these accorded in every way with the tenets that were, on Siren's own admission, those of Chinese architecture of the golden age: "At the peak of its evolution, the roofing seems freed from its support, for the more it juts out from the building, the deeper the patches of shade that set it apart." Far from being deprived of meaning or being reduced to a simple, inconsequential ornament, the "cloud" as decorative motif would thus rather have overdone its active obliteration of all articulation between walls and roof, these being separated from each other by simple spacing—which is what the construction itself tended toward from the outset.

a

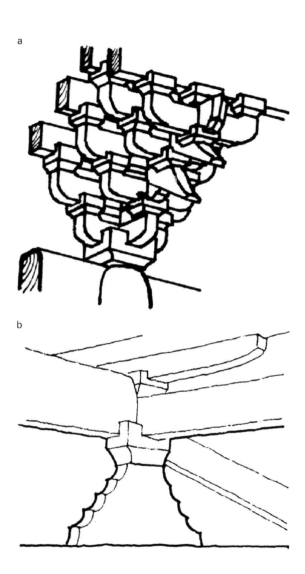

b

14.13a, b
Elaborate systems of brackets support the roofs
of Chinese pavilions. Courtesy the author.

The reading Siren proposes of the evolution of building in wood is a good example of the functionalist ideology then reigning even within the field of archeology. I have said elsewhere how much this ideology, which found its most complete expression at the time in Viollet-le-Duc's *Lectures on Architecture*, seems to me beside the point when compared to the strictly structuralist inspiration of the *Dictionnaire raisonné de l'architecture française*—with the result that, on the conceptual plane, a marked opposition is set up between structure and decor, the latter routinely seen as a mask or veil thrown over constructive reality. Hence the importance of Diller + Scofidio's discourse: here, it is no longer a matter of disguising or camouflaging the structure but of somehow getting it to levitate. In the case of Blur, the attempt was helped by the fact that the authors stuck obstinately to the notion of a structure set on the water and apparently cut loose from all anchorage.

It is not going too far to say that nothing could be more opposed to the moral we might draw from the somewhat Chinese fable dreamed up by Diller + Scofidio than sticking to the categories inherited from art history and considering the cloud that emanated from the structure and blurred its contours as a superfluous detail, a bit of decor or ornament. If there was an added element, then it formed an integral part of the structure in the sense already described—in which the structure only made sense by producing the addition (the "supplement," in Derrida's terms) in order, in turn, to disappear into it. This fits perfectly with the remarks of Robert Smithson, whose catoptric excursions into the Yucatán I took care to evoke earlier: "Contrary to affirmations of nature, art is inclined to semblances and masks. . . . Only appearances are fertile; they are gateways to the primordial. Every artist owes his existence to such mirages. The ponderous illusions of solidity, the non-existence of things, is what the artist takes as 'materials.' It is this absence of matter that weighs so heavy on him, inciting him to invoke gravity." Further, to finally dispose of the problematic of the media (but not with that of the medium): "Artists are not motivated by a need to communicate; travel over the unfathomable is the only condition."[26]

The reference to Chinese architecture is intended to highlight the quality of a centuries-old architecture that had no real permanence and which would wipe itself out without leaving any ruins. This just happens to correspond to one of the purest and least contestable seams of the modernist heritage. Siren remarked further that the only lasting architecture China ever produced was the Great Wall, the sharpness of the contour that gave its shape, its figure, to the *Empire du milieu* having in no way been corroded by history. *To travel over the unfathomable*: Being dismountable and having shed all terrestrial foundations, the cloud machine was no less a thing of great beauty—a beauty connected in some strange way, in its radiance, to the image given to the concept by another Ripa (Cesare, this time) in his *Iconologia* of 1593. For Ripa, beauty was a woman undressed, with her head lost in a thick cloud of ovoid shape. He writes, "There is nothing as hard to talk about in a mortal language; it cannot be looked at without our being dazzled."[27] Nor, I would add, without our being affected in our corporeal, physiological being. I have spoken, still in relation to Blur, about a kind of "pneumatic" beauty (from the Greek *pneuma*, meaning "breath"): The pleasure, both physical and spiritual, we felt in passing through this fog that seemed to have no density, only to emerge here and there into the open air, could only be compared to the feeling of the first aviators navigating among the clouds, out in the open sky. A pleasure that was not only optical in nature but, indeed, was pneumatic, proceeding from what used to be called the revolutions of the "breath" in Chinese aesthetics: revolutions that were not reduced to nebulous or vaporous effects but which could manifest themselves just as well, as the scholar painters insisted, in a brushstroke

14.14
Diller + Scofidio, Blur Building, Exposition Pavilion,
Swiss Expo, Yverdon-Les-Bains, 2002. Breathing in
Blur. Courtesy Diller Scofidio + Renfro.

and its evanescence, its blurring, if not its effacement, seen as constructive in terms of structure, just as in the fable delivered in Blur, all the more ineffaceable in that it was entirely fictional.

NOTES

INTRODUCTION

1. Hubert Damisch and Stephen Bann, "Hubert Damisch and Stephen Bann: A Conversation,"*Oxford Art Journal* 28, no. 2 (2005): 159.

2. Jacques Derrida, "Structure, Sign, and Play," in *Writing and Difference*, trans. Alan Bass (Chicago: University of Chicago Press, 1978), 280.

3. Ibid.

4. Yve-Alain Bois, Denis Hollier, Rosalind Krauss, and Hubert Damisch, "A Conversation with Hubert Damisch,"*October* 85 (Summer 1998): 3–4.

5. Ibid., 8.

6. Hubert Damisch, *The Origin of Perspective*, trans. John Goodman (Cambridge, MA: MIT Press, 1994), 446; *L'Origine de la perspective*, 1987.

7. Hubert Damisch, preface to *De Ledoux à Le Corbusier: Origins et développement de l'architecture autonome*, by Emil Kaufmann (Paris: Éditions l'Équerre, 1981), 20. Translated and published in this volume as "Ledoux with Kant."

8. Damisch, *The Origin of Perspective*, 446.

PROLOGUE: NOAH'S ARK

1. Jacques-François Blondel, "Architecture," in *Encyclopédie, ou Dictionnaire raisonné des sciences, des arts et des métiers*, vol. 1, ed. Denis Diderot and Jean Le Rond d'Alembert (Paris, 1751), 617.

2. Ibid.

3. "Modern," in *Encyclopédie*, vol. 10 (Paris, 1765): 601.

4. Blondel, "Architecture," in *Encyclopédie*, vol. 1 (Paris, 1751), 617.

5. Karl Marx and Friedrich Engels, *Les luttes de classes en France, 1848–1850: Le 18 brumaire de Louis Bonaparte*, trans. Gérard Cornillet (Paris: Éditions sociales, 1948), 173. Translated from the German by Eden Paul and Cedar Paul as *The Eighteenth Brumaire of Louis Bonaparte* (New York: International Publishers, 1926).

6. Blondel, "Architecture," in *Encyclopédie*, vol. 1 (Paris, 1751), 617.

7. Ibid.

8. Ibid.; emphasis in original.

9. Ibid.

10. Ibid.

11. Leo Strauss, *Droit naturel et histoire*, trans. Monique Nathan and Eric de Dampierre (Paris: Éditions Plon, 1949). Originally published in English as *Natural Right and History* (Chicago: University of Chicago Press, 1953).

12. Eugène-Emmanuel Viollet-le-Duc, *Entretiens sur l'architecture*, vol. 1 (Paris: Q. Morel, 1863), 175. Translated by Henry Van Brunt as *Discourses on Architecture* (Boston: J. R. Osgood, 1875).

13. Blondel, "Architecture," in *Encyclopédie*, vol. 1 (Paris, 1751), 617.

14. "Proportion," in *Encyclopédie*, vol. 3 (Paris, 1765), 468.

15. Ibid.

16. Ibid.

17. Daniele Barbaro, in Vitruvius, *I dieci libri dell'architettura* (Venice, 1556), quoted in Rudolf Wittkower, *Architectural Principles in the Age of Humanism*, 2nd ed. (London: A. Tiranti, 1952), 64.

18. Plato, *Republic*, 10.602d.

19. See Pierre-Maxime Schuhl, *Platon et l'art de son temps (arts plastiques)*, 2nd ed. (Paris: F. Alcan, 1952).

20. See Erwin Panofsky, *Perspective as Symbolic Form*, trans. Christopher S. Wood (New York: Zone Books, 1991).

21. Blondel, "Architecture," in *Encyclopédie*, vol. 1 (Paris, 1751), 617.

22. "Composition," in *Encyclopédie*, vol. 3 (Paris, 1753), 769.

23. "Construction," in *Encyclopédie*, vol. 4 (Paris, 1754), 92.

24. Ibid., 4:94.

25. Blondel, "Architecture," in *Encyclopédie*, vol. 1 (Paris, 1751), 617. *Architectus* is from the Greek *arkitekton*, with the sense of architect, builder, and (more particularly) engineer specializing in naval building. See Aristotle, *Metaphysics*, 1.1.ii.

26. Abbé Edme-François Mallet, "Arche," in *Encyclopédie*, vol. 1 (Paris, 1751), 607.

27. Ibid.

28. Le Corbusier, *Toward an Architecture*, trans. John Goodman (Los Angeles: Getty Research Institute, 2007), 153. Originally published as *Vers une architecture* (Paris: Éditions G. Crès, 1923), 75.

29. Le Corbusier, *Toward an Architecture*, 156–157; *Vers une architecture*, 78–79.

30. Le Corbusier, *Toward an Architecture*, 158; *Vers une architecture*, 80.

31. See Roland de Vaux and Bernard Couroyer, *La Genèse* (Paris: Éditions du cerf, 1952), 57, note b.

32. De Vaux and Couroyer, *La Genèse*, 58, note c.

33. Le Corbusier, preface to *Précisions sur un État présent de l'architecture et de l'urbanisme* (Paris: G Crès, 1929), v. Translated by Edith Schreiber Aujame as *Precisions on the Present State of Architecture and City Planning* (Cambridge, MA: MIT Press, 1991).

34. André Masson, quoted in Manfredo Tafuri, *Teoria e storia dell'architettura* (Rome: Laterza, 1973), 111. Translated by Giorgio Verrecchia as *Theories and History of Architecture* (New York: Harper & Row, 1980).

35. See Reyner Banham, *Theory and Design in the First Machine Age* (Oxford: Butterworth Architecture, 1960), 166.

36. See Carmine Benincasa, *Architettura come dis-identità: Teoria delle catastrofi e architettura* (Bari: Dedalo libri, 1978).

37. Le Corbusier, *When Cathedrals Were White: A Journey to the Country of Timid People*, trans. Francis E. Hyslop Jr. (New York: Reynal & Hitchcock, 1947). Originally published as *Quand les cathédrales Étaient blanches* (Paris: Éditions Plon, 1937), 3.

38. See Peter Sloterdijk, *Im selben Boot: Versuch über die Hyperpolitik* (Frankfurt: Suhrkamp, 1993).

1   AUJOURD'HUI, L'ARCHITECTURE

1. Le Corbusier, *Vers une architecture* (Paris: Éditions G. Crès, 1923). Translated by John Goodman as *Toward an Architecture* (Los Angeles: Getty Research Institute, 2007).

2. See Paul Valéry, "Eupalinos, ou l'architecte" (1923), in *Œuvres*, vol. 2 (Paris: Gallimard, 1960). Translated by William McCausland Stewart as *Eupalinos; or, The Architect* (London: Oxford University Press, 1932).

3. G. W. F. Hegel, *Aesthetics: Lectures on Fine Art*, vol. 2, trans. T. M. Knox (Oxford: Clarendon Press, 1975), 636.

4. Samuel Beckett, *Waiting for Godot*, act II. [In the English script, Estragon says "Critic!" not "architect."]

5. René Descartes, *Discourse on Method*, trans. John Veitch (New York: Cosimo, 2008), 17 [translation modified].

6. Plato, *Timaeus*, 29a–30b.

7. Plato, *Philibus*, 55d–56c.

8. Hegel, *Aesthetics*, 2:624.

9. Claude Lévi-Strauss, *Structural Anthropology*, trans. Claire Jacobson and Brooke Schoepf (New York: Basic Books: 1963), 69 [translation modified].

10. See Maurice Merleau-Ponty, *L'œil et l'esprit* (Paris: Gallimard, 1964), 9ff

11. Johannes Kepler, dedication to the first edition of *Mysterium Cosmographicum* (Tübingen, 1596), quoted in Werner Heisenberg, *The Physicist's Conception of Nature*, trans. Arnold J. Pomerans (London: Hutchinson, 1958), 74.

12. Kepler, *Mysterium Cosmographicum*, chapter 2, 23; quoted in Heisenberg, *The Physicist's Conception of Nature*, 79.

13. Plato, *The Sophist*, 265c.

14. Philibert de l'Orme, *Le Premier tome de l'architecture*, 2nd ed. (Paris, 1569), fol. 2v.

15. Kepler, *Mysterium Cosmographicum*, quoted in Gérard Simon, *Kepler: Astronome, astrologue* (Paris: Gallimard, 1979), 406.

16. Valéry, "Histoire d'Amphion," in *Œuvres*, 2:1277–1283.

17. Kepler, *Mysterium Cosmographicum*, quoted in Simon, *Kepler*, 406.

18. Valéry, "Eupalinos," in *Œuvres*, 2:93.

19. Johannes Kepler, *The Harmony of the World*, trans. A. M. Duncan, (Philadelphia: American Philosophical Society, 1997), book 4, chapter 1, 304.

20. See Yvon Belaval, "Une drôle de pensée de Leibniz,"*Nouvelle Revue Française*, no. 70 (October 1958): 754–768.

21. The first edition of Vicenzo Scamozzi's treatise *Dell'idea dell'architettura universale*, which was published in Venice in 1615, is located at the turning point between two ages of theory: the Renaissance, which it appears to close, and the classical age, which it opens—the "idea" of an architecture being less im-

portant (the term is already to be found in Zuccaro and in Lomazzo) than the assertion of its universality.

22. "The structures are not immutable, either in their number or in their form; it is quite possible that the further development of mathematics will augment the number of fundamental structures by revealing the fecundity of new axioms, or of new combinations of axioms. We may take it for granted that there will be decisive progress in the *inventions* of structures, to judge by those which have produced the structures presently known. Of course, the latter are by no means completed buildings, and it would be very surprising if the full essence of their principles was already exhausted. Thus with the aid of these indispensable qualifications one can better understand the internal vitality of mathematics, that which gives it both unity and diversity; like a great city whose suburbs never cease to grow in a somewhat chaotic fashion on the surrounding lands, while its center is periodically reconstructed, each time following a clearer plan and a more majestic arrangement, demolishing the old sections with their labyrinthine alleys in order to launch new avenues toward the periphery, always more direct, wider and more convenient." Nicolas Bourbaki, "The Architecture of Mathematics," in *Great Currents of Mathematical Thought*, ed. François Le Lionnais, vol. 2, *Mathematics: Concepts and Development*, trans. Charles Pinter and Helen Kline (New York: Dover Publications, 1971), 34 [translation modified]. Note the extent to which, thirty years later, Bourbaki's language shows itself to be dated, and sympathetic, even in its handling of metaphor, to a concept of urbanism that (for now) is no longer accepted.

23. Ferdinand de Saussure, *Course in General Linguistics*, trans. Roy Harris (La-Salle, IL: Open Court Publishing Company, 1983), 176.

24. Vitruvius, *De Architettura*, book 2, chapter 8.

25. Maurice Merleau-Ponty, *Signs*, trans. Ricahrd C. McCleary (Evanston, IL: Northwestern University Press, 1964), 39 [translation modified].

26. Pierre Francastel, "Note sur l'emploi du mot 'structure' en Histoire de l'art," in *Sens et usage du terme structure sans les sciences humaines et sociales*, ed. Roger Bastide (The Hague: Mouton, 1972).

27. Immanuel Kant, *Critique of Judgment*, trans. James Creed Meredith, rev. Nicholas Walker (Oxford: Oxford University Press, 2007), 151.

28. Saussure, *Course in General Linguistics*, 122.

29. Ibid., 131.

30. Ibid., 128.

31. "In tota re aedificatoria primarium certe ornamentum in columnis est." Leon Battista Alberti, *De re aedificatoria* (Florence, 1486), 6.13.

32. Hegel, *Aesthetics*, 2:641ff.

33. "Et perpetuam muri partem." Alberti, *De re aedificatoria*, 1.10.

34. Hegel, *Aesthetics*, 2:668.

35. Ibid., 2:671.

36. Le Corbusier, *Toward an Architecture*, 220.

2 THE COLUMN, THE WALL

1. See Eugène-Emmanuel Viollet-le Duc, *Entretiens sur l'architecture* (Paris: Q. Morel, 1863–1872), 2:13.

2. "The whole matter of building is composed of lineaments and structure." Leon Battista Alberti, *De re aedificatoria* (Florence, 1486), 1.1.3. Translated by Joseph Rykwert, Neil Leach, and Robert Tavernor as *On the Art of Building in Ten Books* (Cambridge, MA: MIT Press, 1991), 7.

3. See Vitruvius, *De architectura*, 2.8.

4. See Anthony Blunt, *Artistic Theory in Italy, 1450–1600* (London: Oxford University Press, 1962), 6.

5. See Erik Forsmann, *Säule und Ornament: Studien zum Problem des Manierismus in den nordischen Säulenbüchern und Vorlageblättern des 16 und 17 Jahrhunderts* (Stockholm: Almqvist & Wiksell, 1956), 46.

6. "Render a toutes choses les propres raisons concernantes les matiere." Leon Battista Alberti, *L'architecture et art de bien bastir*, trans. Jean Martin (Paris: J. Kerver, 1553), fol. 101.

7. See Rudolf Wittkower, "Alberti's Approach to Antiquity in Architecture," in *Architectural Principles in the Age of Humanism* (London: A. Tiranti, 1952), 33–56.

8. "In tota re aedificatoria primarium certe ornamentum in columnis est." Alberti, *De re aedificatoria*, 6.13.94; Alberti, *On the Art of Building*, 183. "Tum et tota in re aedificatoria nihil invenes quod opera et impensa et gratia praeferas

columnis." Alberti, *De re aedificatoria*, 1.10.13; Alberti, *On the Art of Building*, 25.

9. See Marcel Reymond, *Brunelleschi et l'architecture de la renaissance italienne au XVième siècle* (Paris: H. Laurens, 1912), 6ff.

10. Alberti, *De re aedificatoria*, 7.10.13; Alberti, *On the Art of Building*, 219.

11. Alberti, *De re aedificatoria*, 10.17.

12. "Quando ipsi ordines columnarum haud aliud sunt quam pluribus in locis perfixus ad apertusque paries." Alberti, *De re aedificatoria*, 1.10.13.

13. Compare, for example, the classical connection between the façade of Santa Maria Novella and that of San Miniato-al-Monte. See Wittkower, *Architectural Principles*, 34–37.

14. "Arcuatis imitationibus debentur columnae quadrangulae. Nam in rotundis opus erit mendosum ea re quod capita arcus non ad plenum in solido columnae substitutae assideant." Alberti, *De re aedificatoria*, 7.15.113; Alberti, *On the Art of Building*, 236.

15. See Wittkower, *Architectural Principles*, 36.

16. See Guilio-Carlo Argan, *Brunelleschi* (Milan: A. Mondadori, 1955), 76–77.

17. See Alois Riegl, *Die Entstehung der Barockkunst in Rom*, ed. Arthur Burda and Max Dvořák (Vienna: A. Schroll, 1908), 44–45; and Rudolf Wittkower, "Michelangelo's Biblioteca Laurenziana," *Art Bulletin* 16 (1934): 113–218.

18. Johann Wolfgang von Goethe, *Italian Journey, 1786–1788*, trans. W. H. Auden and Elizabeth Mayer (Harmondsworth: Penguin Books, 1962), 64.

19. "Parietem dicimus omnem structuram quae a solo in altum surrexit ad ferendem onus tectorem." Alberti, *De re aedificatoria*, 1.2.3–4.

20. An analysis attentive to the vocabulary used by Alberti's successive translators would illustrate the gradual expansion of the semantic field of the concept "structure" from the fifteenth century on. Jean Martin sticks fairly closely to the Latin terminology, whereas James Leoni (who produced the English translation of 1726) systematically translates the word *structura* as "work," or more simply as "wall," reserving the term "structure" for the figure, form, or plan of a building, and even for the building itself ("the whole structure") or for a certain type of building (e.g., "public structures," the temple regarded as "the most honorable structure," etc.).

21. See Paul-Henri Michel, *Un idéal humain au XVième siècle: La Pensée de L. B. Alberti* (Paris: Belles Lettres, 1930), 98–139.

22. "Edificare, non plasmare." See Maria-Luisa Gengaro, "L'architettura romana nella interpretazione teorica di Leon-Battista Alberti,"*Bollettino del Reale Istitutto di Archeologia e Storia dell'Arte* 9 (1941): 37–42.

23. See Wittkower, "Michelangelo's Biblioteca Laurenziana," 214.

24. Alberti, *De re aedificatoria*, 7.11.

25. Alberti, *De re aedificatoria*, 3.6; Alberti, *On the Art of Building*, 69.

26. "Sed corticis infarcinamentorunque inter se ratio pro structurae varietate varia est." Alberti, *De re aedificatoria*, 3.6.36.

27. "Sunt et inter primarias parietum partes uel in primis praecipuie anguli et insertae conceptaeque seu pilae, seu columnae, seu quid uis istiusmodi: quod qui dem substinendis trabeationibus arcubusque, tectorum illic columnarum sunt loco: quae omnia appellatione ossium ueniunt." Alberti, *De re aedificatoria*, 3.6.36.

28. "Quae autem inter has primarias partes intercurrunt atque extenduntur, recte complementa nuncupabantur." Alberti, *De re aedificatoria*, 3.6.36.

29. Alberti, *De re aedificatoria*, 1.10.

30. Ibid., 3.12.

31. Ibid., 3.8.

32. Ibid., 2.10.

33. "Quin et columnam ipsam diffinisse cum iuvet, fortassis non ineptae esse eam dicam firmam quamdam et perpetuam muri partem excitatam ad perpendiculum ab solo, immo usque ad summum tecti ferendi gratia." Alberti, *De re aedificatoria*, 1.10; Alberti, *On the Art of Building*, 25.

34. Alberti, *De re aedificatoria*, 1.12.

35. Ibid.

36. "Sunt et apertionum stantia hinc atque lic labra: quae angulorum columnarumque insimul natura sapient." Alberti, *De re aedificatoria*, 3.6.

37. "Nam esse arcum quidem non aliud quam deflexam trabem: et trabem quid aliud quam in transversum positam columnam." Alberti, *De re aedificatoria*, 3.6; Alberti, *On the Art of Building*, 69.

38. "Arcum dicimus trabem esse flexam." Alberti, *De re aedificatoria*, 3.13.

39. Alberti, *De re aedificatoria*, 1.5.

40. Ibid., 10.17.

41. Alberti, *De re aedificatoria*, 10.16; Alberti, *On the Art of Building*, 359.

42. "Appingentur praeterea ornamenti gratia atque item utilitatis ad parietem supra coronas primas aliae insuper columnae maximae quadrangulae: quae in substitutas primarias columnas mediis centris acquiescant. Nam confert quidem quod feruata ossium soliditate et aucta operis honestate pondus atque impensa parietis maxima ex parte leuigabitur." Alberti, *De re aedificatoria*, 7.15.114.

43. Philibert de l'Orme, *Le Premier tome de l'Architecture*, 1.8, quoted in Viollet-le-Duc, *Entretiens*, 1:365.

44. "Ordines ordinibus crebis traductis kapidum nexuris coadjugato." Alberti, *De re aedificatoria*, 3.11. "De illinendo pariete." Alberti, *De re aedificatoria*, 3.11.61; Alberti, *On the Art of Building*, 77.

45. Alberti, *De re aedificatoria*, 1.10; Alberti, *On the Art of Building*, 25.

46. "Insigne urbis ornamentum extare ubi civium copiam." Alberti, *De re aedificatoria*, 7.1.96.

47. Even before the fifteenth century, as P. H. Michel opportunely reminds us, "grammar" had started to free itself from the logic of extended meaning and to look at the word no longer as the immutable sign of an idea but as a provisional approximation. Alberti himself was extremely interested in the linguistic renaissance distinguished by the names of Lorenzo Vallan Decembrio and others—so much so that he played an active role in it and devoted a treatise to it, now lost. See Michel, *Un ideal humain*, 150ff.

48. See Leon Battista Alberti, *De pictura/On Painting*, bilingual Italian/English edition, ed. Martin Kemp, trans. Cecil Grayson (London: Penguin, 1991).

49. See the first plan for San Sebastiano (Mantua, 1460), as reconstructed in Wittkower, *Architectural Principles*, 52, fig.7.

3   COMPOSING WITH PAINTING

1. Leon Battista Alberti, *De pictura/Della pittura*, bilingual Latin/Italian edition, ed. Cecil Grayson (Rome: Laterza, 1975), 8. Translated by Cecil Grayson and edited by Martin Kemp as *De pictura/On Painting*, bilingual Italian/English edition (London: Penguin Classics, 1991), 35.

2. Alberti, *De pictura*, 2.26; Alberti, *On Painting*, 61.

3. Alberti, *De pictura*, 2.26; Alberti, *On Painting*, 61.

4. "In tota re aedificatoria primarium certe ornamentum in columnis est." Leon Battista Alberti, *De re aedificatoria* (Florence, 1486), 6.13. Translated into Italian by Giovanni Orlandi as *L'architettura* (Milan: Edizioni Il Polifilo, 1966), 2:521. Translated into English by Joseph Rykwert, Neil Leach, and Robert Tavernor as *On the Art of Building in Ten Books* (Cambridge, MA: MIT Press, 1991), 183.

5. See Alberti, *De re aedificatoria*, 6.2.

6. Alberti, *De re aedificatoria*, 6.2; Alberti, *On the Art of Building*, 156. Quoted and commented on by Françoise Choay, *La Règle et le modèle* (Paris: Éditions du Seuil, 1980), 116. Translated as *The Rule and the Model*, ed. Denise Bratton (Cambridge, MA: MIT Press, 1997), 91.

7. See Jacques Derrida, *Of Grammatology*, trans. Gayatry Chakravorty Spivak (Baltimore: Johns Hopkins University Press, 1976), 145.

8. Alberti, *De pictura*, 2.30.

9. Ibid., 2.31.

10. Ibid., 2.33.

11. Ibid., 2.38.

12. Alberti, *De re aedificatoria*, prologue, fol. 1.

13. Ibid., 1.9.

14. See Peter Eisenman, *Fin d'Ou T Hou S* (London: Architectural Association, 1985), fol. 4.

15. Alberti, *De pictura*, 3.55; Alberti, *On Painting*, 89 [translation modified]. For more on this, see Hubert Damisch, *A Theory of the Cloud: Toward a History of Painting*, trans. Janet Lloyd (Stanford: Stanford University Press, 2002), 116–117.

16. See Alberti, *De re aedificatoria*, 7.7. For advocates of cement, the molding will constitute one of the stumbling blocks of modernity, while at the same time it will be, for them, situated at the junction between construction and architecture, with the obligatory reference to the idea of composition: "Contour modulation leaves the practical man, the bold man, the ingenious man behind; it calls for the plastic artist." Le Corbusier, *Toward an Architecture*, trans. John Goodman (Los Angeles: Getty Research Institute, 2007), 247. "La science de la modénature a disparu en même temps que celle de l'architecture. Actuel-

lement, les recherches de construction et d'organisation occupent entière-
ment l'esprit de l'architecte; de plus, la science de la composition est si égarée
que seuls les problèmes plastiques principaux ont pu, jusqu'aujourd'hui, être
étudiés et résolus de manière satisfaisante." [The science of contour modulation has disappeared at the same time as the science of architecture. These
days, construction and organization research occupies the architect's mind
entirely; moreover, the science of composition is so far lost that only the central plastic problems have been able, untill now, to be studied and resolved
in a satisfying manner]. André Lurçat, *Architecture* (Paris: Sans pareil, 1929),
170.

17. See Derrida, *Of Grammatology*, 295.

18. See James Leoni, trans., *The Architecture of Leon Battista Alberti in Ten Books*
(London, 1726), 143.

19. On the column considered as a bone, see "The Column, the Wall," chapter 2,
this volume.

20. See Ferdinand de Saussure, *Course in General Linguistics*, trans. Roy Harris (London: Bloomsbury Academic, 2013), 145. Times change; we now talk
about *paradigmatic* relationships, whereas Saussure referred to *associative*
relationships.

21. For more on this, see Hubert Damisch, *The Origin of Perspective*, trans. John
Goodman (Cambridge, MA: MIT Press, 1995).

22. See Rudolf Wittkower, "Brunelleschi and 'Proportion in Perspective,'"*Journal
of the Warburg and Courtauld Institutes* 16, no. 3/4 (1953): 275–291; reprinted
in Rudolf Wittkower, *Idea and Image: Studies in the Italian Renaissance*, ed.
Margo Wittkower (New York: Thames and Hudson, 1978), 125–136.

23. See Jacques Derrida, *Edmund Husserl's Origin of Geometry: An Introduction*,
trans. John P. Leavey Jr. (Stony Brook, NY: N. Hays, 1978). Also see Damisch,
The Origin of Perspective, 95.

24. Alberti, *De re aedificatoria*, 2.1; Alberti, *On the Art of Building*, 34. On the notion
of "architecture in perspective" as developed by Jacques-François Blondel in
the entry on "Architecture" in the *Encyclopédie*, see "Prologue: Noah's Ark,"
this volume.

25. Alberti, *De re aedificatoria*, 1.1; Alberti, *On the Art of Building*, 7.

26. See Choay, *The Rule and the Model*, 95n109.

4 PERRAULT'S COLONNADE AND THE FUNCTIONS OF THE CLASSICAL ORDER

1. "Registre ou Journal des délibérations et résolutions touchant les bâtiments du roi," compiled by Claude Perrault (April–May 1667), in *Description historique de la ville de Paris et de ses environs*, by Jean-Aimar Pigagniol de la Force, vol. 2 (Paris, 1765), 260.

2. See Michel Foucault, "Order," in *The Order of Things: An Archaeology of the Human Sciences* (New York: Pantheon Books, 1971), 50–57.

3. Claude Perrault, ed. and trans., *Les dix livres d'architecture de Vitruve* (Paris: 1673), 98n1.

4. Vicenzo Scamozzi, quoted in Perrault, *Les dix livres d'architecture de Vitruve*, 37n2.

5. Perrault, *Les dix livres d'architecture de Vitruve*, 9.

6. See Louis Hautecœur, *L'histoire des châteaux du Louvre et des Tuileries* (Paris: Van Oest, 1927), 171–174.

7. See Jean-François Blondel, *Architecture française*, vol. 4 (Paris: 1756), 54.

8. "A royal palace should be sited in the city center, should be of easy access, and should be gracefully decorated, elegant, and refined, rather than ostentatious. But that of a tyrant, being a fortress rather than a house, should be positioned where it is neither inside nor outside the city. . . . An appropriate and useful guideline, which will lend the building dignity, will be to construct it in such a way that, if a royal palace, it should not be so large that it is impossible to throw out any troublemaker, or, if a fortress, not so constricted that it resembles a prison more than the apartment of a fine prince." Leon Battista Alberti, *De re aedificatoria* (Florence, 1486), 5.3. Translated by Joseph Rykwert, Neil Leach, and Robert Tavernor as *On the Art of Building* (Cambridge, MA: MIT Press, 1991), 121–122.

9. "Nunquam fuit multitudo non referta malis ingeniis." Alberti, *De re aedificatoria*, 5.4; Alberti, *On the Art of Building*, 122–123.

10. "[Bernini] created the loggias so that the King could go up and down in a closed carriage, which made them into places where troublemakers could hide behind the columns he made to support the vestibule." Paul Fréart de Chantelou, *Journal du voyage du Cavalier Bernin en France* (Paris, 1885), 85. As Colbert noted, "It is necessary to take careful note that, in the seditious times

that almost always occur in the ghettos, not only can kings be secure but the quality of their palace may serve to hold the people to the obedience they owe" (Colbert, quoted in Hautecœur, *L'histoire des châteaux*, 155).

11. Perrault, *Les dix livres d'architecture de Vitruve*, 70n1.

12. See the plans published in André Chastel and Jean-Marie Pérouse de Montclos, "L'aménagement de l'accès oriental du Louvre,"*Monuments historiques de la France* 12, no. 3 (July–September 1966): 176–249.

13. Legrand and Landon, who witnessed the opening up of new windows under Napoléon I, report that they "found fully built and arched bay windows and the masonry for the niches that replaced them, formed of light partitions. . . . We cannot quite divine the reasons that prompted Perrault to do away with [the windows]. Perhaps he realized too late that they did not correspond to those of the interior of the courtyard. Or perhaps he thought that in closing them up he would give his peristyle more tranquility." Hautecœur, *L'histoire des châteaux*, 175. According to Hautecœur, it is likely that Perrault was hoping to imitate the blank walls of antique temples at the back of his peristyle. But again, is that really a peristyle?

14. See Blondel, *Architecture française*, 4:25. As a lithograph of Baltard's shows, a provisional gallery was set up on the edge of the Cour Carré, in Year IX of the Republic, to house the exhibition of the products of industry.

15. Perrault, preface to *Les dix livres d'architecture de Vitruve*, viii.

5 THE SPACE BETWEEN

1. Eugène-Emmanuel Viollet-le-Duc, "Restauration," in *Dictionnaire raisonné de l'architecture française du XIe au XVIe siècle* (Paris: Bance, 1854–1868), 8:14–34.

2. Victor Hugo, "Note Added to the Definitive Edition (1832),"*Notre-Dame de Paris*, trans. A. J. Krailsheimer (Oxford: Oxford University Press, 1999), 8–11.

3. See Pol Abraham, *Viollet-le-Duc et le rationalisme médiéval* (Paris: Vincent, 1934). A summary of this work appeared with the same title in *Bulletin monumental* 93 (1934): 69–88.

4. Henri Focillon, "Le problème de l'ogive,"*Bulletin de l'Office International des Instituts d'archéologie et d'histoire de l'art* 3 (March 1935).

5. Viollet-le-Duc, preface to *Dictionnaire*, 1:vi.

6. Ibid., 1:x.

7. See, for example, Viollet-le-Duc, "Style," in *Dictionnaire*, 8:474–497.

8. Even by his greatest advocate, Focillon himself. See Focillon, "Le problème de l'ogive," 52.

9. Viollet-le-Duc, "Pilier," in *Dictionnaire*, 7:151.

10. Ibid., 7:171.

11. "Just as when one sees the shape of a leaf, or an animal's bone, the whole plant or creature can be inferred, so on seeing a section one can infer architectural features," and from a single feature, one can infer the whole building. Viollet-le-Duc, "Style," in *Dictionnaire*, 8:486.

12. Viollet-le-Duc, "Cathedrale," in *Dictionnaire*, 2:324.

13. Viollet-le-Duc, "Construction," in *Dictionnaire*, 4:1.

14. Viollet-le-Duc, "Style," in *Dictionnaire*, 8:486.

15. See Claude Levi-Strauss, *Structural Anthropology* (New York: Basic Books, 1963).

16. Abraham, *Viollet-le-Duc et le rationalisme médiéval*, 58.

17. Focillon, "Le probléme de l'ogive," 46–48.

18. See Eduardo Torroja, *Philosophy of Structures*, trans. J. J. Polivka and Milos Polivka (Berkeley: University of California Press, 1958).

19. Viollet-le-Duc, "Construction," in *Dictionnaire*, 4:1.

6 FROM STRUCTURALISM BACK TO FUNCTIONALISM

1. Eugène-Emmanuel Viollet-le-Duc, "Colonne" [Column], in *Dictionnaire raisonné de l'architecture française du XIe au XVIe siècle* (Paris: 1854–1868), 3:491.

2. Viollet-le-Duc, "Fût" [Shaft], in *Dictionnaire*, 5:563.

3. Viollet-le-Duc, "Style," in *Dictionnaire*, 8:500.

4. Viollet-le-Duc, "Astragale," in *Dictionnaire*, 2:10–13.

5. Viollet-le-Duc, "Abaque" [Abacus], in *Dictionnaire*, 1:1–3.

6. Viollet-le-Duc, "Chapiteau" [Capital], in *Dictionnaire*, 3:480–544.

7. Viollet-le-Duc, "Échelle" [Scale], in *Dictionnaire*, 5:149.

8. Viollet-le-Duc, "Pilier" [Pillar], in *Dictionnaire*, 7:173.

9. See "The Space Between: A Structuralist Approach to the *Dictionnaire*: Viollet-le-Duc as a Forerunner of Structuralism," chapter 5, this volume.

10. Philippe Boudon, Hubert Damisch, and Philippe Deshayes, *Analyze du Dictionnaire raisonné de l'architecture française du XIe au XVIe siècle* (Paris: A.R.E.A., 1978).

11. Claude Lévi-Strauss, *Structural Anthropology*, trans. Claire Jacobson and Brooke Grundfest Schoepf (New York: Basic Books, 1963), 68–69.

12. Eugène-Emmanuel Viollet-le-Duc, *Entretiens sur l'architecture* (Paris: Q. Morel, 1863–1872), 1:175.

13. Viollet-le-Duc, *Entretiens*, 1:78.

14. Viollet-le-Duc, *Entretiens*, 1:213.

15. David Hume, *A Treatise of Human Nature*, ed. L. A. Selby-Bigge (Oxford: Clarendon Press, 1888), 299.

7 LEDOUX WITH KANT

1. Bertolt Brecht, "Ce que nos architectes doivent savoir," in *Les arts et la revolution* (Paris: L'arche 1970), 143.

2. *Allgemeines Lexikon der bildenden Künstler von der Antike bis zur Gegenwart*, comp. Ulrich Thieme and Felix Becker, vol. 23 (Leipzig: Seemann, 1928), s.v. "Ledoux."

3. Immanuel Kant, *Critique of Pure Reason*, ed. and trans. Paul Guyer and Allen W. Wood (Cambridge: Cambridge University Press, 1998), 108 [translation modified].

4. Emil Kaufmann, *Trois architectes révolutionnaires* (Paris: Edition de la S.A.D.G., 1978), 137.

5. Jacques Derrida, *Edmund Husserl's Origin of Geometry*, trans. John P. Leavey Jr. (Stony Brook, NY: N. Hays, 1978), 178.

6. Claude-Nicolas Ledoux, *L'architecture considérée sous le rapport de l'art, des moeurs et de la législation* (Paris, 1804); quoted in Emile Kaufmann, *Von Ledoux bis Le Corbusier* (Vienna: Passer, 1933), 43.

7. Jean-Jacques Rousseau, *Contrat social*, 3.10, quoted in Kaufmann, *Von Ledoux bis Le Corbusier*, 42.

8. Ledoux, *L'architecture*, quoted in Kaufmann, *Trois architectes révolutionnaires*, 162.

9. Ledoux, *L'architecture*, quoted in Kaufmann, *Trois architectes révolutionnaires*, 162.

10. Kaufmann, *Von Ledoux bis Le Corbusier*, 38.

11. "The new ruling class should not begin its construction work with the construction of three million individual houses, nor slightly more comfortable housing barracks, but with that of large-scale residential buildings." Brecht, *Les artes et la revolution*, 144.

12. Theodor W. Adorno, *Minima Moralia: Reflections from Damaged Life*, trans. E. F. N. Jephcott (London: Verso, 1951), 38.

13. François Furet, "The French Revolution Is Over," pt. 1 in *Interpreting the French Revolution*, trans. Elborg Forster (Cambridge: Cambridge University Press, 1977), 1–80.

12. Walter Benjamin, "Theses on the Philosophy of History," in *Illuminations*, ed. Hannah Arendt, trans. Harry Zohn (New York: Harcourt, Brace & World, 1968), 261–262.

13. Leon Trotsky, *La Révolution permanente* (Paris: Rieder, 1932), 7–8.

14. Emil Kaufmann, preface to *L'architecture au siècle des Lumières*, French trans. Olivier Bernier (Paris: René Julliard, 1963), 14.

15. Meyer Schapiro, "The New Viennese School," *Art Bulletin* 18 (June 1936): 258–266.

16. Immanuel Kant, *Lectures on Logic*, ed. and trans. J. Michael Young (Cambridge: Cambridge University Press), 8.

8   L'AUTRE "ICH," L'AUTRICHE—AUSTRIA, OR THE DESIRE FOR THE VOID

1. Adolf Loos, "Potemkin City" (1898), in *Spoken into the Void: Collected Essays 1897–1900*, trans. Jane O. Newman and John H. Smith (Cambridge, MA: MIT Press, 1982), 95–96.

2. Adolf Loos, "Architektur" (1910), in *Sämtliche Schriften* (Vienna: Herold, 1962), 315; "Architecture," trans. Wilfried Wang, in Yehuda Safran and Wilfried Wang, *The Architecture of Adolf Loos* (London: Arts Council of Great Britain, 1985), 108.

3. Adolf Loos, "Antworten auf fragen aus dem publikum" (1919), in *Sämtliche Schriften*, 372. One can recognize here the title of Karl Kraus's tragedy about World War I (*Die letzen Tage des Menschheit*). But if we are living "the last days of mankind" today, then what of the *future* of the work of art now?

4. Adolf Loos, "Men's Fashion" (1898), in *Spoken into the Void*, 12.

5. In June 1913, Georges Besson published a first translation of Loos's "Ornament and Crime" (1908) in *Les Cahiers d'aujourd'hui*, later reprinted by Paul Dermé in *L'Esprit nouveau*, vol. 2 (November 1920).

6. In all cases in which the term *ego* appears, the author used the French *moi*, which refers also to "me" or the "self" more generally and corresponds to the German *ich*.—Trans.

7. Robert Musil, *The Man without Qualities*, trans. Sophie Watkins (New York: Vintage, 1995), 28–29.

8. Ibid., 4.

9. Karl Kraus, *Dicta and Contradicta*, trans. Jonathan McVitty (Urbana: University of Illinois Press, 2001), 42.

10. Adolf Loos, "Ornament and Crime," in *The Architechture of Adolf Loos*, 103.

11. See Heinrinch Kulka, *Adolf Loos: Das Werk des Architekten* (Vienna: A. Schroll and Co., 1931).

12. In 1857, Owen Jones had already prefaced his *The Grammar of Ornament* with a picture of the tattooed face of a Maori woman, accompanied by this revealing commentary: "In this very barbarous practice the principles of the very highest ornamental art are manifest, every line upon the face is the best adapted to develop the natural features . . . the ornament of a savage tribe, being the result of a natural instinct, is necessarily always true to its purpose." Owen Jones, *The Grammar of Ornament* (London: Day and Son, 1856). Loos clearly must have been familiar with Jones's book, in which the notion of ornament was already the object of heavy criticism, just as he would have known the writings of Gottfried Semper. See "Science, Industry, and Art" (1852), in Gottfried Semper, *The Four Elements of Architecture and Other Writings*, trans. Harry Francis Mallgrave and Wolfgang Herrmann (Cambridge: Cambridge University Press, 1989), 130–167. Jones, like Semper, was very much struck by the presentation of a Maori village reconstructed at the international exhibition at London's Crystal Palace in 1851, for which the inhabitants had been specially brought over.

13. We must recognize another probable source of Loos's ideas on the "felonious" nature of ornament and various forms of tattooing: Lombroso's writings on delinquent man, the "palimpsest body," secret languages, and "anti-

languages," which had a great influence in their time. *Palimseti dal Carcere*, published in 1888, constitutes one of the most fascinating works that can be found on tattooing among delinquents (despite the limited number of copies that were published). Cesare Lombroso, *Palimseti dal Carcere, Raccolta unicamente destinata agli uomini di scienza* (Turin, 1888); "Gerghi nuovi," in *Archivio di psichiatra, scienza penale e antropologia criminale*, vol. 9 (Turin, 1888); *L'uomo delinquente in rapporto all'anhropologia, alla giurisprudenza e alla psichiatria* (Turin, 1897). For a recent, if superficial, contextualization, see Ernesto Ferrero, *I gerghi della malavita dal'500 a oggi* (Milan: Mondadori, 1972).

14. Loos, "Ornament and Crime," 100.

15. Ibid. The same "puritanism" that made Loos assimilate ornament to "crime" also led him to work toward the reform of typography, by eliminating from his text (as one can see from the preceding citations) the accumulation of capital letters with which German bedecks all nouns—and with them any residual trace of ornamental calligraphy, which he considered "barbaric," like the "Gothic" writing the Nazis were to bring back to a place of honor. In doing this, Loos relied on the authority of Jacob Grimm: "If we have rid our houses of their gables and their projecting rafters, and have removed the powder from our hair, why should we retain such rubbish in our writing (*warum soll in der Schrift aller Unrat bleiben*)?" Cited in Loos, *Spoken into the Void*, 2.

16. Loos, "Architecture," 104. Translation modified.

17. Manfredo Tafuri, *Architecture and Utopia*, trans. Barbara Luigia La Penta (Cambridge, MA: MIT Press, 1976), ix.

18. Manfredo Tafuri, *Theories and History of Architecture*, trans. Giorgio Verrecchia (New York: Harper and Row, 1980), 84. I would not follow Tafuri's analysis to the end, however. According to Tafuri, the effect of Loos's project resulted from the extraction of a "linguistic" element (the column) from its context and from its transfer to another context, to a scale beyond any norm. In fact, the column monument was nothing new, and Loos was playing on this symbolic autonomy, long conquered by the column relative to its "linguistic," syntagmatic, and paradigmatic functions, by enlarging the monument to the dimensions of the skyscraper.

19. Loos, "Architecture," 108.

9 ORNAMENT TO THE EDGE OF INDECENCY

1. Adolf Loos, "Ornament and Crime" (1929 revision), in *Ornament and Crime: Selected Essays*, trans. Michael Mitchell (Riverside, CA: Ariande Press, 1998). First written 1908.

2. As an example, see Reyner Banham, *Theory and Design in the First Machine Age*, 2nd ed. (New York: Praeger, 1967), 88–97.

3. See Le Corbusier, *The Decorative Art of Today*, trans. James Dunnett (Cambridge, MA: MIT Press, 1987), 135. Ripolin is a brand of paint.

4. Ibid., 118.

5. Ernst Gombrich, *The Sense of Order: A Study in the Psychology of Decorative Art* (Ithaca, NY: Cornell University Press, 1979), 19–20.

6. "Quasi ad inspirciendum delectationis causa." Cicero, *Orator*, 37.

7. Ibid., 65.

8. Ibid., 152.

9. Ibid., 50.

10. Ibid., 155.

11. Frances A. Yates, "The Three Latin Sources for the Classical Art of Memory," in *The Art of Memory* (London: Routledge and Kegan Paul, 1966), 17–41.

12. "Sed quandam neglegentia est diligens." "Legantia modo et munditia romanebit." Cicero, *Orator*, 78.

13. Ibid., 80.

14. Cesare Lombroso, *Palimsesti del carcere: Raccolta unicamente destinata agli uomini di scienza* (Turin: Bocca, 1888).

15. Eugène-Emmanuel Viollet-le-Duc, *Entretiens sur l'architecture*, vol. 2 (Paris: Q. Morel et Cie, 1872), 177.

16. Ibid., 185.

17. Auguste Choisy, *Histoire de l'architecture*, vol. 2 (Paris: Éditions Vincent Fréal, 1954), 469–470.

18. Gabriel Jouveau-Dubreuil, "L'Architecture," in *Archéologie du sud de l'Inde*, vol. 1 (Paris: P. Geuthner, 1914), 169.

19. Viollet-le-Duc, *Entretiens*, vol. 1 (Paris: Q. Morel et Cie, 1863), 82.

20. Ibid., 1:80. Passage translated in *The Architectural Theory of Viollet-le-Duc: Readings and Commentary*, ed. M. F. Hearn (Cambridge, MA: MIT Press, 1990), 85.

21. Charles Percier and Pierre-François-Léonard Fontaine, "Discours préliminaire," in *Recueil de décorations intérieures* (Paris: 1812), quoted in Gombrich,
The Sense of Order, 32–33.

22. Viollet-le-Duc, *Entretiens*, 1:80.

23. See "L'Autre 'Ich,' L'Autriche—Austria, or the Desire for the Void: Toward a
Tomb for Adolf Loos," chapter 8, this volume.

24. Heinrich Kulka, *Adolf Loos: Das Werk des Architekten* (Vienna: Anton Schroll,
1931).

25. Le Corbusier, *Decorative Art of Today*, 12.

26. Ibid., 84.

27. Ibid., 79.

28. Ibid., 114.

29. Ibid., 18.

30. Le Corbusier clarified in the preface to the book's 1959 edition: "Page 99,
third line. The phrase 'expressing the construction' (*accuser la construction*)
means 'emphasizing construction' (*mettre en valeur la construction*)." Le Corbusier, *Decorative Art of Today*, xix.

31. Ibid., 134.

32. Georges Duby, *Saint Bernard, l'art cistercien* (Paris: Arts et métiers graphiques,
1976), 94.

33. Karl Marx, "The Dual Character of the Labour Embodied in Commodities,"
in *Capital: A Critique of Political Economy*, vol. 1, trans. Ben Fowkes (London:
Penguin, 1976).

34. Le Corbusier, *Decorative Art of Today*, 49.

35. Ibid., 96.

36. Leon Battista Alberti, *On Painting*, trans. John R. Spencer (New Haven, CT:
Yale University Press, 1956), 67.

37. Ibid., 64.

38. Leon Battista Alberti, "Ornament," in *On the Art of Building in Ten Books*, trans.
Josephy Rykwert, Neil Leach, and Robert Tavernor (Cambridge, MA: MIT
Press, 1988), 183.

39. Françoise Choay, *The Rule and the Model: On the Theory of Architecture and Urbanism*, ed. Denise Bratton (Cambridge, MA: MIT Press, 1997), 121.

40. Ibid., 156.

41. Ibid., 204–205.

42. Alberti, *On Painting*, 3:89. See Hubert Damisch, *A Theory of /Cloud/: Toward a History of Painting*, trans. Janet Lloyd (Stanford, CA: Stanford University Press, 2002), 116–117.

43. See "The Column, the Wall," chapter 2, this volume.

44. Gombrich, *Sense of Order*, 34–35.

45. Henri Matisse, "Interview with Dorothy Dudley," in *Matisse on Art* (Berkeley: University of California Press, 1995), 110–111.

46. Henri Matisse, "Notes of a Painter," in *Matisse on Art*, 38.

47. Henri Matisse, "Transformations," in *Matisse on Art*, 128.

48. Matisse, "Notes of a Painter," 38.

49. Marcel Mauss, "L'art et le mythe d'après M. Wundt," *Revue Philosophique de la France et de l'Étranger* 66 (July–August 1908); reprinted in Mauss, *Oeuvres*, ed. Victor Karady (Paris: Minuit, 1969), 197.

50. Wilhelm Wundt, "Die Sprache," in *Völkerpsychologie: Eine Untersuchung der Entwicklungsgesetze von Sprachen, Mythus und Sitte*, vol. 1 (Leipzig: Engelmann, 1904), 220; cited in Mauss, "L'art et le mythe," 200.

51. Mauss, "L'art et le mythe," 199.

52. Gottfried Semper, *Style in the Technical and Tectonic Arts, or, Practical Aesthetics*, trans. Harry Francis Mallgrave and Michael Robinson (Los Angeles: Getty Research Institute, 2004), 219.

53. Joseph Rykwert, "Semper and the Conception of Style," in *The Necessity of Artifice: Ideas in Architecture* (New York, Rizzoli, 1982), 124.

54. James Février, *Histoire de l'écriture* (Paris: Payot, 1959), 20–23.

55. Wundt, "Die Sprache," 186, cited in Mauss, *L'art et le mythe*, 199.

56. Meyer Schapiro, "Nature of Abstract Art," in *Art of the Twentieth Century: A Reader*, ed. Jason Gaiger and Paul Wood (New Haven, CT: Yale University Press, 2003), 30.

57. Owen Jones, *The Grammar of Ornament* (London: Day & Son, 1865), 13–16; emphasis mine.

58. Bronisław Malinowski, *Coral Gardens and Their Magic* (London: Routledge, 2002).

59. Sigmund Freud, *Three Essays on the Theory of Sexuality*, trans. James Strachey (New York: Basic Books, 2000), 23.

1. Sérgio Ferro, Chérif Kebbal, Philippe Potié, Cyrille Simonnet, *Le Couvent de La Tourette* (Marseille: Parenthèses, 1987).

2. Colin Rowe, "La Tourette," in *The Mathematics of the Ideal Villa, and Other Essays* (Cambridge, MA: MIT Press, 1976), 85–203.

3. Sigfried Giedion's statement, "Construction plays the role of the subconscious," from his *Bauen in Frankreich, Eisen, Eisenbeton* (Leipzig: Klinkhardt & Biermann, 1928), was quoted by Benjamin in the following context: "Just as Napoleon failed to understand the functional nature of the state as an instrument of domination by the bourgeois class, so the architects of his time failed to understand the functional nature of iron, with which the constructive principle begins its domination of architecture." Walter Benjamin, "Paris, the Capital of the Nineteenth Century," trans. Howard Eiland and Kevin McLaughlin, in *Walter Benjamin: Selected Writings*, vol. 3, *1935–1938*, ed. Howard Eiland, Michael W. Jennings, and Gary Smith (Cambridge, MA: Belknap Press, 2002), 33.

4. Minutes of a meeting dated April 23, 1955, Archives de la Fondation Le Corbusier, quoted in Ferro et al., *Le Couvent de La Tourette*, 29.

5. Iannis Xenakis, "The Monastery of La Tourette," in *Le Corbusier*, ed. H. Allen Brooks (Princeton, NJ: Princeton University Press, 1987), 143–162.

6. Ferro et al., *Le Couvent de La Tourette*.

7. Ibid., 41.

8. "In conceptual art, the idea or concept is the most important aspect of a work. When an artist practices a form of conceptual art, this means all planning and decisions are made beforehand and the execution is a perfunctory affair. The idea becomes the machine that makes art." Sol LeWitt, "Paragraphs on Conceptual Art," *Artforum* 5, no. 10 (Summer 1967): 79–84; reprinted in Alexander Albero and Blake Stimson, *Conceptual Art: A Critical Anthology* (Cambridge, MA: MIT Press, 2000), 12.

9. Alison Smithson, "Couvent de La Tourette, Éveux-sur-l'Arbresle, near Lyon, France," *Architectural Design* 28, no. 11 (November 1958): 482.

10. Le Corbusier, interview with the Dominican community (October 1960), "Le Couvent Sainte-Marie de La Tourette construit par Le Corbusier," in *L'Art*

sacré, nos. 7–8 (March–April 1960); reprinted in Jean Petit, *Un couvent de Le Corbusier* (Paris: Cahiers Forces Vives-Editec, 1961), 28–29.

11. Le Corbusier, "Conversation avec Savina," in *Aujourd'hui*, no. 51 (1965): 98; quoted in Stanislaus Von Moos, *Le Corbusier: Elements of a Synthesis* (Cambridge, MA: MIT Press, 1979), 282.

12. Petit, *Un couvent*, 20.

13. On the subject of "slopes," Jacqueline Salmon writes this to me: "It seems hard not to see Ronchamp, because there they [slopes] are more complex and do not have the same function as at La Tourette. They are there to enlarge the visual space. Without any relationship to the terrain, practically flat. The floor of the nave has been dug out of the ground from the entrance right up to the altar, where it then rises again. But in contrast the ground sinks again toward the back and in particular along a different axis at 45 degrees only to die away toward a secondary altar. There is nothing remarkable apropos in Le Corbusier's drawings published in different books." Personal communication, undated.

14. Petit, *Un couvent*, 28–29.

15. Ibid.

16. Philippe Potié's otherwise excellent little monograph, *Le Couvent Sainte-Marie de La Tourette* (Paris: Fondation Le Corbusier, 2001), 59. Note the resonating effect of the date of publication of this booklet and the title of Stanley Kubrick's film *2001: A Space Odyssey*, in which a parallelopedal UFO plays the role we are all familiar with.

17. Ferro et al., *Le Couvent de La Tourette*, 13, 31.

18. Le Corbusier, interview with Dominican community, quoted in Petit, *Un couvent*, 28.

19. Le Corbusier apparently never tired repeating: "Composition begins with the roofline, a great wide horizontal, and ends with the downward slope of the ground on which the building rests by means of pilotis." Echoing this paradox, I cannot resist recording here an anecdote that José-Luis Sert told me years ago. After months of work during which Sert consulted Le Corbusier several times a day about the slightest problem posed by the Carpenter Center building site at Harvard, from the position of a door knob to the texture of a form, the day of the inauguration arrived, followed by a visit to the building

during which Le Corbusier did not utter a word. Sert finally broke the silence by asking him what he thought, to which Le Corbusier replied: "Perfect, everything is perfect, but why did you put it the wrong way round?" Sert was stunned and thought Le Corbusier might be having a dig at him as a way of paying him back for his excessive zeal—unless La Tourette is the beginning of an answer to that question.

20. Edmund Husserl, "Foundational Investigations of the Phenomenological Origin of the Spatiality of Nature: The Originary Ark, the Earth, Does Not Move," trans. Fred Kersten, in Maurice Merleau-Ponty, *Husserl at the Limits of Phenomenology*, ed. Leonard Lawlor (Evanston, IL: Northwestern University Press, 2002), 117.

21. Ibid., 126.

22. Edmund Husserl, "The World of the Living Present and the Constitution of the Surrounding World That Is Outside the Flesh," trans. Bettina Bergo, revised by Leonard Lawlor, in *Husserl at the Limits of Phenomenology*, 151.

23. Petit, *Un couvent*, 20.

24. "*It is a great modern word. Architecture and urbanism are all about circulation.*" Le Corbusier, *Précisions, sur un état présent de l'architecture et de l'urbanisme* (Paris: Éditions Vincent Fréal, 1960), 128.

25. Frances A. Yates, *The Art of Memory* (London: Routledge and Kegan Paul, 1966).

26. Ferro et al., *Le Couvent de La Tourette*, 49.

27. Edmund Husserl, "Notizen zur Raumkonstitution,"*Philosophy and Phenomenological Research* 1, no. 1 (1940–1941): 21–37.

28. Husserl, "World of the Living Present," 150.

11 THE SLIGHTEST DIFFERENCE

1. Le Corbusier, *Toward an Architecture*, trans. John Goodman (Los Angeles: Getty Research Institute, 2007), 220; emphasis in original.

2. Manfredo Tafuri, *Teorie e storia dell'architettura* (Bari: Laterza, 1973), 112; *Theories and History of Architecture*, trans. Giorgio Verrecchia (New York: Harper and Row, 1980), 91.

3. See Le Corbusier, *Toward an Architecture*, 117–130.

4. Peter Eisenman, "miMISes Reading," in *Eisenman Inside Out: Selected Writings 1963–1988*, ed. Mark Rakatansky (New Haven, CT: Yale University Press, 2004), 194.

5. Le Corbusier, *Toward an Architecture*, 219.

6. Ibid., 113.

12 ARCHITECTURE AND INDUSTRY

1. Benedikt Huber and Jean-Claude Steiegger, eds., *Jean Prouvé, Une architecture par l'industrie* (Zurich: Éditions d'architecture Artemis, 1971).

2. Ibid., 8.

3. Ibid., 14.

4. I will not expand here on the relationships between the modern movement and industry. Let me just say that it is no accident that the first buildings designed according to industrial construction standards were not residential buildings but factories. Industry no doubt expected greater profits from the "design" ideology than from practices that, deliberately or otherwise, went against the accepted division of labor. That was, in any case, the line jointly taken by the members of the Deutscher Werkbund, who were unsparing in their support for the same *Führer* who shortly after strove to persuade German industrialists that one of the strongest bastions of the established order was the so-called traditional thatched cottage.

5. "L'avenir lui révéla cruellement sa confiante ingénuité" (The future was to show how naively trusting he had been). Huber and Steiegger, *Prouvé, Une architecture par l'industrie*, 193.

6. Ibid., 24.

7. Ibid., 203.

8. Figures put forward by Jean Prouvé within the framework of his teaching at the Conservatoire national des art-et-métiers, 1970–1971. The reference to the Bauhaus experiment is instructive for what it reveals about the opposition between the interests of so-called light industry—the processing industry—represented by the institution's backers, and those of heavy industry, in which Nazism found solid support.

9. William Marlin, "The Evolution and Impact of a Teacher,"*The World of Buckminster Fuller, Architectural Forum* 140 (January–February, 1972): 72.

10. Huber and Steiegger, *Prouvé, Une architecture par l'industrie*, 23.

11. Ibid., 11.

12. Projects by Georg Muche and Richard Paulick. See Hans Maria Wingler, *The Bauhaus*, ed. Joseph Stein, trans. Wolfgang Jabs and Basil Gilbert (Cambridge, MA: MIT Press, 1969), 417.

13. Walter Gropius, *Scope of Total Architecture* (London: G. Allen & Unwin, 1956), 15–16.

14. Sigfried Giedion, *Walter Gropius, l'homme et l'œuvre* (Paris: Albert Morancé, 1954), 193–200.

15. Huber and Steiegger, *Prouvé, Une architecture par l'industrie*, 30.

16. Ibid., 142.

17. In a feature film made by Jean-Marc Leuwen for the Plastic Arts Department of ORTF (Office de Radiodiffusion Télévision Française), Jean Prouvé agreed (at my insistence) to step up to the blackboard—a drawing board as it happened—to give us a few moments of his teaching again. There is a really beautiful edited version of this in circulation, twenty minutes long end to end. Since then, the course has been published in its entirety, all of Prouvé's drawings having been found.

18. Huber and Steiegger, *Prouvé, Une architecture par l'industrie*, 25.

19. Indeed, Le Corbusier was so persuaded by this that he included Prouvé in the preliminary studies for the Cité Radieuse in Marseille.

20. Huber and Steiegger, *Prouvé, Une architecture par l'industrie*, 185–186.

21. A public and stupefying demonstration of this is provided by the Corning Glass Center in New York, which is visited in order to "deconstruct" a number of naive associations when it comes to architecture.

22. It is no longer a question here of scaffolding—another cherished metaphor of structural theory—because the skeleton itself serves as scaffolding at each stage of the building process, just as it once did in the Greek temple.

23. Huber and Steiegger, *Prouvé, Une architecture par l'industrie*, 203.

24. Ibid., 108.

25. Royston Landau, *New Directions in British Architecture* (New York: Studio Vista, 1968), 77.

13 ARCHITECTURE IS . . .

1. Gillian Naylor, "De Stijl: Abstraction or Architecture?" *Studio International* 190, no. 977 (September–October 1975): 98–102.

2. "In tota re aedificatoria primarium certe ornamentum in columnis est." Leon Battista Alberti, *De re aedificatoria*, trans. G. Orlandi (Milan: Edizioni Il Polifilo, 1966), 6:3.

3. "Prese l'architettto, se io non erro, pure dal pittore gli architravi, le base, i capitelli, le colonne, frontispici e simili tutte altre cose." Leon Battista Alberti, *De pictura*, ed. Cecil Grayson (Bari, 1975), 48.

4. Greg Lynn, *Animate Form* (New York: Princeton Architectural Press, 1999), 41.

5. Jean Dubuffet, *Prospectus et tous écrits suivants*, ed. Hubert Damisch (Paris: Gallimard, 1995), 1:636n176.

6. Ibid., 241.

7. Jean Dubuffet, "Edifices" (1968), in *Prospectus*, 3:342.

8. "The time has come for architects to respond to questions—notably the question of restoring to architecture its character of art, long ago forgotten. Of art, and what that notion connotes of caprice and invention, the architecture of our time is dismaying—completely devoid of imagination, dependent on sordid considerations of economics and on the least effort, relying strictly on the rectilinear, on such a poor invention as the parallelepiped box." Letter from Dubuffet to Marcel Cornu, January 12, 1969, in *Prospectus*, 3:497n51.

9. Jacques Derrida, "Point de folie—Maintenant l'architecture," in *Psyché: Inventions de l'autre* (Paris: Galilee, 1987), 480.

10. Ibid.

11. Roland Barthes, "Sur le cinema," interview with M. Delahaye and J. Rivette, *Cahiers du cinema* 147 (September 1963). Reprinted in *Le grain de la voix, interviews* (Paris: Seuil, 1981), 22.

12. Hubert Damisch, "Le signe et la fonction," in *Modern'signe: Recherches sur le travail du signe dans l'architecture moderne* (Paris: CORDA, 1977), 2:13, a report on the research carried out by Le Cercle d'HistoireTheorie de l'art de l'Ecole des Hautes Etudes en Sciences Sociales in the account of the Department of Architecture.

13. Derrida, "Point de folie," 517.

14. "[The question] of what it is that projects in front or in advance in the project (projection, program, prescription, promise, proposition) of everything that belongs, in the architectural process, to the movement of throwing, or of being thrown (jacere, jacio/jaceo). Horizontally or vertically: foundations for the erection of an edifice that always jumps toward the sky—there where, in an apparent sense of mimesis, there was nothing." Ibid., 514.

15. Walter Benjamin, *Das Passagen-Werk* (Frankfurt: Suhrkamp, 1982); French trans., *Paris, capitale du XIXe siècle: Le livre des passages* (Paris, 1989), 182; English trans., "Iron Construction," in *The Arcades Project*, trans. Howard Eiland and Kevin McLaughlin (Cambridge, MA: Belknap Press, 1999), 160.

16. *The Arcades Project*, 155.

17. Ibid., 162.

18. From *Tower with Figures*, Dubuffet continued to say that the work was not conceived "with a view to furnishing a lodging in the form actually in use in our homes," but as "an occasional home for retirement and reverie." Dubuffet, *Prospectus*, 3:336.

19. Paul Valéry, "Histoire d'Amphion," a lecture read at a concert performance of *Amphion* at the Université des Annales, January 14, 1932. First published in *Conferéncia*, August 5, 1932.

20. Walter Gropius, "Architect—Servant or Leader?," in *Scope of Total Architecture* (London: G. Allen & Unwin, 1956), 94.

21. See Manfredo Tafuri, *Architecture and Utopia*, trans. Barbara Luigi La Penta (Cambridge, MA: MIT Press, 1976).

22. Peter Eisenman, *Recent Projects*, 25, as quoted in Fredric Jameson, *The Seeds of Time* (New York: Columbia University Press, 1994), 170–171.

23. Jameson, *The Seeds of Time*, 143–144.

24. Session of December 30, 1926, as quoted in Frederike Huygen, *Het mueum Boijmans van Hannema: Gebouw, geschiedenis, architectuur* (Rotterdam: Museum Boijmans Van Beuningen, 1992), 78.

25. Adrian Dannatt, *United States Holocaust Memorial Museum: James Ingo Freed* (London: Phaidon Press, 1995), 5.

26. *The Architecture and Art of the United States Holocaust Memorial Museum* (Washington, DC: United States Holocaust Memorial Museum, 1995), 9.

1. "But yesterday I made the first negatives other than matter-of-fact records—negatives with intention. A quite marvelous cloud form tempted me—a sunlit cloud which rose from the bay to become a towering white column." Edward Weston, *The Daybooks of Edward Weston*, 2nd ed., ed. Nancy Newhall (New York: Aperture, 1990), 14.

2. "Life here is intense and dramatic, I do not need to photograph premeditated postures, and there are sunlit walls of fascinating surface textures, and there are clouds! They alone are sufficient to work with for many months, and never tire." Ibid., 21.

3. Mark Wigley, "The Architecture of Atmosphere," in *Daidalos* 68 (1998), 18.

4. Ibid., 25.

5. Le Corbusier, *Toward an Architecture*, trans. John Goodman (Los Angeles: Getty Research Institute, 2001), 109.

6. "Adunque l'orlo e dorso danno suoi nomi alle superficie." Leon Battista Alberti, *Della Pittura* (Florence: Sansoni, 1950), book 1, section 5. For the English translation, see Leon Battista Alberti, *On Painting*, trans. John R. Spencer (New Haven, CT: Yale University Press, 1966), 45.

7. Edmund Husserl, *The Origin of Geometry* (Stony Brook, NY: N. Hays, 1978). First published in 1939 as *Frage nach dem Ursprung der Geometrie als intentional-historisches Problem*.

8. Paul Valéry, "Eupalinos, ou l'architecte" (1923), in *Œuvres*, vol. 2 (Paris: Gallimard, 1960). For the English translation, see Paul Valéry, *Eupalinos; or, The Architect*, trans. William McCausland Stewart (London: Oxford University Press, 1932).

9. See my *L'Origine de la perspective* (Paris: Flammarion, 1987). For the English translation, see *The Origin of Perspective*, trans. John Goodman (Cambridge, MA: MIT Press, 1992).

10. Antonio di Turchio Manetti, *Vita di Filippo Brunelleschi*, ed. D. Robertis and G. Tanturli (Milan: Il Polifilio, 1976). For the English translation, see Antonio di Turchio Manetti, *The Life of Brunelleschi*, trans. Catherine Enggass (University Park: Penn State University Press, 1970). See also my *Théorie du /nuage/. Pour une Histoire de la peinture* (Paris: Éditions du Seuil, 1972), 157–171. For the

English translation, see *A Theory of /Cloud/: Toward a History of Painting*, trans. Janet Lloyd (Stanford, CA: Stanford University Press, 2002).

11. Robert Smithson, "Incidents of Mirror-Travel in the Yucatan" (1969), in *The Collected Writings*, ed. Jack Flam (Berkeley: University of California Press, 1996), 119–133.

12. Elizabeth Diller and Ricardo Scofidio, *Blur: The Making of Nothing* (New York: Harry N. Abrams, 2002).

13. Ludwig Wittgenstein, *Culture and Value*, ed. G. H. von Wright, trans. Peter Winch (Chicago, IL: University of Chicago Press, 1984), 41e.

14. Jacques Lacan, *Le Séminaire*, livre IV, *La Relation d'objet* (Paris: Éditions du Seuil, 1994), 48.

15. Diller and Scofidio, *Blur*, 3.

16. Henri Atlan, *Entre le cristal et la fumée. Essai sur l'organization du vivant* (Paris: Éditions du Seuil, 1979).

17. John W. Cloud, *Steel for Bridges* (Philadelphia, PA: 1881).

18. See Wolf D. Prix and Helmut Swiczinsky, *Coop Himmelb(l)au Austria: From Cloud to Cloud* (Klagenfurt: Ritter, 1996) and *Construire le ciel* (Paris: Centre Pompidou, 1993).

19. See Experiments in Art and Technology (E.A.T.), *Pavilion*, ed. Billy Klüver, Julie Martin, and Barbara Rose (New York: Experiments in Art and Technology, 1978).

20. I am referring here to the work conducted by Pierre Rosenstiehl at the Centre de mathématiques sociales of the Ecole des Hautes Etudes, Paris, under the title of "taxiplanie."

21. Walter Gropius, *The New Architecture and the Bauhaus*, trans. P. Morton Shand (Cambridge, MA: MIT Press, 1965), 30.

22. Matteo Ripa, *Views of the Chinese Imperial Palaces and Gardens–Jehol*; 1713). There are eight known copies of this album, one of which is in the collection of the Canadian Centre for Architecture in Montreal.

23. See Lai Sing Lam, *Origins and Development of the Traditional Chinese Roof*, Mellen Studies in Architecture, vol. 5 (Lewiston, NY: Edwin Mellen Press, 2001).

24. Oswald Siren, "Histoire des arts anciens de la Chine," in *L'Architecture*, vol. 4 (Paris: G. van Oest, 1929), 24.

25. Lam, *Origins and Development*, 51.

26. Smithson, "Incidents of Mirror-Travel," 132.

27. Cesare Ripa, *Iconologia, overo Descritione delle imagine* (Rome, 1593). For the English translation, see Cesare Ripa, *Iconology* (New York: Garland Publishing, 1979).

INDEX

Page numbers in italics refer to figures.